From Time to Time

HANNAH TILLICH

From Time to Time

STEIN AND DAY/*Publishers*/New York

The author gratefully acknowledges the editorial assistance of Grace McGraw-Smith. The author also wishes to thank Maria Pelikan for translating the verses originally written in German.

First Published in 1973
Copyright © 1973 by Hannah Tillich
Library of Congress Catalog Card No. 73-79225
Designed by David Miller
Printed in the United States of America
Stein and Day/*Publishers*/Scarborough House, Briarcliff Manor, N.Y. 10510
ISBN 0-8128-1626-9

SECOND PRINTING, 1974

Contents

CHILDHOOD

YOUTH

MARRIAGE

CHILDHOOD

Prelude

☙

THE WORD

When out of the heart's own chaos
The word arises—a white dove—
To wing across desolate landscape of despair,

When fountains of ecstasy fall back
Into the heart's abyss
In quest of a clear-cut Yes or No,
A great deal, indeed, gets lost on the way.

THE RETURN OF THE "I"

THE BIRDIE GAME

Essentially, it was a question of proving: "I am. I alone am; the others are not." I had to say No to the others. I negated the others and refused to be in touch with them, for then I existed. The moment I admitted the reality of the others, I vanished.

It was like the game my father had played with me when I was a child, a game of "Now I am here, now I am not here." The "I" in the game was a paper "birdie" glued to my father's finger. He sat across the table from me, his hands on the table rim, and the finger with the birdie on it swung up and down in rhythm with the other fingers pressed against each other on the table rim, hiding the loss of the birdie finger. My father sang out, "Now I am here, now I am not here," as he swung his hands up and down. I gasped in astonishment. I imagined the birdie had flown far away into foreign countries and then back again with his cry, "Now I am here."

"Now I am here." Triumphant return of the "I."

THE FATHER OF THE OLD WOMAN

The "I" was also there when I was with others and spoke without waiting to be spoken to.

It was there when I talked to the great mountain of my father and while his arms and hands were stretching out to receive me. It was there while I climbed the steep hills of my father and hid my face in the woods of his reddish beard.

But this was not always a case of just the "I" anymore. Sometimes he called my two sisters to him and I stood at the foot of the mountain and watched them being lifted up, one at a time, into the scraggly hair near his chin. I then forgot that it was not "I" being raised high in the air, screeching joyously. I became my sisters, one after the other. I left "myself," a childish heap, on the ground at my father's feet and abandoned my physical unity for the elation of being lifted and swung. I left myself standing on the floor like an empty cocoon and turned into a butterfly, fluttering happily in my father's arms—an enchanted butterfly of empathy.

THE I REFOUND

"And then," said the old woman, "you lost my 'I' on the road, after you had made use of it as if it were your own."

"We used to enjoy an exchange," said the old man, "I dreaming your dreams, you thinking my thoughts."

"That may have been so, but you made me forget that it was 'I' who participated in your thoughts; you made me invisible to myself. You made me forget who said that. It was only when I separated myself, when I went off and lay down under a shady tree, paying no attention to your angry exhortations to go on—only then did I see my 'I.' And now it was either lying on the sunbaked road, or hobbling like a rainbow-feathered bird with weak wings. Ah, it was sickly! You went on walking angrily ahead, without me. I caught my 'I' then, and took it back into me—my right eye, my left eye, and my center 'I.' I experienced the shock of being whole again."

"What is so wrong about guessing other people's wishes?" asked the old man.

"The freedom of being 'I,'" she exclaimed.

"Freedom," muttered the old man, "did you say 'freedom'?"

THE CHRIST CHILD ON THE CEILING

"What is your concept of truth?" asked the old woman.

"Truth," replied the old man, "is interaction. What is 'truth' here is not necessarily 'truth' there."

"If I carry a child, I carry a child, and that is the truth."

"You confuse 'truth' with 'fact,'" he said, "Truth is a lie. That I know."

"Truth has to be two," she responded, "or even three. If it is only two, there is still no witness."

"Truth is the circle of light on the ceiling. Truth is the greatest secret of all. I watched my father reading by the light of a kerosene lamp, which was hanging from the ceiling. The flame made circles on the ceiling, as it flickered through the milk-glass cylinder. The milky dome made soft, vibrating, starlike shapes around the circle of light, as the lamp swung from its metal chains. It was shortly before Christmas. I exclaimed to my father that I had seen the Christ Child up there on the ceiling, in the pattern of sunlike rays. My father's faith must have been disturbed. Nobody, according to his religious beliefs, could ever have seen the Christ Child. He pounced on me, a five-year-old child, with fierce words. He forced me, whimpering and feverish, to call what had been my innermost truth a lie. But in my heart, I knew better. Truth was hidden deeper than my father's anger could reach."

"Nevertheless," she declared, "you do need 'two' for a fact. Could you make your father understand, when you grew up?"

"Oh him," said the old man, "I escalated him into one who was eyeless, earless, speechless, invisible, and finally nameless. He became the great question mark of truth."

THE SEESAW

The old woman sat on the seesaw and sang. She bounced up and down. The old man sat at his end, balancing forcefully. He sang too. He sang his song, she hers. They did not take turns, but sang at the same time, mingling their melodies. Clouds scudded across the sky. Trees around the playground bent to the gusts of autumn wind, which also drove the leaves across the playground in sudden spurts. The great bridge towered in the distance.

The old man hummed and rumbled on, out of tune. He muttered words between his teeth, "Father, mother, sister, brother, I do not have anybody anymore in this world." He sounded happy.

The old woman swung her feet in heavy shoes, vigorously sending the seesaw up into the air. She sang out of tune, too. "Full fathom five my father lies. Of his bones are corals made. Nothing of him that doth fade, but doth suffer a sea change, into something rich and strange."

"What are you singing?" the old man called across to her. But she had changed the tune. "My mother who me slew, my father who me ate, my sister the Marleniken, who picked up all my bonekens, kiwitt, kiwitt, what a beautiful bird am I—Shakespeare and Grimm's fairy tales," she shouted back at the old man.

"Let me down," he called.

The old woman slowed the movement of the seesaw. She sat still in the high seat while the old man got off cautiously. She braked the fall of the board as her own weight brought it down to the ground. He had let go of his empty seat and was walking back to the house without waiting for her.

THE REALITY SLAP

"Ah," said the old woman, entering his room without knocking, "the old torture game." The old man had pushed the buttons on his custom-made screen. There was the familiar cross shooting up the wall. "So fitting for a Christian and a theologian," she sneered. A naked girl hung on it, hands tied in front of her private parts. Another naked figure lashed the crucified one with a whip that reached further to another cross, on which a girl was exposed from behind. More and more crosses appeared, all with women tied and exposed in various positions. Some were exposed from the front, some from the side, some from behind, some crouched in fetal position, some head down, or legs apart, or legs crossed—and always whips, crosses, whips.

"Ugh!" she exclaimed, "how sick and bored I am with all your imaginary tortures. I bet you have never hit a woman in real anger in all your nonvisionary life. You've never given me a real slap, anyway."

"What are you talking about?" queried the old man.

[14]

"You don't know how good it is to receive an honest-to-goodness slap."

"An honest-to-goodness slap in a real-life situation," the old man mused. "You never would have stood for it."

"But I did," she said, "and I loved it. I was in a plane flying in an area where there were tornadoes. It was like being on a ship in a storm. Turbulence knocked the cocktail glass out of my hand. I was very scared. In panic, I turned to my companion in the next seat, put my hand out to him for comfort and whimpered, 'I'm scared.' 'Stop that,' he said, and he gave me a firm slap on my outstretched hand."

"What did you do?"

"I did nothing. I stopped being hysterical. I sat quietly and I was no longer afraid."

"What did he say?" asked the old man.

"He said he felt he had to give me a countershock, and he had."

The old man turned off the screen. "A reality slap, eh?"

THE BORDERLINE

"Why do you always remain on the borderline?" asked the old woman. "Why can't you decide between Yin and Yang, between the mountain and the deep blue sea? I made my decision long ago. I belong to the deep blue sea."

"Why should I decide?" retorted the old man nastily. "I don't know where I belong. Besides, indecision allows for freedom."

"Up to your old tricks," she said. "Freedom, my eye! When I was seventeen, I wanted to be everything, male and female, a self-sufficient hermaphrodite. But you know something? You severed my Yin and Yang. I became submerged in femaleness."

"I don't want to be submerged in either," he said.

"Why don't you want to be the mountain? Why won't you be the man for the woman in me?"

"Poppycock," said the old man. "You are not all woman either. You like to climb mountains too, don't you? You are your own male and female, too."

"We shall meet on the borderline," she cried. "You will come to me from wherever-that-is. I shall rise out of the deep blue sea and join you."

"I shall embrace you," declared the old man. "I shall balance on the rope with you and we'll be two eternal ropedancers."

[15]

"We'll do a jig on the rope," promised the old woman.

"We'll rise into the air," they pledged together. "We'll fly over the deep blue sea and the steep mountain in an Ariel embrace."

KAIROS

"Kairos," the old woman said. "I understand Kairos to mean the irrevocable moment of decision, destiny—the moment in which one has the exacting knowledge of being called to act, having crossed the borderline between dreaming doubt and assurance. It is the moment of the 'green light' for the hero, the now and the here. In it one does the unique, the unrepeatable deed. You turned Kairos into a rosary of enchanting moments. You made kai-roses for everybody. How can there be a democratic Kairos? A hero is not democratic."

"The human race has a long history," replied the old man. "There are many periods in which man has felt 'en kairo.'"

"There is only one period for me," she said. "Make your game, choose your number."

"Choosing is an exclusion."

"I like to be exclusive," she declared. "I choose."

The old man held out a rosary. "Choose."

The old woman snatched the rosary, breaking the chain. Beads rolled everywhere.

"Choose one," said the old man and sniggered.

"Too much mass-produced equality," she scoffed. "Each bead should be different from the others. How is it possible for me to choose?"

"That's what I think," he said, "individuality, individuation. . . ." He turned away.

"I never win," mused the old woman. She laughed a soft laugh at his retreating figure and turned the other way.

FEAR

"How afraid you are of everything!" exclaimed the old man. "Whenever we went for walks in the mountains, across the fields, or among the hills, you were afraid of dogs that barked at you. You shook with fear."

"We were always trespassing on private property," responded the old woman.

"You were also afraid of airplanes," he said.

"I got used to those, except when there was good reason to be frightened—when we flew through violent storms, or close to a volcano, or lost power in one engine, or when the visibility was zero."

"Then there was the hurricane," he recalled. "How afraid you were of that!"

"Yes, I was. I had to take our five-year-old son up ninety-nine steps from the beach where you were racing along joyfully with the wind. As I opened the door of our cottage, a tree crashed to the ground, so close it almost struck us. Of course I was afraid."

"You should have kept a good distance from trees," he said maliciously.

"There was good reason for fear," she insisted.

"There was good reason for ecstasy," he countered.

"Ecstasy of destruction," she said.

"Ecstasy of life force," he replied.

"I remember the other hurricane. We were in the long, narrow cottage and I shook as the house shook. Then came the sudden stillness. There was no wind at all as the eye of the storm passed over us. I shook with fear again when the winds came on from the other direction, billowing out the curtains. I remember how I sat whimpering on the steps."

The old man said, "I wrote."

"And you drank," she reminded him.

"Yes, drank and slept."

"But in the early morning, before sunrise," she said, "you ran down the steps, into the yard and onto the street, screaming in the terror of a nightmare. The morning was cool and blue. There was a gentle breeze, nothing to fear."

SECOND BEST

"I pity you so very much," said the old man, with tears in his eyes.

"You pity me," replied the old woman, "for all the things you have done to me. You pity me."

"I don't know if it's because of things I have done to you, but because you are unhappy, so deeply unhappy."

"You called me 'second best,'" responded the old woman, "never 'best,' never your true love."

"As to 'second best,'" he said, "that was only a cosmic reservation."

"It was indeed," she said. "You wrote poems for our guests; you celebrated each one of them. Everyone felt more beautiful, more witty, more lovable; everyone except me. I was only celebrated as the person in gray workaday clothes—the person celebrated for daily drudgery. I was Cinderella without the glass slipper. You gave me no golden presence. I was only the Ugly-Wugly!"

"You were my reality and my necessity," he said. "You were my bridge across the seasons, my continuity in past, present, and future."

"I served you," she countered. "I served you in order that we might celebrate life together, but you turned away from me and followed other women. And when I break down and weep, you pity me."

"Another's unhappiness is a reason for pity."

"Once," said the old woman, "I sat at the feet of one of your women friends, who was dying of cancer. I saw our mutual brother, Death, sitting on her armchair. I sat down at her feet, fully aware of the fact that she had estranged you from me. Was that the same pity you felt for me?"

"Pity," he said, "is such a multiple feeling. How can you describe it?"

"I can," she cried. "I hated her so much, I dreamed that I destroyed her. I was frightened at my own dream-pleasure, feeling her dying under my hands. There was something in that dream and something in sitting at her feet—she in such misery—that superseded my hatred and pity for her, and even my suffering for her sake."

"Something like that," agreed the old man, in a dreamy voice. "Images of hate and love coexisting, overcome by compassion."

SELF-LOVE

The old man walked to the mirror, stopped, looked at his reflection. "Phooey," he exclaimed.

"How can I love you," the old woman cried, "when you hate yourself?"

"You never want to look in a mirror," he retorted. "You won't let yourself be photographed."

"Only by my grandson, but I do like myself as that funny little child with a runny nose and tousled hair. Don't you like to see the little boy, hopping merrily downstairs?"

"My father loathed the way I hopped downstairs. He hired a sergeant to teach me not to hop," said the old man.

"What about the little boy who saw the Christ Child on the ceiling?"

"My father called me a liar for that," he said.

"And the boy who built dream-castles with his building blocks?"

"Somebody stole the blocks."

"You are saying 'phooey' to the wrong person," she said. "Don't you hate that thief for stealing your toy? You should hate your father for denying you your vision of the Christ Child and for insisting that you learn a different walk, instead of your joyful hop."

The old man was silent.

"Tell me about your mother," she asked.

"She took me away from my toys every afternoon to go for a walk. Besides, she had a glass eye. She died of cancer. She put an awful lot of clothes on me, homemade clothes. How I hated them! Every year they let the seams out of the sleeves and pants. They did not want me to have new clothes."

"In spite of your becoming a new person every year," she sympathized, "you still had to wear old clothes."

"Tell me about your parents," he asked.

"We were a large bunch of sisters and brothers. For me, my parents were a bag full of fun and trouble. I did as I liked, since nothing ever prevented either trouble or fun. I lived my life in a state of confusion. Tell me about your sisters."

"I threw them into the bushes," the old man said. "I handcuffed them."

"And how about your friends among the boys at school?"

"I always tried to sit in the last bench, behind the other boys. I imagined I had a machine gun and mowed them down. I shot them down in rows, bang, bang, bang."

"So," she said, "it was 'bang, bang, you're dead;' that must have been fun for you."

"Fun galore."

LOVE STORIES

"I remember," said the old woman, "how you did not let me stay in the same hotel with you."

"I wanted to be free," explained the old man. "I had lived in that city before I ever met you. It was my city."

"But every morning," she said, "you telephoned me. You seduced me over the telephone, me, your wife of many years. I was just another woman for you. I wore the mask of a stranger."

[19]

"What's wrong with seducing your wife over the telephone?" he asked. "I like to play. I turned you into a stranger to make you more seductive."

"But I myself love the well-known," sighed the old woman. "I am happy with continuity, with certainty. I liked the familiarity of you, the known lines of your face, your everyday ways. I did not want to be treated as a stranger."

"You should have felt flattered. I played each time with a new image of you and each time it was a breakthrough. The known is exhaustible. I looked for the unknown in you."

"But you wouldn't go along with me," she cried, "when I tried to find a way other than infidelity, a way wherein you would not always be running to other women and I to other men. I wanted it to be a circle that embraced you and your lover and me and mine, a circle of four, not a struggle of one against one. I wanted to enclose us, not divide us."

"To me, such a foursome is imprisonment. I wanted to escape to a secret and return to you."

"I remember," she said, "how you pretended you did not know you were caressing a woman friend who was sitting on one side of you, while I sat on the other."

"What is wrong with that?"

"Nothing, except that later you insisted with great intensity that you had never done such a thing, that you never would do such a thing in my presence. But I think you did it, knowing you did not want to know, trying to hide it from yourself, pretending you were ignorant of what you did. You were like the Nazis, who pretended innocence and at the same time enjoyed the terror caused by their double game. You had played on my naïveté so many times, but this time I saw through you."

"Naïveté," observed the old man, "is not innocence. Perhaps true innocence would have defeated the devil of the double game."

"Yes, but I fell from innocence, after so many years of abused naïveté."

DEMONS

"The rats follow the Pied Piper even into the black river," the old man said.

"You were my Pied Piper once," cried the old woman. "I did not follow you all the way." She added, "You have to know the tune, or you will be destroyed."

"What is your tune then?" he asked.

"Have a sense of direction; live with simplicity; keep your self-awareness; let your right hand know what your left hand is doing."

"That would be catastrophic," he exclaimed.

She continued, "A cool sheet at night; cool dreams, cool thinking."

"These last years of understanding," asked the old man, "to whom do we owe them?"

The old woman thought about this question. She could not answer it. She said, "All you need to understand is where you are going."

"I am going away from understanding," said he. "I am returning to the inexhaustible springs of the subterranean depths."

"The god Odin found his wisdom there," she replied. "He gave up one eye for wisdom. The man Goethe found his way there. An inscription reads: 'Drink and perish. If you survive, you do so at your own risk.' And it is true," she added, "you do not need the tune there—if you survive, you are the tune."

THROUGH THE LOOKING GLASS

There was my mother and there I was, leaning on the door, watching her sew on the machine. There I was, another time, giving her flowers. She looked pale and misused. There I was, five years old, refusing to give thanks for the birth of my younger brother. There I was, alone with her, for once without competition. I looked through the windowpane that separated me in time from the images of myself. I was sixteen now, and tall; my mother seemed tiny. I stood, looking down at her. She was talking. She said she was never bored with him. "Him" was my father and her husband. She said they laughed a lot together. He had a name for every one of his toes and could wiggle all of them. I thought about my toes. I could wiggle them all, too, but I had never given them names. She said, "After all, the one who comes first with me is my husband. Children are very nice, but. . . ." She called him "my man" in German.

I must have developed my mannish ways at that time. I would let my girl friends go ahead of me with a gesture—those earlier years, when I pretended to be a boy. My brothers and their friends would play Indians with me. I saw myself, twelve years old, being tortured as they chased me with spiders. (They could touch them. They were the masters, the ones my mother loved.) A few years later, I was fourteen or fifteen, playing Indians with the girls in my class. I was photographed, looking like a chief in my brother's pants, hating my father in youthful sincerity, because I wanted to be a man to my mother.

My first sense of physical love, the first sexual feelings after masturbation. There was the young, high-breasted woman who taught me the essentials of my body and my father's body, things my mother had never taught me. She also taught me about kisses and the varieties of physical delight. She made me aware of the difference between the man's germinal ways and the woman's sensual lips. (At that time, my childlike parts were still hairless.) Now, I saw myself more than twenty years later, a grown woman, being taught again. This time my teacher was a man who was like a father to me. He was sixteen years older and he washed my hair and body. He taught me that special sexual cleanliness. He used to say that the suicides in Monte Carlo stank, if they were ladies, but that if they were whores, they were clean and sweet-smelling. He gave me lessons in how to kiss and fully enjoy all kinds of stimulation. He showed me how delightful it was to watch a male organ become aroused and the sweetness of opening lips. He taught me that women were goddesses and men were gods.

There, behind the windowpane of my thoughts stood Dionysus-Poseidon, with his strong, wet, hairy limbs. Heinrich had a high forehead and a wide space between his thin eyebrows, which arched over melting brown eyes. Aroused, he smelled like heliotrope. I was sitting at his feet at one of our first social gatherings. At that time, it was fashionable to sit on the floor. His hand hung over the arm of a heavy leather chair. I opened my hand underneath his and collected the golden drops, which I imagined flowing from his fingers. We fell in love. I asked my husband to permit us to make love and he did. My lover made me grow up. He made me stop being afraid and taught me a new way to write poetry, to understand art. He talked to me about his personal philosophy, which was a whole world. He taught me to heed the subterranean streams uniting our bodies and souls. He cut my hair in an archaic Greek-goddess fashion. We were never married.

Now I was seeing the image of my first husband, the one who had to propose to me three times, and even then it was still wrong. I was a child-woman then, hiding my intellect. (This was before Heinrich had made me aware of my own dignity.) I pretended to be what my first husband wanted me to be, the body beautiful. He drew, painted, and worshiped me. For him, I was the little woman; he pampered, spoiled, and ruled. It was by walking through the door of my intellect that I left him. When I did, I deserted one of the most loving souls, with whom I could easily have spent a lifetime of good living, hard work, rough jokes, care, and affection. He might have become a great artist. After I left him, he still became a good teacher. He married a girl who bore a physical resemblance to me, but who didn't have my restless mind. His large, thirsty eyes would drink me in whenever our paths crossed. He would have taken me back any time.

Now I was seeing Paulus, the man with the golden mouth, who looked like a Riemenschneider carving in his earlier years. He had a body like a Gothic statue, lean, from the hungry years of World War I. His face was finely carved, with a well-shaped mouth over animallike teeth. He was the desperate child of the century, who dared to give word to dreams of disaster and hope, carrying on to an ecstatic "yes," in spite of his philosophy of the demonic, of Kairos. He preached the agony of death in war, instead of heroism. He knew about compassion and dared to ask for social justice. He called on ecstasy as the tremulous instigator of sacred action. He dared open "the doors of the deep" to the monsters of his convulsed wishes and unfulfilled desires. By boldly naming them and showing their faces, he coined a new philosophical-theological language. Courageously, he pushed the image of God beyond the concept of heaven. By dematerializing and depersonalizing Him, he threw the weight of sin and grace back upon the human soul. He said "yes" to his own being.

He was the magician of the mind, as my first husband was the magician of the eye, and my lover, the teacher of humanity.

I was eager to become a human being, but what set me on fire was the spirit and the mind. Heinrich was responsible for my becoming as human as I ever became. Paulus was the fulfillment of my cosmic-mindedness. We were both exposed to demons. I struggled against my id, which wanted to destroy my rational self-awareness. Perhaps my salvation was that I fought for a conscious, personal self, though I always felt in danger of becoming the matter on which another person's mind fed. I fought for survival as an independent center. My desire was to become my own constellation.

Paulus was a cosmic power. There was no danger of his becoming submerged. It was easy for him to call the demons by name. He transformed the terrifying thicket into the crystalline forests of his mental vision. We were tied together by our common ability to walk in those forests. Even though I could not call the demons as he did, I *knew* his name and he would be lost if I forgot to *call* his name. I was his shelter. He was never mine, because he could never protect. He was ecstasy and despair, with no discrimination. For him, everything was power and force. The seduction of women was not a matter of individual attraction. It was an act of submission to the power of the female. He transmuted his personal experience by shaping it into golden words meant for a world audience. He forsook life for the word. His knowledge of love was not personal. He dove into it and then formulated its cosmic aspects with words. Mother Earth gave Paulus the final power, that of transgressing life for the sake of the spirit. He was an eternally suffering, Christian saint.

A Japanese Zen master, sitting with him in earnest confrontation, once described him as "not one of the enlightened yet." He still made the distinction between "good" and "evil." The Zen master had banned good and evil in his world, acquiring physical immobility and perfect quietude. He listened with the inner ear and would not permit demons to enter his five orifices. He was not tortured by nightmarish dreams. He had found the dissolution of his "koan." Paulus lived in fear. His nervous body was tense; his desires many. His fingers would fiddle with a pebble from the beach, a silver coin, or a paper clip. He breathed unevenly and sighed heavily, an ever guiltridden Christian in distress. His was the *Temptation of Saint Antony* in Grunewald's altar, attacked by demons. His solution was to *suffer* the demons, take them into his being and describe them in words. He was the martyr of the mind. The Zen master talked to him about "austerity" of the mind. But out of the ecstatic shambles of Paulus's mind came his visions of the coming, his penetration of the present, his knowledge of the past, and his compassion and understanding. Only rarely, when watching the constant motion of the ocean waves, did he find the onemindedness of nonbeing. Occasionally he found it in terror, but never in quietude.

Compassion came to him during the First World War, when he participated in death on the battlefield as a minister tending the soldiers. There he experienced no hostility. He broke his nationalistic ties and became a citizen of the world. He met brothers of the mind in every country and transgressed every borderline of spirit and soul. He was always aware of the two sides of every question. The temple of the Zen master had a dragon painted on the ceiling. When he showed us in and Paulus saw the dragon, Paulus lay down before the dragon. The Zen master felt that was the proper thing for him to do.

At the time, I thought the dragon was a beautiful, powerful being, who made me feel strong and exuberant. I did not feel threatened by his power, I participated in it.

Finally, in his last days, Paulus was able to glimpse nonbeing. When he walked, a slim, white-haired wisp of a man now, over the lawn of his garden at the sea, Death watched him from the branches of every tree. Death silently enclosed him, whispering to him softly and pointing out a new borderline to be crossed. When he touched the leaves of his rhododendron bushes, still green and juicy, he knew he belonged to the other side. When he looked at the apples that had fallen from the tree, he knew they would soon be invisible to him. The knowledge of death came to him and he was able to weep about leaving this earth to enter nonbeing.

FROM THE INDIAN DIARY

The night after I saw the Dalai Lama, I dreamed somebody was trying to choke me. I must have been in the grip of my own elbow, having folded my arm too tightly around my neck. I awoke, having prayed in deep sorrow, "Our father, who art in heaven." I said it in German, *"Unser Vater, der Du bist im Himmel."* I had had fear before falling asleep. I awoke in the morning feeling different. I cried softly, feeling that much had been dissolved through my visitation with His Holiness, the Dalai Lama. Much later I remembered that the dream—being choked by my own elbow—must have been an echo and dissolution of the birth trauma, which might have had to do with my having been nearly strangled in my own umbilical cord at birth. . . .

Rothenburg

At 9:30 or 9:40 on a Sunday morning in May, while the church bells rang, my father cut the umbilical cord that had been strangling me. The first thing I felt was my father's hands. I had shot out of my mother's tummy so violently that I tore her insides. I was the third child, a boy and a girl ahead of me. There would be another sister and two more brothers. When I was five, I refused to pray, to give thanks after the birth of my second brother.

We lived on the upper floor of a small-breasted old town house that overlooked a spacious church plaza. We had two more rooms downstairs. Once I fell over the bannister. I landed in a perambulator parked at the foot of the stairway. I survived.

My father brought home a pine marten, which lived in the attic above our apartment. Playfully it rolled me down the stairs to our apartment—that was sheer fun.

When I toddled down the stairway, I came first to the outhouse, which served both floors, on the landing between them. It had a cold wooden toilet seat and the refuse was carried through a metal pipe directly into the ground. It was smelly. Under the stairs on the main floor was a shed for toys, bicycles, and old things, and beside it, the door to our living room, with its stuffed green armchairs fringed to hide the legs. Next to that was another bedroom.

If I opened the entrance door, which was heavy for me, I could descend a few stone steps to the cobblestone street at our doorstep, which opened out into the church plaza. To the right, the road led down to the river past our friends', who owned the grocery store where we could buy candy for a penny, where we might even get candy as a present without spending our pennies. I did not play beyond the big plaza.

Next to our house on the left was a small wooden door in the stone wall, through which I walked up a few steps into our own back yard. A tree grew there that my mother said she had planted, a penny tree. I'd better watch, she said, there might be pennies growing on it.

My elder sister and brother caught daddy longlegs. They tore off the legs and watched them ploughing about bodilessly, while the warty round bodies, which seemed to smell evil in my mouth, lay twitching. I was scared of spiders, crying bitterly on seeing one over my head on the ceiling of my sleeping corner. I called my father to remove it, which he did willingly. My older brother, and later his friends, took pleasure in teasing me because of my fear of spiders, running after me, shouting, "A spider! A spider!" which aroused such terror in me that I once ran off the road into a field of nettles and was badly stung.

Once in a while after my sister and brother must have entered school, I took my small wooden-framed blackboard and a silvery milk-crayon in a pencil box. I passed by our yard on the left, I passed by the big entrance of the next house, which was meant for carriages but was no longer used. I rang the bell, the door was opened, my shoes clattered on the spacious hall's stone floor inside. On the left was the entrance to a chamber where the sun shone through white lace curtains, breaking into rainbow colors through the many-faceted crystal paperweight on the desk.

Behind the desk, my friend, a slim, white-haired, retired old minister, received me graciously. I sat down on a child's chair, took out my utensils and wrote. He may even have taught me. The theme was the crystal, the sun, and peace—perhaps even a few letters of the alphabet.

My brother Roland, about four years older than I, called my sister and me to come, first one and then the other, into the bicycle shed under the stairway. She went first, while I peeked through a crack in the woodwork. Magarete, his girl friend, stood by my brother, who ordered my sister to pull up her skirts. Margarete spanked my sister's naked fanny with her hands while Roland stood by. My sister came out. I went in to be spanked.

My mother spanked me, too, after she found a hard brown ball on the floor, which I had somehow lost on the way to the toilet. I was also a bedwetter—an agreeable sensation when it happened, usually in my sleep during a dream, very disagreeable when I awoke and found myself cold and wet, especially since I stayed right there, trying to dry the wetness with my own bodily warmth.

Around the time of the christening party for the new baby, for whom I had refused to offer a prayer of thanksgiving for my mother, my father told me to get some of the especially good water, fresh from a nearby well. I broke the decanter on my way home, swinging it and accidentally knocking it against the church wall. I did not show up throughout the afternoon.

Before we came to Wippershain, my father took us first to Dresden, but we stayed there only one night. He was supposed to become the director of a boarding school in Dresden. He had made it clear that he would take over only if there were no lice in the buildings of the school he intended to buy. The director had sworn that the school was clean.

However, in the evening when my father made a tour with a lamp to look at the children sleeping in the different rooms of the main building, he found, as he put it, that every single child was sticking his fanny out from under the covers, and every fanny was covered with lice bites.

Unfortunately, my overcautious father had not signed the contract yet, so the next morning the director, who therefore had no obligation to him, simply asked him to leave the premises. My father would have been entitled to a considerable compensation had he signed the contract before he discovered the lice.

Instead of Dresden, we found ourselves in Kassel again. After a time, my father accepted a position in a small village of 498 people, two stores, one inn, one teacher, and one minister. My father became the minister. He would later become superintendent of schools of several parishes, where he would also preach.

My father was a hunter and a fisherman and a gardener. He was a woodcutter, too. He would take us into the woods a half hour's walk from our house. Then, when we were standing very still, he would call a deer for us, making bleating noises on a green leaf torn from a birch. The deer would come bounding through the trees. We could all see it. My father never killed while we were around.

My father became a farmer in Wippershain. We had pigs. One of them was called Fritz. We all knew Fritz laughed with pleasure when my father came to scrub him clean and sprinkle him with water. We cried when Fritz was slaughtered at our house, but later we enjoyed eating him anyway. My mother wanted to have turkeys as well as chickens. My father bought them for her. After the ugly little turkeys had popped out of their brown-flecked shells, he taught them to eat hard-boiled chicken eggs. Once in a while we had scrambled turkey eggs. The turkey roast tasted different from the roast goose we used to have at Christmas time.

My father bought a horse for our carriage. He let the small boys ride on it. He let it walk around the yard. It would put its head through our dining room window for its piece of sugar or carrot.

Every Sunday, and sometimes on weekdays, my father had to be a minister. He preached in the church next door. The farmers and their wives came to hear him. During Advent and for the Christmas Eve celebration, the church was lit by candles fastened to the benches with clothespinlike attachments carved of wood. The minister's family had their own stall behind a thin wooden lattice—to look through into the church. We had to go often. Sometimes I sat crying through the whole service; before me in the latticework a spider was weaving its web or catching a fly. My brother beside me did not kill it. He enjoyed my fear.

My father had funny names for all of his children, and for his wife. He called me "Eskimo" because of my slanted eyes, my high cheek bones, and my wide mouth. He said my mouth would stretch all around my head when I was happy—it was good the ears were there to stop it. He also called me "Glaucopis Athena," the owl-eyed Athena, because he thought I had such big owl eyes.

My mother was a foreigner. She came from America. She was not tall, she had black hair, her skin was slightly yellow. She liked to wear pretty housecoats. She had a seamstress who came to our house to sew for her and for us children. When we outgrew our old coats, we had new coats instead of the old ones let down, we had new dresses, new hats, and new shoes. My older sister had green shoes with a single strap that buttoned.

When one of my brothers had warts all over his body, my mother counted them. Then she took a silk thread and tied it in as many knots as she had counted warts. She went to the roof of the house when the moon was waning and threw the silk thread from the roof. She did not talk about it. The warts disappeared.

My mother had her own dream. When she dreamed of nursing a sickly child, there would be trouble.

My mother gave me a silk American flag to play with, blue and white and red, with many stars. It became one of my secret treasures. She said I was the daughter of an Indian chief and herself.

When she was sick, we had a Fräulein who spread so little butter on our sandwiches that we could scarcely wait for our mother to return. She spread a thick layer of butter on our sandwiches.

My mother had played the piano in America. My father had no piano for her. She did her finger exercises on a chair so as not to get out of practice. Later, her mother—my grandmother—gave her a grand piano. Then she played Beethoven and Mozart. I danced to the music behind her, in our parlor with the green-fringed chairs. I was sixteen years old then.

My mother's mother smelled of violets. She wore taffeta dresses and little hats trimmed with mauve flowers and tied with a silk ribbon. As a young girl she had left Kassel for New York because she could not marry the boy she loved. She was the daughter of a postmaster. The whole town called her the beautiful Louise from Kassel. Her husband-to-be first saw her in a courtyard in New York, where she was taking care of children. He, too, came from Germany. He married the *schöne Luischen,* and when she came back to her home town in Germany, after my grandfather had died, my father met my mother in Wilhelmshöhe. They were soon married.

My mother liked to read books. She locked her books in a glass cabinet, but she sometimes left it unlocked. When I was fourteen or fifteen, I read some of them—*Pan* by Knut Hamsun, Tolstoi, Wassermann's *Kaspar Hauser,* Zola, Ibsen, and many more.

Interlude

ᶳ

COMMENT WRITTEN AT SIXTEEN

My fear of spiders, which belonged from my earliest youth, led to most terrifying experiences. The mere word, spider, could frighten me into running as if chased by a ghost. I had the insane fear that I never could escape the monstrous warty beast, which in my fantasy grew into gigantic size. Even later, when my reason controlled my feelings, I could not rid myself of this fear. It seemed like Fate, approaching pitilessly, impossible to shun, a grizzly fate, sitting cunningly, steadfastly in the corner of the room, certain to be aroused in its own time, to make its way straight to me.

Such was the darkness that attacked me, a dangerous animal, before which I was helpless and paralyzed. Gray bats crouching in the deep crevice of my soul, flapping out on gray rainy days in ghostly ugliness. In this landscape of my soul belonged my experience with the tramp in the cemetery, which unlocked a door, showing me what until now I had only recognized as a terrifying black cave.

It was on an afternoon in early fall, when the tramp looking for work had been asked to clear out the refuse on the garbage heap of the new cemetery. He had remarked, when he came into the kitchen during lunch time, that somebody ought to come and take away, or look at, the nest with the baby mice he had unearthed. Naturally, I went and stood feet apart beside the dirty tramp, who knelt down beside me. Suddenly I felt his hand on my white drawers, and higher up on my stomach. He asked me whether one could not open the panties. I stood stiffly, my whole body tightened in a fearsome convulsion I had never before experienced. A frantic anxiety gripped me. I said no and left, forcing myself to go slowly at first, then racing, arriving at the house breathless. I hid in a dark corner until supper time, feeling again and again the same tense convulsion, which I would never lose. It cut with frightening sharpness, with harsh clarity through my fantasy world, which until then had had no such sensation.

Much later, as a grown woman, having borne a child, when my husband had gone traveling for a month and I had started painting again, I painted my own birth and many scenes from my childhood that I seemed to have forgotten until that time. I painted, too, in a somewhat hypnotic stupor, the scene that I wrote about when I was sixteen—myself standing beside the kneeling tramp, his hand between my legs, and I smiling broadly, the tramp having the face of my father.

STRANGE ENCOUNTERS

I met my father in a dream.
He is a little boy,
he is somewhat supercilious,
and very very spoiled.

He has three older sisters
who button his pants for him.
He is a show-off
and a tale-teller.

We are of one age, I sit at his side.
He dances around me, ignorant of fate.
He will beget me without knowing
that we have met before on an unborn star.

I met my mother in a dream.
She is but a little girl.
Her panties are longer than her skirts—
that was the fashion of the time.

She is quieter than her sisters,
looking at me with doe-eyes.
She feels I will be her child.
I feel she will become my mother.

At dream-hour we smile at each other,
walking arm-in-arm on friendly roads,
blooming at the same age,
filled with mutual affection.

"I am going to make you cry."
"You will hurt in time to come.
But nothing disturbs our dream-love.
We are twins from unborn stars.

Wippershain

From the first-floor window of our parish house, I looked out onto the garden where my father had planted tulips near the wire fence with the new door, which separated the garden from the old cemetery and the small village church with the plump, short tower. I walked through the cemetery with the two tombstones facing each other that were so old their inscriptions were unintelligible. Their tops were rounded and we children climbed on them, using them as horses in our game of "knight."

In the old cemetery grew one of my sacred objects, shared with no one: a red-and-white striped rose on a small rosebush. I never told the others about the laburnum tree, either. It was in the new cemetery beyond a neglected-looking door of thin boards. Nor did I tell them about the silken bark of the birch tree, which I peeled off the trunk, carried home, and hid under my silk American flag, after writing mysterious signs on it. When the laburnum tree was in bloom, I climbed into it. From there, hidden from the world, I could look down on the wax palms and wax leaves of discarded wreaths the caretaker had thrown on the garbage heap. I took a few of those home, too.

My most secret place was in our yard close to the old cemetery, in the "little wood," an assembly of twelve odd young pines with long silky threadlike needles. I collected coal cinders from the refuse heap in the yard and large and small slag stones—blue and shimmering with molten glass in all sorts of baroque convolutions, shiny, black warty toad-skin features, dark blue glossy frog eyes. With these

I built a castle with a moat and a sacrificial altar, adding a shiny piece of broken blue glass for the priest and smaller, glittering cinders and stones for the knights, the people, and the king. Here I reenacted the events of a tale of great significance to me.

I had taken a book from my older brother, reading it secretly, locked in my room where no one could reach me, before returning it, to the howls of my brother and the two young boarders, who had tried to keep it as their secret. The book's title was *The Grandson of the Kings*. The hero, who does not know he is the grandson of the king, is taken prisoner by Indians, who transport him to their sacrificial altar in the pyramidal temple in the jungle of Guatemala. There, he is restrained by powerful hands while the priest opens his shirt, lifting a knife to thrust it into the prisoner's heart. The priest's hand is stayed when he sees, tattooed on the prisoner's chest, the sign of the kings. The hero is not killed. Instead, he becomes the leader of his people, the last king with the sign.

When I was about sixteen, a spiritualist who had studied the East Indian scriptures told my family that he had seen the sign on me. I never doubted it.

When I played with the boys, we went to the lake further away from home, reached by a shortcut through the fields. There, hiding behind the overhanging grassy border, we caught salamanders as they swam into the shallow water. I once caught a five-legged salamander. It frightened us and we killed it on a flat stone, smashing it with another stone. After seeing its blood, we must have been overwhelmed by the lust to kill. We caught and killed many of the male salamanders with their proud crests.

Another common playground was "the trench," an assembly of rocks that we had collected and arranged to resemble a wall of defense. It lay on a strip between two acres belonging to us, shaded by a black thorn bush near the top of a slope. To attack us, the enemy had to come from below, in full view. We smoked there, too; my brother wheedled me into stealing the cigar ends my father kept in a box, to smoke later in his pipe. They deserted me often. I would run after them, howling with fury.

A boy came from the city, the son of friends of my parents. He kissed me in the dark hallway, before we went in to supper. My brother and the two boarders invited him to play Indians. They tied me to a tree and shot spears and arrows at me. I howled. They ran away. The city boy turned back and untied me before he followed the others. I waited for him the next morning in the courtyard sunshine, lying on the roof of our carriage beneath the dining-room window. I heard my mother say to his mother, "She seems to be in love with him." I could not be found when it came to saying good-bye. I hid in a tent in our back orchard until the crunch of the wheels and the clattering of the hooves disappeared into the distance.

Once I got genuinely lost, causing my parents some anxiety. I was allowed to walk out of the village to meet my oldest brother, who was then in a boarding school and came home for weekends. When the May bugs were swarming in the trees through a tender night, I got carried away running after them. I forgot where I was, in the ecstasy of celebrating spring with the May bugs.

When the weather was bad, I played with Otto. Otto was a doll that had lost its hair. I created a wig for him, stuffing the curly, hairy roots of an onion plant into the gaping hole of his head. I turned him into a sailor, making a cardboard ship, sewing and hacking away with scissors and knife, building sails, a rudder, and an oar. My father liked it.

On rainy days we played Robinson Crusoe in the big room among the benches for the village kids who came for instruction before confirmation. We made a stage with the benches, from which we recited poems—"The Fisher," "The Lorelei," "Erlkönig," and other ballads —acting them out. I had found the illustrated works of Goethe. I read about Amor and Psyche, Orestes and Pylades. At night, before going to sleep, I donned towels arranged in a fancy way, pretending to be one of the persons illustrated, a prisoner, hands tied together at my back, with a delicious feeling of surrender.

I read avidly. My father tried to constrain me to fifty pages an evening. When he discovered me at my hundredth page, I clowned, saying, "I will read nothing tomorrow." My father gave us a periodical that described the biblical stories in children's language. My uncle and aunt in Berlin sent me the first biographies of Botticelli, Rafael, Michelangelo, Andrea del Sarto, and many others. I read little of the text, but studied the reproductions. I started drawing in Botticelli's style, exploring the nude body underneath the folds of gowns—girls, for the most part.

In winter we raced down the steep hills of nearby meadows on

[39]

a home-made wooden sled. The road to Hersfeld was so drifted over with snow that the men from our village who worked there and had to get through piled up snow walls so high that a horse and carriage disappeared between them.

I must have been twelve when we left Wippershain for Gelsenkirchen in Westfalen.

Wilhelmshöhe

Wilhelmshöhe was grandmother and grandfather—and no parents, lake frogs, green tree frogs hopping in the streets after a rain, picking up chestnuts in the morning on the slopes of the park of the emperor, Heck (short for Hector), the bowlegged yellow-haired dog with the beautiful eyes and the long dangling ears, frog-training in the pergola near the entrance of the villa, which belonged to my grandparents.

Wilhelmshöhe meant the building honoring Hercules with a statue of the hero on top, which we called "The Hercules," water streaming down the multitudinous wide steps, and the big fountain at the foot, which would suddenly gush up, spraying rainbow-colored water blown by the wind. If you had not been clever, you were caught in the spray.

Wilhelmshöhe was the Palm bath, where I once nearly drowned trying to swim at the deep end. Wilhelmshöhe was the "heath" before the door of my grandmother's apartment, on the topmost floor directly under the roof, where I tortured a lizard with a grass palm, where I played with my younger brothers, sewed all sorts of clothes for their bears—called the "Wooks"—and told them stories I invented of dwarfs and fairies, bears and adventures.

Wilhelmshöhe was reading about the hunchback girl who was poor and miserable, who was adopted by a family of children without parents, who put their house in order, washing and mending the dirty bed linen, cleaned, and cooked the children's meals. The story "Pick Up What God Puts Before Your Door" made me eager, for the first time in my .childhood, to participate, instead of trying to

[41]

butt in, raving, and being offended. I must have been almost twelve by then.

Wilhelmshöhe was my father's dream of the bull that chased him around a tiny house in the park where the chestnuts grew. It seemed to have been a real story. He ran into the house, banged the door shut, and was saved.

As to the frogs, we children collected them after a rain on the downhill road to the "Lac," the artificial lake in the emperor's park. We took them home to the pergola and put them on the wet wooden table. We watched my oldest brother train them to hop over sticks on the table. We were going to make a circus, but when the sun shone again we all ran off in different directions, playing new games.

As to Heck, the lazy, tottering old dog was my friend. He was squashy and furry and soft all over. I remember sitting on him, rubbing my inner thighs in his fur with great pleasure, while my aunt watched with a quizzical expression. I stopped, though it had felt delicious. I must have been five at the time.

When my grandfather died, my grandmother moved to the apartment on the heath. She liked to comb my hair with a very narrow comb, weaving it into tiny braids.

I had seen my grandfather after his death, though the grown-ups had forbidden it. I sneaked into the room where he was laid out. He looked peaceful and unchanged. I liked him even then. I used to sit on his lap. He would take my finger, guiding it from his forehead and nose down to his yellowish, stained beard (unless my grandmother had washed it). When my finger arrived at his mouth, he would snap noisily and I would draw back, screeching in delighted terror. Or he played Hop Hop Rider, putting me on his knee before his mountainous stomach, throwing me up with an unexpected shrug, holding me firmly with his hands. He always sat in the same armchair, close to a window.

Wilhelmshöhe was the electric tram, which ended at my grandparents' villa. There it turned around, moved forward slightly, and stopped for ten minutes before going downhill again to Kassel. We kids were permitted to ride down in the car to the official stop. The driver and the ticket seller gave us green and pink stubs from the tickets they sold to the passengers. They were treasures.

When I was about fourteen, my Wilhelmshöhe widened out into Kassel. We took the tram down the hill to the museum, where I saw my first Rembrandt—Saskia, all in red, and "Rest on the Flight into Egypt," with the drawn red curtain. There was a Rubens—a voluptuous goddess crowning a voluptuous hero—and there were the marble bath inscribed to Napoleon, a marble frieze, and lush bathtubs. In one of my dreams of escape I took flight to Kassel.

Gelsenkirchen

Gelsenkirchen—I watched our furniture being carried from the van through a shaded street. The house seemed heavy, the air dark. Beside my elder brother and sister and me, stood a boy and girl we had just met. The girl's hair was hanging loose with a ribbon fastened on top in a bow. They asked in a conspiratorial whisper, "Are you Protestant or Catholic or Jewish?" I did not know. My sister or brother answered something. The new friends were Jewish.

My father, who had been supervising several school districts in and around Wippershain, had been appointed to establish new school districts here. We soon moved from the dark house into a new, light apartment on the upper floors of a modern building. The nursery wallpaper had a "Struwelpeter" design. We ate in the vestibule. A long, narrow passage led from it to the bedrooms. My parents' bedroom and the living room were separate, to the right of the entrance. My younger brothers ran down the hall naked, abundantly happy, their small penises flying.

I daydreamed in endless repetition two stories I had read. One was about a murderer, a retarded man (with reddish beard) who had raped and killed a child. He had received his punishment and served his term. He returned to the village where he had grown up and had committed the rape. He became the devoted pet of the village kids. The grown-ups seemed to have no fear that he would repeat his crime. Everybody trusted him more than any man living in the village.

The other story was about a lover who had killed his beloved, not because he hated her, but because he wanted to possess her more than union could have accomplished. I became the victim and the aggressor of the story by turns, always strangling with my hands, or being strangled by pressing, dark fingers around my neck, pressing and pressing unto final annihilation. The strangling of the umbilical cord at my birth had turned into a nightmare.

Rika, our nanny, took the younger kids and me on a daily walk. She woke us in the morning, braided our hair, washed our faces and hands, tied our shoelaces, put my dress over my head, buttoned it in the back. I stood like a stone, unwilling to cooperate, emitting a shriek when I felt the comb hit a snarl in my hair. Rika gave us breakfast, fed us supper, put us to bed. We had a second maid, Minna, the cook and housekeeper, who was older. She had just finished school; she had heavy breasts. I wondered at her white skin. In my book, servants were made of wood.

One Sunday, Rika took me to her parents' house in the foundry region. We took a tram. It must have been an hour's ride. Things grew blacker and blacker around us—rows of dirty red-brick houses, each with steps and a bench before its entrance and a few feet of black lawn between it and the street; in back, a chicken coop and pig stall. I ate *Streusselkuchen*. On the way home I saw the sky reddened by burning furnaces, towers of fire. I gasped.

My mother fell ill. The doctor recommended that she take the waters at Bad Homburg. My father had to stay with his work. The two maids took care of us. We did not see much of my father. One day after school I ran to find Rika. She had said, "Do not go into my room." I went anyway. I found my father lying on her bed in dirty clothes, with a swollen face, snoring. I closed the door and fled. Rika must have taken him in when he came home the night before, dead drunk. It was my first acquaintance with my father's weakness.

Hamm in Westfalen

The three-story house had been divided to accommodate two families. We had the two upper floors, which we reached by a broad wooden stairway with heavy banisters. It was on a fashionable avenue lined with three rows of old linden trees, leading to the park. There, on wide lawns, stood groups of red-leafed beeches among the green oaks. Beyond the park, the River Lippe curved. Behind our house, an open field was crossed by a small, dirty brook in which we caught polliwogs and the "man-eating larvae" of the dragonfly. Unaware of their ferocity, I put them in my new aquarium. I found my fish eaten, bits of their bloody corpses floating in the reddened water.

On the borders of the Lippe, exploring, my younger brothers and I found blue and white and red pebbles, bits of mica, which could be separated into transparent panes simulating glass. Crystals glittered in some of the dull rocks.

I noticed my mother looking tired and depressed. Her face looked yellowish-brown. She sat at her sewing machine. After Minna had left she had so much more to do. I ran out into the fields and picked a bunch of grasses and wildflowers for her.

I felt angry with my father, who had betrayed me. My older sister had complained about me. I must have been very nasty to her. My father insisted that I tell her I was sorry, which I did with malice in my heart. After my apology, I ran upstairs to our bedroom. From my drawer, I took my most prized possession, a children's sewing machine my older sister had given me, which I kept wrapped in the silk flag of the United States that my mother had given me.

[47]

Crying and moaning with fury and sorrow, I tore and bent the machine to pieces in revenge for my father's treachery and my sister's tattling.

I entered a private school for girls—daughters of lawyers, teachers, and business people. Often in the morning on my way to school, I met a husky boy, the son of a judge. I blushed deeply, passing him on the other side of the street.

I liked two teachers especially. One was my French teacher, who wore a pince-nez and had untidy hair and an obsession with French grammar. She drove us hard. There is a story that I went to her with two other goodie-goodie girls to confess that we had all cheated on some test. Miraculously, it had no other consequences than a furious willingness to learn and to be honest and in her favor.

The other teacher was a tall, beautiful woman with hair covering her ears in black wings. She always wore black. Her story was that she had lost her betrothed in a duel. She greeted every child by bending her head and swaying her body to the hips in a graceful gesture. She taught history and German. I wrote long essays in both subjects, which were marked A, except for atrocious handwriting. She gave me foreign stamps. Once she offended me by being too strict in some small matter. I did not forgive her until she came to me, put her arm around my shoulders, and gave me some stamps.

Once a week I went to a parish to be prepared for my confirmation. I had to go to the Sunday service to hear the minister's superintendent preach. I had become very antichurch. A few years earlier, on a Good Friday, I had hidden in my father's study under his desk on a fur rug, crying bitterly as I read the story of the crucifixion, suffering it. Now I was in rebellion against the Bible texts the minister had us learn by heart. I did not understand them, refused to have them explained to me, refused to even try to understand them. I did not want to hear the minister preach. Since I was forced to go to church, I sat and counted the flakes of paint drifting down from the high Gothic ceiling onto the heads of the congregation.

I resented the minister's habit of overlooking the mistakes of the children from the private school and being sour with the students from the public school. The air smelled sweaty. We sat on hard benches. I chose as my companion in receiving the communion an ugly, unpleasant-looking child with a long, red, dripping nose. Her deep brown eyes were the eyes of a gazelle. I never participated in the Lord's Supper again. My confirmation verse was Colossians 2: 6 and 7, "As you have accepted Jesus Christ, walk with him, be rooted and lifted in him and firm in the faith you have been taught and be in your faith abundantly grateful."

I took sick after the confirmation. My parents suspected pneumonia. The doctor tried to check my lungs, telling me to take off my undershirt. I cried hysterically. He gave up. It was summer and I sat in the pergola in the back yard. I painted with water colors and wrote stories. One water color was called "The Domestic Tyrant," and another one was of a water nymph struggling in the nets of two dwarf fishermen. I painted a bunny-fairy, a young lady in an old-fashioned lilac crinoline, sitting in our blooming lilac tree, two immense bunny ears sprouting out of her head.

Liseolotte, beautiful, tall, graceful, and full-bosomed, with delicate ankles and wrists, was my friend. Her dark brown hair hung loose around her face with its soft brown eyes and soft-lipped mouth. She was deeply melancholic and wildly flirtatious. Her party dresses were flimsy elegance; she wore patent-leather shoes. She walked for hours with me on thin soles, confiding that she enjoyed the pain the frail shoes on stony roads caused her. I could not yet understand her being flirtatious. Patent-leather party shoes would have been unthinkable for me. I was petrified at the sight of the male, or clumsily wild, treating him as I would have treated a younger brother.

Liseolotte and I were disturbed by our growing femaleness —developing breasts and broadening hips. When I felt for the first time my hips changing from the slenderness of childhood, I was intensely frightened. I thought that babies might come from those growing, fleshy cushions. I confided to Liseolotte my question of where children came from. She said hesitantly that she believed they came out of the womb of the mother. I countered her statement with the belief that they might come out of eggs, but never directly from their mother's womb. Liseolotte was silent. We both felt our bodies painful. We walked along the old town wall. We stood trembling in the dusk of her room, embracing, feeling each other from breast to knee. She loved me as a trembling maiden loves her young knight, who knew so much less about the world of the soul, about male and female. She exchanged stories with me—fairy tales; she gave me tiny drawings of young women in fluttering clothes or young men in knights' armor. I gave her my stories about two children who drown in the lake at sunset, trying to walk across the sun's golden image in the water, to reach their heaven. Liseolotte's mother did not like me. I excited her daughter toward the romantic, the abnormal. She could not know that I was also a ruthless ball player and good at hide-and-seek.

We wrote long letters after I departed. Liseolotte got married; the letters ceased. I visited her many years later. She was living in a village as the wife of a schoolteacher, who did not like my visit. It excited her too much. Liseolotte must have had troubles with her glands. Her body was abnormally large. She cried when she talked to me. She still talked about Elaine, her favorite maiden from the story of King Arthur. In her ungainly body, the memory of the fairy tales we had confided to each other while we were Botticelli-like, fluttering young girls, still persisted. I found myself bewildered and saddened in her presence. She was still Elaine the beautiful, waiting for her lover (having borne children to her schoolteacher husband on the side). She knew nothing about her husband or her children. They knew nothing about Liseolotte, except her inability to live. She accompanied me to the bus wrapped in a woolen shawl. She had no coat. She wept. I left.

Hedwig had coarse yellow hair, a coarse pink skin, white eyelashes and eyebrows. She had broad ankles and heavy legs. She was sturdy. Her brother was dark, curly-haired, and tall. He once looked at me down his nose, attempting to pull me onto his lap, an enterprise in which I was woodenly unresponsive. Hedwig's mother was coarse-skinned, coarse-haired, with white eyebrows and eyelashes. The father did not exist.

Hedwig's mother invited me to come with them to the coffee garden in the park, not far from the avenue where we lived. When I arrived at their home at the appointed hour, I found Hedwig's mother combing her daughter's long hair with an exceedingly dirty, broken comb. She wore a flowery dress.

In the coffee garden we all sat down at a table near the orchestra, which was playing popular music at intervals. Among the small group of players was a short, foreign-looking man with a Roman profile, as Hedwig's mother explained to me, and curly hair. He played the cello. He played two solos, Italian melodies, perhaps "Santa Lucia" and another one equally popular. Hedwig was swooning. The vibrations of the dark sound, the humming and grumbling, the pleasant growl of the instrument sank into me. The foreign face bent over the cello seemed exquisite. Hedwig and I walked around during the intermission, while the cellist moved about animatedly, making the wide gestures with his hands and arms that seemed to us children from the north so enchantingly free.

[50]

Annie sat at a table next to us with a lady in black. She introduced herself during intermission. She must have watched our fascination with the orchestra. She introduced the cellist to us. I now know that she was dressed with expensive simplicity. Her eyebrows were sickle moons on a high forehead over gray eyes, her light hair piled under an expensive yellow straw hat with a black velvet ribbon. She invited me to her aunt's house, where she was visiting, and I went for a short time. We exchanged poetry, she encouraged me to write to her. I confided in her without hesitation. My timidity was gone, as were any suspicions. I submitted trustingly and unquestioningly. She was the dream come true; I was hers.

It was my first visit alone with people who were not friends of my parents. Annie lived in an old patrician home with heavy furniture and gleaming silver tableware on the credenza, dark oil portraits, green plants in windows with lacy curtains and heavy drapes. She led me upstairs to her room, a simple, elegant studio with a desk, two beds, several windows overlooking the river, hills, and the town garden.

It was Pentecost. Annie had two brothers, one of whom was continuing in his father's business, the other a glamorous poet, a student who roamed the university. Annie was invited to the social activities of the fraternities. She told me about dances she attended. We would go together on an outing on Sunday. She showed me the red rose she was painting in oils on a white velvet background for one of her friends. We slept together in her room, our two beds side by side. She had a tub brought up to her room filled with warm water. I scrubbed myself, hesitating when I found her staying on and watching me.

In the evening she took off my nightgown, drew me gently into her bed, kissed me, and told me about the secrets of physical love. She put my lips to her lips, she taught me to kiss not only with my awkwardly responding lips, but deep, and still deeper. She taught me to touch her private parts, she made me feel the wonder of searching fingers and hands pressing into my own parts. She drew my face gently between her opening legs, teaching me the kiss of intimacy into the salty depths of her innermost flesh. She told me about the male seed and the female egg, about intrusion, growth, and birth. I found myself responding to her night-long caresses, until exhaustion made me fall asleep.

When I returned home after my ten-day visit, I was a different person. I wrote her often. She answered often, in the beginning.

I sent her poems, she sent me love poems written to her men. Then she did not write for a long time. She had gone to Italy, trying to escape with her lover. Another friend and her brother brought her back. A duel was fought for her. She was betrothed to the man who had fought the duel, abandoning or having been abandoned by her former lover. Word finally came that she had committed suicide. First the black-rimmed announcement, then a gentle letter from her mother, and lastly a letter from the glamorous brother, the only one who knew about Annie and myself. He wrote that despair had gripped her when she tried to destroy the love letters of her lover with whom she had fled to Italy, reading them one by one. She had taken sleeping pills.

Annie had given me physical knowledge, but I kept her in my world of fairy tales. Nothing of my newly gained knowledge filtered into my daily life with my family or at school. I seemed to have locked the experience away in a waterproof and soundproof compartment of my own subterranean world. I was not yet ready. When one of my aunts who was visiting us asked me cunningly whether I knew where babies came from, she received a bland face and no answer. It was she who had pointed out to my mother that, in one of my newest fairy tales, I had reproduced parts of old tales as my own. I had not been conscious of it. I was fifteen years old.

Postlude

ANNIE

Walking restless over the grounds
as night circles by,

walking away from the mound
where my dead love lies,

shivering through hours—
no place to cry.

My love in her coffin
sings a lullaby.

OUR FLAGRANT DESIRE TO LIVE

Our flagrant desire to live
Knowing about Death—
Have we not become possessed
To celebrate the feast of life,

A terse and greedy beast
Holding Death at bay,
Forfeiting heaven's joys
For ecstasies of flesh?

YOUTH

Prelude

TO WILHELM E.

My eyes unlocked the doors of love for you,
Long hours waiting.

My lips reshaped my new-taught smile for you,
Come you tomorrow?

How many days have followed many nights
In timid craving?

You always passed me by in any light
And I must sorrow.

THE DIARY OF A WITCH (1929)

All day long I've lain beside the sea. Jellyfish, drifted near the edge, are rotting in the sand. The waxing moon brightens the evening. I am lying in the sand, smoking a cigarette and staring into the moon. It floats above the sea, descending slowly; the sand sends up sparks, then goes dark again, as the gentle waves recede, glittering in the path of the moon.

A kind of paralysis overcomes me, and my eyesight is unnaturally acute; the sea sends a red glow far into the sky; the air becomes watery, greenish, forms waves, washes around me as the ocean does when I swim in it. The moon-bowl clicks open, a wide black ribbon emerges from it, the two halves of the bowl fit themselves back together. The black ribbon comes floating toward me, it parts the fog, paddles toward me with huge, curving strokes, floats in front of me, half shadow, half shape: a Negro with his feet and legs swathed in veils up to the middle of his body. In a whisper he asks for my command. I don't know when I've called him. I had been staring into the moon and wishing for power over the body and the life of a man. I say quickly, "I want him." The Negro emerges more distinctly from the swaying veils. "For time and eternity?" he asks in a whisper. I hesitate. I search for a different way to formulate it, cannot find one. At last I declare with great resolve, "For time and eternity." The Negro disappears, I lie still; he reappears, howling with laughter and grimacing hideously. He throws up his arms and vanishes into the darkness.

I am lying beside the sea. I feel my breath, the breath of wind and waves. Inexplicable things seep into me with the sifting sand, which I can no longer get out of my clothes, my hair. Inexplicable things come out of me; I observe myself, splitting up, dividing into two or three sections.

I walk along the beach; algae and stones form a dark rim along the ocean, showing how high the water reached yesterday. Sand makes grinding sounds beneath my feet, it is warm, there is no wind. Laughter drifts from the beach chairs. I walk to the next bay, lie down and stare into the moon. It is veiled, black clouds move around it, slowly covering it. A part of the sky is still free, the big dipper shines, shooting stars sink from air to air. Along the horizon, sky and water mingle in that strange way that instantly makes me feel beside myself. I lie still and want to transform myself, my breath has the rhythm of the waves pounding the beach evenly with hollow sounds, but I am not transformed. Instead, my body slowly becomes illuminated from within, it becomes milkily translucent, I am looking into a gentle cave with rising and falling tides. In my right breast I see a moonstone that makes my body radiantly transparent. I try to disperse myself, but am reassembled; a voice within me whispers, "The Negro shall bring him here." I feel I can command the Negro; the stone gives me the power—the same power bestowed by the moon. . . .

The moon floats above the ocean, framed in clouds. To avoid the strong wind, I sink into a beach chair. I see a white kerchief come fluttering out of my mouth; it spreads, takes on the shape of a moving cloud and flies against the wind. I see it float away, then the rhythm of the waves embraces me, my consciousness slips into the moon-kerchief. I feel the red smoke coming, it is a delicate shimmer in the air but I cannot guess its meaning. I float directly above the ground just high enough so that I do not mingle with the earth fragrances, and I wait for a long time, immobile in the ice-cold air. A furious wind compresses my veil kerchief, wrings it, hurls it upward in rags; I want to be divided into atoms; a pale shimmer—the moonstone's light—reaches me; I spread myself and whisper into myself, "The Negro must obey me." The Negro appears, emerging from grotesque cloud formations. I begin to fly, I see the luminous smoke I had lost, I am not sucked in, I make myself light, I penetrate solid objects, sink down into a room. The moon looks in through the open window.

"See the moon," says a voice, and another, a male voice, answers. Sound of kisses; I hover above a bed. The two people are naked. It is he and a woman. I see only her face, thrown back, her black hair falls away from her forehead, forms a dark puddle on the silken pillow. She is in ecstasy, she sighs convulsively, her small hands press into the man's back. He buries his face in her throat, covers her body; I feel his body tremble in spasm and I know that release is near. I sink down through him as finely dispersed dust, I sink into her, I fill her entirely; over her face I place the mask of my own features. I surround her womb with my own breathlike, veillike substance, and I feel him pour himself into me and am intoxicated. The woman makes strangling sounds beneath my mask. I look at him with my eyes; my hair, my light hair, is spread over her black hair. I see rosy birds fly out of his mouth, then I collapse, dissolve. With my last bit of strength I command, "Carry me home." I dream that the Negro is taking me into his arms. Cradled in his arms I fly over smoking cities, over the open sea; he smiles at me and whispers: do you still have the moonstone? I answer, Yes. I fall asleep and waken on the beach, feeling deeply perturbed. My first thought is for the moonstone. I look into myself; the moonstone continues to glow undiminished within me; it seems to have become larger, more solid. I get up, the moon has set, I have been out too long. Numbed, reeling, I reach my room and sleep for a long time. When I wake up, the sun is high in the sky.

Neukölln

Rixdorf, a workers' suburb of Berlin, had had its name changed to
Neukölln. It had acquired a reputation for being slovenly. My father,
together with another superintendent of schools, had been assigned
by the government to organize the district's school. We rented a
big apartment on an upper floor of a large old house on the main
thoroughfare. In front, overlooking the street, were the spacious
dining room, the parlor, and the study. My parents' bedroom down
the hall was sandwiched between my younger brothers' room and
the room I shared with my older sister. We slept together.

I completed my last year of high school in a private institution
in Neukölln. I remember there a pleasant, dark and bosomy teacher
laughing merrily with the whole class when she called me to the
blackboard to solve some problem in mathematics that was a mystery
to me. I clowned my way through the new surroundings, not minding
being laughed at and getting along rather well with my new friends.

When I had finished school, my parents agreed to let me study
art but not, as I had hoped, at the academy. They insisted on a
school that would give me a teaching degree. When my father and
I went with my drawings—mostly illustrations of my stories—to see
the director of the King's School of Art, the director decided I would
have to prepare for entrance by attending a private course in drawing
from nature, which in this case meant drawing pots and flowers.
Moreover, I would have to attend the first-year course twice, which
was merely a preparation for the ensuing three-year course. I was
too young.

In retrospect, it seems strange that my parents agreed to the arrangement. For six months I went to a private studio with pencil and eraser.

At home I drew illustrations for my stories. I took myself for a model, trying to get the perspective of my face in full view looking up.

I had become critical of my father. Feeling that he restricted my younger brothers, I made myself their protector and defender. When he came home drunk, my father could be querulous and I enraged him with my criticism, usually over the dinner table at night, where he believed children should speak only when spoken to. Once he ordered me out of the house. When I persisted in taking him seriously, he finally had to ask me to stay. On another occasion, I helped my mother quiet him down.

His worst drinking bout was during the celebration of the emperor's birthday, which included a big dinner at the town hall. I leaned out of the living-room window, waiting for him to come in sight—tall, red-haired, swaying. When he did, we children vanished into our bedrooms, leaving my mother with him.

Sleeping beside their bedroom for the first time in our childhood, my sister and I heard their lovemaking. If he came home and my mother refused to cooperate, he could get insensibly furious.

Very late one night we heard my mother threatening to call the police. I banged at the door connecting our bedrooms. My father grew more enraged at that, and I could hear him trying to come after me. Finally there was silence; my mother came into our room trembling, with an ashen face. He had fallen asleep. She told me to leave for school at once and to return home late. It was a chilly prespring dawn. I walked to school through the Tiergarten, Berlin's famous park near Unter den Linden, passing the Spree on my way to Alexanderplatz, rejecting with a touch of contempt the thought of suicide. By the time I went home in the late afternoon, it was dark. My sisters and brothers were huddled together. The maids fed us supper. My parents had left on a trip. On their return a few days later, there was no mention of the incident. I don't know if my father even remembered it.

On another night my mother opened the door between our bedrooms to announce she would sue for divorce. She then went into the living room where she sank down on the roomy old sofa as if faint. When my father embraced her lovingly, she revived. Divorce was not mentioned again.

[62]

Despite all this, the family had glorious times together. My father loved his brood and adored his tiny wife. My brother Hellmuth, in his early teens, used to lift her in his arms to prove his strength and affection. During the gay times we would call my mother "Husch'chen," that is, "Little Hush-Hush."

We had big, festive Sunday dinners with huge roasts of beef, veal, or game, of goose or chicken. My mother's foot would be on my father's knee under the table. There were wine, luscious desserts, and gay moods. My father brought home baskets full of fruit—strawberries, peaches, apples, cherries. For Christmas he bought the tallest tree that would stand in the high-ceilinged living room. He decorated it with beeswax candles, which breathed the sweetest, golden summer-afternoon honeyed fragrance. On the wide-spanned branches he hung chocolate rings sprinkled with colored grains of sugar, rings of tasty white-and-brown striped cake, golden stars, and silver strands. It was a tree big enough for our dreams.

In one of her confiding comments, my mother recited to me a poem that she felt expressed her husband in his happy moods. Each verse ended with the refrain, "The happiness-bearing friend returns to the city." She felt he was the center of joy and pleasure wherever she went with him. He shone with a lust for life, whereas she was somewhat retiring and found it difficult to show her emotions.

ART SCHOOL

I started art school in 1911, having completed the preliminary courses. I lived at home, but I came under the influence of young men and women who worked and played together, of teachers, of the city—which opened up to me—and of museums, private galleries, theaters, and new books, none of which my parents could control. I received a monthly allowance. Nobody bothered to inquire how I spent what remained after my initial expenses for food and train fare and art materials had been paid out. Any larger needs were to be taken care of with additional money. My parents were not particularly careful with money—they were rather pleasantly sloppy. My father was downright irresponsible when he was under the weather. My mother would try to get him to pay household expenses—maids, children, schools, and so forth—and keep her own money for extracurricular affairs. She would sometimes say with a sigh, "Now I will have to sell another bond," which meant for the family that peace was restored after a spending spree. We were not supposed to talk, or know, about money. In later years, I used to say to Paulus, "Life does not have to be bothersome, if you can throw in a hundred marks to balance every month's miscalculations," which seemed to be my way of handling finances.

I ate badly, of course, and bought books and theater tickets.

The art school was in the greasy center of the city of Berlin. It was more an old barn than it was a school, with ugly dirty gray classrooms and shabby benches, chairs, and easels for our drawing boards. From the school's entrance, a wide stairway with iron banisters swung not ungracefully to the upper floors. Walking with the crowd of students up and down those steps reminded me of the paintings of Schlemmer's young men and women on a stairway. But his painting was gayer.

We had special classrooms for history of art, a room with individual blackboards where we learned how to draw, and demonstration rooms in which to practice geometry, painting, and drawing. On the uppermost floor was the cafeteria. There, even during the war, one could buy a concoction of chocolate to drink with a soggy square of rum-flavored cake.

Classes would be partly mixed during the war, when men and women generally worked together. The students ranged in age from seventeen years up. I was only fifteen.

At the end of my student years I bought photographs of all my teachers so as never to forget how hideous they all looked—and perhaps not only to me. There was one interesting sardonic face, the teacher of the artcraft course.

Another young teacher, who taught us lettering, held our attention. We tried to invent script for applied art with pens of all sorts and ink of all colors, developing decorations out of pen strokes. One of our assignments was to design a calendar. I took the opportunity to draw my youngest brother in the nude. It was not among the three best in the class. Later I copied my own poems in script on parchment paper for my friends. Still later, under Heinrich's influence (a man who was to mean much to me), I developed my own handwriting in a somewhat stylized script.

The professor of art history aroused our enthusiasm for the Renaissance. One of our tasks was to select a favorite painting in a museum and draw it from memory, filling in the colors. It taught me to inspect the surface of a painting inch by inch. Slowly I got the feeling of various periods. I selected as my favorite painting "John on Patmos"

[64]

by Bosch. My husband had the original in the museum copied before our exodus to the United States. It was in his room until he died.

In drawing, I developed a graceless line, but I got to the essentials and was sharp at proportion. Painting with water colors was torture. The female teacher of the course, who looked like a flabby white pussycat, was full of misgivings about any individual approach to color. She wanted us to find the contours of light and shadow on an object and apply the so-called palette dirt for the shadow. I used a wild purple shadow on one of the houses we painted as an outdoor study. This was not so good.

In my third year, when at last I entered the higher echelons of the school, I found myself on bad terms with a goat-bearded, middle-aged, unshaven teacher, who took pleasure from pressing his hands into the shoulders of his victim, beard stubbles against her cheek, ostensibly to attain the same view as that of his pupil while criticizing the work. Everybody complained. I suggested we complain to the director. Some of the older students did and as a result the old goat must have had a hard time. He got even with me through one older student who told him about my sitting in dark corners with my girl friend. Suspecting us of lesbianism, that student also reported that I had said I would fool my family on the emperor's birthday, a holiday, by pretending to meet with boys but actually going off with my girl friend.

One morning soon afterward, my father telephoned from his office at city hall, asking me in a peculiar hoarse voice where I had been on the emperor's birthday. I said firmly that I had been at home. My father asked again, adding that my art teacher was at his office. I repeated that I had been at home. I knew he had not been at home—he had been drunk that day. Nobody checked it further. My claim went undisputed.

Later, I asked Gelen to prepare a ready answer to the same question, in case of any further inquiry. I told a lie, to make it clear there was no lesbianism between my friend and me. I considered my lie a triumph of truth. In some muddled way, though, there was truth in the accusation of "loving my friend with an undue love," not physically, but in the sense that I identified with her. She had been lucky enough to have received advances from the boy I had confessed to her I was in love with, and she had responded gleefully and mischievously with all the ardor of newly discovered sex. Gelen had introduced him to me.

His classmates had asked the boy again and again if I were his

[65]

sister, the likeness between us was so extraordinary. Gelen flirted with him. I fell in love with him, never attempting to come too close to him, but imitating his walk, his way of bending his head to one side, his way of moving his hands, and smiling with curved lips—the same Cupid's bow as mine. After he had kissed her, I sought her out like a hungry bird, picking at the reminders of his caresses in her. She used it for sweet torture every so often, enjoying my blush at the mere mention of his name. She had arranged dancing lessons, which they taught together. He danced with me, smilingly pointing to my thumb, which never rested on his hand but stuck forlornly in the air, while he held me tight for the tango. He tried to talk to me but I was unresponsive; in fact, I was terrified speechless near him. At the farewell party when he finished school, he plucked a red rose from a bush in the garden of the hotel restaurant and gave it to me. The moment I reached home I wrote him that I loved him. I posted the letter that same morning.

In August the war came. I reeived a letter from him with a photograph in uniform. He wrote that I had given him more joy than I could have known. He wanted to know me better. A few months later, in nasty winter weather, another letter arrived, this one from Russia, with an unknown name on the envelope and in an unknown hand. His sergeant wrote that he had given him my address, asking him to inform me if he should not come back from a mission. He seemed to have had a premonition of his own death.

For months I walked around like a living ghost. It was as if I, too, had died and was also rotting in a grave in Russia. I would sit before the mirror, imagining the lines of his face on my mirror image. Twice I experienced the miracle of his likeness blotting out my features in my reflection. His actual face smiled at me, undiluted by my own crying image. Clearly and unmistakably, I saw his eyes, his mouth, his hairline, and his smooth forehead, while my image in the mirror vanished, and after tears of misery, I shed tears of happiness. This vision saved me from self-destruction.

My friend Gelen gave me *The Picture of Dorian Gray* by Oscar Wilde, the book that woke me from the haze of my childhood fairy tales. She cast me in the role of Dorian, while she took over that of the witty Lord Henry, who seduced Dorian to the higher and lower passions. We "lived" Dorian and Lord Henry. Strangely enough, it remained an aesthetic experience. The moralistic ending of the story concerned us as little as the sinister ending of Don

Giovanni in Mozart's beloved opera. The hero carried the image; the bitter ending seemed inconsequential.

I took to Tolstoi much later, but at eighteen Dostoevski spoke directly to me. He was the diver into the deep, where I found my own world again.

I began studying literature on my way home from school, starting with the beginnings of German literature, as all good, thorough Germans would do: the Edda, the Nibelungen songs, Tristan and Isolde, Parsifal, up to Walther von der Wogelweide, "Horribilicribifax" by Opitz, and into the next centuries. I would sit in a folding chair in my tiny room, a green rug my aunt had given me at my feet, surrounded by a bookcase with my books, a small desk Nora had given me, and the hard couch on which I slept. I was never able to think of my books from a librarian's point of view, and it made me very unhappy later on, when Paulus tried to assemble them, according to library rules, into his voluminous library. My library contained favorites only, and I refused their regimentation.

My mother did not object when I invited Carl to our apartment. He used to take me home from the philharmonic concerts, after waiting for me outside of the concert hall.

Carl wanted to be photographed, for some reason or other, but although his father was not lacking for money, Carl was poor. So I arranged it, including paying for the pictures, which a professional friend of mine was to take. She photographed his profile, his full face, his figure in a new tuxedo, and even the palms of his hands, at his request. He was beautiful like the emperors on the coins of the early Romans.

Although Carl's breath was foul, nobody minded. Lotte and I loved his spiritual being. When he described to us in detail his sexual relationship with another girl, whom we knew, we drank it in as the message of one poet to another. Carl read us innumerable poems of cosmic import. He put one of my poetic images into one of them, on the assumption that I would be proud to give *him* something of *my* imagination. I was. Once, I wrote twelve poems about a cosmic couple and their individuation. Carl read it and sighed—he could never finish anything.

Lotte met a gymnastic teacher, Lydia, whom she brought into our circle. We all fell in love with her. She was beautiful indeed, like the blond angels in an Italian Renaissance fresco. I invited Lydia and Carl to a *Fasching* party at the apartment I shared with my sister, my parents having departed for Marburg. Carl arrived very late because of an evening job. Meanwhile, I had dragged Lydia into a small tent I had built in one of the rooms, while the other guests were making merry in an adjoining room. I kissed her, I embraced her. She seemed stunned and I whispered that she should not tell anyone about it. She did tell Carl, however, who appeared in my quarters some days later to accuse me of having seduced his future wife and to demand the return of the negatives of the photographs my friend and I had taken of him. I laughed at him while I destroyed the negatives before his eyes. He left in helpless wrath; the prophet's cloak had fallen from his shoulders. I rejoiced.

It wasn't until after World War II that I next heard from him. He wrote to ask me for help, proposing that he translate my husband's works. I never replied. But when I returned to Germany some years later, I visited Carl and his wife Lydia, the beautiful gym teacher. She was still beautiful. She was supporting him and their son with her job. They lived in an old castle through the generosity of the owner, who had given them ample space in the lofts of one wing, as well as access to the communal kitchen. During the time of the Nazis, they had both worked in a race research center. Because of their extraordinary beauty, they were considered living examples of racial purity, they traveled much, and were received by worshiping crowds. After the breakdown of Nazism, they found their castle refuge. Carl was still bewildered whenever he encountered hostility for having participated in the Nazi movement. Of course, he had known nothing about concentration camps. I refrained from comment. His breath was still foul, his poetic cycle was still unfinished, and he was still confused.

Albert walked past the gray cement walls with firm steps, crossing the schoolyard. He arrived at the windowsill, low enough to sit on, where a triumvirate of friends known as the three Hannahs had established their domain at lunch time. There was Gelen in a black smock embroidered with bouquets of flowers, her triangular brows above narrow eyes and heavy jowls. Her upper lip looked slightly swollen. Her hands were well formed, if not small. It was easy for her to get acquainted with boys at school; her father held high military rank and she had acquired some social grace. The second Hannah, called "Zäsky," was a country doctor's daughter. She was overly tall, overly thin, her pimply skin covered with freckles. She had a preoccupied, far-away look and an engaging ugliness. She wrote poetry, drew extraordinarily well, and had a disarming laugh whenever she was detected in some negligence. The third Hannah, I was called "Wernerken." I wore a blue smock with tiny over-all pattern and my ash-blond braids were twisted around my head. I was taller than Gelen, shorter than Zäsky, thinner than Gelen, plumper than Zäsky. I was what used to be called a slim, full-bosomed blond.

Albert had been introduced to us by Gelen, of course. On this occasion he walked right up to me, lifted my chin, and looked at my neck. "It's true," he said and departed in his white smock, the constant pipe between his lips, his well-polished shoes clicking over the cement floor. I never polished my shoes, I preferred them dirty, whereas Albert went so far as to carry an extra handkerchief for cleaning his. He was one of the best students in the upper grade. On festive occasions he wore a gray flannel suit with a butterfly cravat. He was taller than I. His big brown eyes, beneath a heavy forehead, with their thick straight brows could be gay with laughter. Short brown hair covered his round skull. His hands and feet were broad, and not sensitive.

Emil, another student, had told Albert about the fine white hair under my chin. Emil was in love with me. He had written me a passionate letter describing me from head to foot. It seemed to me extremely funny to be told I was beautiful. I did not feel beautiful. Always slow to recognize my physical advantages, I laughed at his letter.

Emil was to go with us on the hike to Rügen—there were the three Hannahs, Emil, Albert, and an older youth. Nobody remembered who had first planned it, but to Rügen we went on a ten-day hike, we girls finally landing at Zäsky's parents' house on the coast.

My mother had objected to the trip when she heard that men were involved. I had developed the technique of asking her permission for outings with men friends when she seemed absentminded, but this time she was alert. I shouted at her, telling her that I would go anyway and that I would lie to her from now on. Mercifully, my parents and the rest of the family departed for their vacation earlier than I could. They rented a room for me so I could finish my art school course, and they didn't object when I presented my invitation from the parents of a girl friend. They gave me a month's allowance and off they went.

I then completed my work at school and off I went. The six of

[69]

us took the train to Rügen. I remember the ocean from the cliffs, from the rocky coast, and from a sandy beach; woods of gray-barked birches in summery green along the shore; and low, thatched houses with tiny windowpanes. Tremendous clumps of hollyhocks as high as the roofs were in bloom in the villages. Sometimes we slept in the hay, the girls in one farmer's barn, the boys in another. Sometimes we slept under the low, straw-thatched roofs in a musty room with the hollyhocks in the front yard.

Albert painted with water colors on a day when we were resting. I stood behind him while he put ribbons of many colors on the paper. When the clutter finally became a landscape, I felt he had painted me into it and that made it an exuberantly happy picture. Once, when we girls were walking on the opposite side of the road from the boys, Albert crossed over, taking my arm for a moment. Tension sprang up—Gelen considered Albert her man. I remained naïve under my hood of disheveled ash-blond braids. The boys took leave of us before we arrived at Zäsky's, dirty, hungry, and tired.

Upon my return home by train, everybody at home seemed relaxed. I participated dreamily in our family life. I was happy too.

Later, when Emil did not return from the front, his friends accused me severely of having sent him voluntarily to his death. He had been on furlough a short time before it happened and had tried in vain to evoke some sign of affection from me. I had been barely civil. On our trip to Rügen, in the group, it had been easy for him to feel comfortable with me. He had given me books with florid inscriptions. He also gave me a melancholic landscape, an almond-shaped, whitish-blue lake between harsh, broomstick trees. The lake seemed an open eye in a gray sky. I had liked it. But there was something in Emil's chemical makeup, something in the design of his face, of his hands, of his bodily bearing, something in the sound of his voice or the smell of his skin to which I could not respond.

There was also something in the line of my first husband Albert's back—in his elongated neck, his sloping shoulders—which did not please me. When he turned his back to me to wash himself, I recall feeling a slight aesthetic discomfort. Perhaps it was one of the reasons I left Albert for a physical shape that gave me delight in its every line and texture. I did love my second husband's face, the shape of his hands, his whole physical being. Even during the years when we nearly separated, I had the same sensation of pleasurable joy when I opened the door for him, returning from a trip or even from his office. Seeing Paulus's face was always glorious to me.

[70]

Nora was the daughter of a rich merchant living in the elegant quarters of what is now West Berlin. She shared an apartment with a benevolent and adoring friend who permitted her other friends. Nora lavished upon me all the wealth of her civilized, educated understanding. Her mother had committed suicide. Nora was to turn away from men, developing the aggressive power of the male sex drive in herself. She would seduce and live with women, except for occasionally giving in to a man. Her upturned nose gave her face an odd expression in spite of its near beauty. She had the most beautiful, slender hands and lovely feet. I gave her much sorrow of passion. Letters arrived that I could not laugh at, but she was incapable of lighting the fire of Eros in me.

Much later, I once asked Paulus to give her one night of love. It seems incomprehensible to me now why I made that request. Perhaps I considered him the divine seed-thrower, bringing fulfillment to each mortal being he took into his arms. Perhaps I hoped he would thereby balance my earlier refusal of her passionate onrush.

I introduced Nora to Uli, devoted friend of our group. Uli always had some new cultural adventure to propose. He would perform a puppet play at my apartment, for which he created the intricate puppets, designed the program, and worked the puppets himself. Soon thereafter, we moved to Nora's spacious apartment, with our performances, where we ourselves became the actors in even more adventurous plays than we produced.

Uli had been my brother Walter's friend, and Walter had introduced us. Uli became the one who was permitted to enter my room, a favor I seldom granted. He never arrived without a flower, a book, a ticket for the opera. He seemed always to have money enough for gifts and expensive invitations. He knew the Berlin night life and he once took me out for the evening in a long, exquisite evening dress he had designed for me. One of his friends made up my face for that adventure. Later, we found out that he was a homosexual and that he took drugs.

Several years later, when he met Uli, Heinrich wanted me to help Uli overcome his homosexuality. I consented to an evening with Uli, putting on my blue linen suit. My hair was straight, in page-boy style. Uli bent me to his wishes; reclining on my bed, he entered me. He visited us some months later, bowlegged in white stockings, checkered plus-fours, and a white jacket. Uli was incredibly ugly with his long spidery fingers, sensitive hands, a drooping nose, a receding chin, and a sagging underlip. His gray pupils swam in his almond-shaped bluish-white eyes. We loved him. It didn't matter to us that he was not a Greek god. On his final visit he brought along a Greek god, who aroused panicky hatred in the citizens of Dresden as we were taking our walk in the park. I wore an elegant, mannish, tailor-made suit with a silk shirtwaist. Uli put his tongue out at some citizens who turned around to stare.

The young god trudged along, arm-in-arm with me, while Uli told me in a voice trembling with passion that he was finally going to marry and set up a household. We sensed the Greek god would be the other member of that household. He was so disarmingly beautiful that, in my usual preoccupation with the values of emotion and beauty, I found no word of caution.

The end was foreseeable. Uli went to Venice, where he dined and wined a last time, but without the Greek god. He then took sleeping pills that freed him forever from all responsibilities. He had stolen much of his father's money. He wrote me a farewell letter. Dark little paintings of whores, nudes carrying handbags and walking through gray city streets, an elderly man holding Uli's head like a Japanese mask under a magnifying glass, two apaches drinking, and a few black avant-garde stories are all that is left of Uli, revealing only half of what he could have said.

My younger sister and my oldest brother had left Berlin, my parents were in Marburg, and my oldest sister and I were sharing an apartment. We were both teaching, I still in my old neighborhood, Neukölln. We occasionally invited Irma, who was my brother's girl friend as well as a friend of my younger sister, along with Uli and others, to visit us. We would read together, discuss, or chat.

One evening at dusk, we sat without lights, Irma in a huddle of friends at my feet. I found myself touching a finger to her lips, against her teeth. With gentle strokes around the outline of her mouth, my finger slipped into the inside of her softly opening cave of love. People around us were talking of poetry; I chimed in, keeping my voice steady, while I pursued my double occupation. A few days later, Irma came to me while my sister was at school. I took her into my room with its wild blue ceiling, which Uli had painted for me, where yellow lemons and bright oranges as well as red-cheeked apples, graced my blue and white Chinese bowl. I fell upon her, wordlessly, kissing her mouth madly, pressing my private parts to hers, experiencing through our clothed bodies all the orgiastic ecstasy I would ever live to feel. I had broken through to orgasm in taking

[72]

the role of a man. She left without having exchanged a word with me. She was dainty. She had the brown eyes of a doe.

THE WAR

The war overtook us in August in Neuendorf, as we lay playfully after swimming—a group of friends and puppy loves—in our usual meeting place, a grassy dell beside the country road to Misdroy (which I learned later was my second husband's vacation seaside resort). Neuendorf was a vacation paradise under pine trees and old oaks. There we met the doctor's children from Stettin and the lawyer's children from Rostock—we, the school superintendent's kids from Berlin. We lived amid the fragrance of pines in family cottages to which we had brought our maids and our bedding and some kitchen utensils. Every morning we walked on roads strewn with soft pine needles to the Baltic Sea, which was gentle with soft lapping water, a white sandy beach under cliffs overgrown with old trees, and a strip of grass and strawberries and flowers. There was a maze of wild growth near our houses to hide in on rainy days. Honeysuckle and meadow flowers made the air sweet. I used to take a walk before meeting the gang, either along the ocean or further inland, where fields of wheat and rye, spread out on wide slopes, swayed in a summer breeze. I would hide myself, lying down for a moment in a furrow between the stalks, intoxicated by the sharp smells of the ripening grain.

When they heard the news of the war, the boys immediately separated from the girls. The world had become a man's world. They sought out their elders for counsel. Every single young man was to join the army. We met on the hill by the road for one short good-bye that same evening, before their departure. We sang our special folk song and dived wordlessly with no personal good-byes into the night. The next morning, as my family took the last train to Berlin, Neuendorf was deserted. The war had us all in its grip.

My parents' special sorrow was my oldest brother, who had been serving in one of the forester regiments, an elegant and expensive enterprise my father had wished him to join. He had sent word that we could meet for a few hours at Berlin's big railroad station, Alexanderplatz. We children were sent out to find him among the crowds of soldiers and civilians. I fluttered around like a bat at night,

[73]

relying on invisible antennas. I discovered him and brought him to the appointed place. He had grown to twice his size since I had last seen him. He was able to spend one short night at home; he left in the early dawn. My parents took up most of his time.

Regiments being channeled to the several fronts passed through the railroad stations. My older sister and I assisted the Red Cross in distributing coffee and sandwiches when the trains made short stops at our station. At that time I saw soldiers; otherwise I would learn very little about the war. There was no bombing of the civilian population. There was no knowledge of what was going on at the front. There was no radio, no television, no communication, except for the government-controlled bulletins. There were letters from my friends, but no descriptions of a battle, a victory or a defeat. Paulus, who was a chaplain in the field during the war, told me later that the chasm between the home and the front was so unbridgeable that soldiers were relieved to return to their positions after a furlough. There seemed to be a vast inability of soldiers and civilians to understand each other.

To us civilians the war meant hunger and cold, no clothes, no shoes, discomfort of every kind, the disruption of a so-called civilized way of life. My hair fell out, my teeth broke. Influenza and coughs seemed unhealable. I tired easily. I had feelings of weightlessness, a certain thin ecstasy, dream fulfillments resembling a fata morgana—an inability to act and a silver-blue, tender sleepiness that made me forget my hunger. I listened to music with a finer ear, I read with greater understanding, great insights seemed to come to me in ecstatic vision. I saw people surrounded by circles of colors expressing their inner being. I became sensitive to other people's suffering. When somebody talked to me I was sometimes swallowed up by his ideas, forgetting myself to extinction, taking his ideas as my own concern and a matter of greatest importance to me. I remember an acquaintance asking me, when I seemed insatiable for his information, "But do you wish to become a scientist?" Identifying had become my way of acquiring knowledge.

At the end of the war, my mother had to be taken to the hospital. She was emaciated from starvation. She invited us to visit her around noon, when she would share with us a soft roll or a bit of meat from her lunch.

My father brought home a pig he had bought from a farmer. He had hesitated for patriotic reasons to go to the black market, but conditions in the city finally became so bad that we were dying from hunger. The pig was worked into its different forms—bacon, sausage, salted meat, roasts, and boiled ham. He must have found some way to have parts of it smoked. We had meat then, and sausages and fat in the evening. I ate my lunch in the government folk kitchen, where the starving population was treated for a few pennies to a dish of the most godawful mixture of a slimy gray stuff—watery potatoes, some occasional bits of nearly invisible meat, and of course turnips in all unappetizing shapes, marmalade, and what not. No sugar, no coffee. Sometimes my father received from one of his schools the leftovers of the American Friends Service Committee's feeding program, which we devoured gratefully.

Our house had a neglected garden with a chicken coop where we kept a few chickens for eggs and occasional meat. One morning, when one of us went to retrieve eggs, he found only the chicken heads laid out side by side in the yard in an elegant curve. It seemed the end of the world to us.

We had to ration our bread allowance. I was acclaimed the "just" one. Every night I weighed the slices of bread for the next morning on a letter scale—paper-thin slices of an unhealthful brown damp loaf. Sometimes my own bread was finished the same evening and I went to school the next morning hungry. Once when I came home late, I found, to my delirious delight, a pot of a sort of porridge. I heated and ate it immediately in the dark of the night. I felt a new person. The next morning I learned that my younger brothers had spent painstaking hours sorting out the oats from the leftover chicken feed, separating it from the chaff, and had then cooked it, dreaming of a good meal all night long. They never forgave the culprit who had unwittingly stole their nourishment. Gelen and I sometimes walked down from the art school to the Potsdamer Platz, visiting several cafes along the way where one could buy a single, incredibly bad piece of cake at a time, with some watery cocoa.

For one vacation, two or three members of our family were invited by my mother's mother, who lived in Munich, to the Bavarian countryside. It was near the high mountains in good fertile farm country. We had everything there—white-flour pancakes, milk and meat, good bread, butter, coffee, and eggs. I walked in open-toed wooden-soled sandals, wearing a blue-gray home-dyed skirt and blouse. My painter uncle was delighted. I had to sit for him for a "flight into Egypt." The last wartime photographs showed my younger sister and myself with skulls on which there seemed to be no flesh.

Clothes were getting scarce. I wore an old brown coat of my

father's, turned by a seamstress who came to the house, with black frog closings to hide the buttonholes. My mother gave me a gray silk blouse with cuffs of old lace. I wore a black velvet hat with a brim. Coming home from a concert on the tram, I remarked to my mother that the girl opposite us in a black velvet hat looked beautiful. She replied ponderously, "I just looked at her and thought how much better you looked in your hat."

It must have been at that time that I decided to take upon myself a woman's fate, a decision made consciously during tortured nights lying under a thin blanket. My Narcissus had died, it was the middle of the war, and I had become hungry and holy. I washed every morning in cold water, I meditated, I read, and I decided, convinced that from then on my assumed fate would take its course—that I would attract men and live the life of a woman or, as I put it to myself, "go through the life cycle of a woman." I was fascinated by Strindberg's dream play, which I saw at least three times, the story of Indra's daughter coming down by her own choice to live the life of a mortal, which ends with the outcry, "It is a pity about humanity."

Within our group, patriotism had petered out. Carl had successfully escaped induction into the army by faking a heart murmur. I was able to give him details and addresses of an escape route for deserters into France. I do not recall whether he used it.

After art school, I went regularly to the public library. Carl had shown me how to secure a card and take out books. He sometimes came in and sat with me, or chatted with me outside on the steps for a moment.

I had fainting spells from hunger, as I sat at my window in the late evening. My bedtime was ten o'clock. I memorized works of the great poets. Lotte and I took long hikes, reciting Stefan George to each other. Occasionally we slept in a hayloft at a farmhouse. On one such occasion, I wrote poetry on my shirttails, having brought no paper along—paper was also getting scarce.

We arranged our life without the men, except for Uli, who was exempted from service. Nora read some of my poems before a small audience. She introduced me to an older woman, a journalist from the Baltic, who was interested in women's reactions to the war. She printed one of my plays, "The Woman and the Redeemer." She was also impressed by some of my poetry of despair.

Two younger Baltic friends joined Nora's circle. Some years afterward, one of these girls, who had married a businessman, caught my second husband's imagination when I introduced them. She later wrote a novelette with a foreword by Thomas Mann in which she satirically described my husband's style when he was "on the warpath." She had received him very enthusiastically in the beginning but had cooled rather suddenly.

Thomas Mann accomplished a similar feat in exploiting Paulus. He had asked my husband for information about the University of Halle, where Paulus had taught. Paulus had reported in good faith, only to find his description of university life turned into a satire in one of Mann's books.

When I finished art school, my father found me a position in one of his schools. I was a good teacher, unorthodox in some ways. I was able to stimulate the children to work—even if I left the class for some time, they remained involved in their projects. In one of my classes of six-year-olds I had a favorite child. When the class formed into pairs after hours, "Miss Werner's" favorite child walked, with the full approval of the class, at the head of the column, hand-in-hand with her smiling teacher. Fortunately my rather unusual methods of teaching lasted no longer than eighteen months, when I married.

THE WAR'S END

The war was over, the revolution was on. Pacifists, Socialists, Communists, and patriots fought one another in the streets. It was sometimes hard to get to my philharmonic concerts on foot (the tram was not running). I waited in doorways and took side streets to avoid the shooting. There were transportation strikes. Carl showed me the bullet holes in the walls of the house he lived in. I walked to the Brandenburger Tor, the entrance to Unter den Linden, where the trucks of the mutineering sailors were parked. The crowd surged back and forth away from the danger of getting caught in the shooting. I moved with them. "Extras" were being offered by all parties.

My brother had come home, leading his company in good order from the battlefield in France, only to find in Berlin a tumultous breakdown in revolution. Crowds were hostile to officers, tearing off their insignia, which the officers had worn with pride as defenders of the fatherland. When my brother first changed into civilian clothes, he ducked into a house when a civilian plane flew over us. Not being able to overcome his wartime responses quickly made him desolate. When I came home, tears in my eyes, and told him the bad news that Liebknecht and Rosa Luxemburg had been murdered, he nearly strangled me—he felt altogether differently about them.

My father had become a victim of the revolution in the red workers' quarters in Neukölln, where the soldiers' and workers' council ruled for a short time. He was dismissed from his office as superintendent of schools. He fought back valiantly and, with the help of some conservative leaders in the ministry, he was assigned to the district of Marburg and surrounding areas, which had to be organized. He had only a few years before retirement.

Lotte asked me to accompany her on a visit to Albert, who was in a soldiers' camp in Brelau. I did. I was glad to help her out with some money. Albert had left his art school sweetheart, a lovely, seductive, dark-haired madonnalike woman. I had often visited the two of them. Lotte's and my visit with him was pleasant. He aroused my femininity, but I felt the occasion was not mine.

Albert had been injured at the front and had not yet returned when the war ended. Lotte asked me to visit him with her a second time. He had not been in touch with her after his return. While we were on the train, she confided to me that she had seen him several times alone in her room over the garage, which her parents had given her and where she was allowed visitors without restrictions. I listened to her as a good white knight. She telephoned Albert from the station. Albert agreed to meet for a walk, not inviting us to his house. He seemed disgruntled at meeting us and I was angry at being treated inhospitably. I was wearing a nice outfit, I felt pretty, and I decided to take my revenge by winning him over. I put him at ease. He responded immediately, taking my arm, chatting amiably, while Lotte trotted ahead of us between white birches and meager pines. I changed the subject from art to my friend. Albert did not rebuke me for my interference on Lotte's behalf. He answered that she was a very sweet kid, that she had met him in Breslau without me after our initial visit and he had found it delightful. But, he said, grasping my arm in a new firm grip, he had never cared for her the way she cared for him. He cared for me, he had cared for me in Rügen, he had invited me out even when he was still seeing his art school sweetheart. He had broken with her. I was the one for him, the only one.

My face flushed, the white knight's visor opened. We stopped talking about Lotte. Albert talked about himself, I listened. I understood that he did not love Lotte. I told her she was not the one he had in mind, trying to be outraged that he had said he liked me best. I could not quite hide my happy excitement, even from myself. Lotte must have understood my flushed cheeks and flashing eyes better than I did.

I met Albert in Neuendorf during my vacation. I was staying by myself at a boarding house that had comparatively good food. I was also expecting another visitor from the old Neuendorf gang, Hermann. Through some miracle, I had got hold of a silky, natural-colored material that was highly flammable. I dyed it cerulean blue and, despite my lack of experience, made it into a long-sleeved dirndl, which was supposed to hide me but did just the opposite, especially since I had little to wear underneath. No stockings, of course, and some sort of wooden-soled sandals. Going barefoot was popular in spite of the unavoidable cuts and infections; it had started during the war.

Albert arrived first. He started painting my portrait in my clinging Piero de la Francesca dirndl.

Hermann's mother told friends that she wished she could tell her son not to visit me in Neuendorf, but it was too late. His family had stressed healthy race conditions for a marriage, when they invited my sister and me to dinner at their comfortable Berlin home. His father was a doctor. Hermann was extra good-looking, intelligent, and intellectual. We had had a good evening and shared many common interests. He came to my boardinghouse room, finding the sketches Albert had made. He looked around thoughtfully. When Albert came in, the two of them had a hesitant, civilized conversation. Hermann, the dark-haired sensitive half-Jew (as I later found out), left, never to return. He suffered during the Nazi period, but survived as a professor somewhere in northern Germany.

When Albert had first arrived, he asked me for the third time to marry him and this time I said yes. It was in one of those sweet, overgrown pathways of the maze where we had played as children, filled with the fragrance of honeysuckle. He kissed me on the mouth. I responded passionately. Later he asked me who had taught me to kiss that way. I was puzzled—I felt I was responding to him. Until then, only girls had opened me up that way. Albert and I had some kissing bouts afterward, though he avoided the ultimate physical contact.

He painted me in the nude on the high cliff between the birch trees and the flowers and tall grass. I had no reluctance in posing for him. Shame, to me, was connected with the sense of not being beautiful. I knew my proportions were all right, my skin had no blemish in its pale ivory color. My hips were narrower than my girl friends' hips, I wore mannish suits well, my breasts were high—a bit to my embarrassment—but they were firm, nothing to worry about. My feet and hands were slender, my second toes still straight and longer than the first toes. I had a certain vanity about my hands, which I had learned to manicure.

When Albert finished his sketch, he fell down in the tall grass, moaning. He called to me to get dressed, which I did, leaving him to his pain. Later he made a woodcut of his sketches, putting the blue clinging dress over my body in the painting and calling it "the blue woman." I personally preferred the nude sketches, which had brought out the shades of my skin—rose and a very light, whitish yellow.

After our Neuendorf vacation, Albert visited my parents. He talked with my father, who wanted to discuss with him his job opportunities, and with my mother about the practical details of our marriage. We decided to marry in August of the following year. I was to go on teaching at my school in Neukölln until then, while Albert would continue teaching in Greiz at a high school that gave him a good monthly salary. We planned to live in Greiz in an apartment let for us in the house of an industrialist with whom Albert had made friends. He had often played the piano accompaniment for the older man's still charming wife when she sang the classical songs of Schubert, Schumann, Brahms, and Wolff.

My mother tried to assemble a trousseau for me, which was difficult just at the war's end. But we did not have to worry about furniture and equipment—the apartment was to be furnished with luxurious beds and every comfort.

Interlude

YOU ENTERED ME

You entered me
—a god entering his house—
and I received you
as one who has come home.

You broke my bread,
I drank of your wine,
we shared a meal
like an old habit.

When your familiar mouth
touched me the first time
I was shaken with
ultimate ecstasy.

Your open gaze revealed,
bathed in heroic light,
the longed-for landscape
of my dreams.

SLEEPING BETWEEN MY BREASTS

Sleeping between my breasts
which dream of mothering and nurture,
you are at rest.
I would open my mother-body
to take you in,
to nurse you, reborn,
peacefully upon my heart;
Till, replete with sucking from my earth-realm,
slumbering in the depth of my embrace,
you break the surface of my bloodstream,
brush the dimness from your eyelids
and begin, all vigor, the new day.

HOW MANY TIMES AT NIGHT

How many times at night when you professed
Your love for me in flesh and blood embrace
Have you committed treason at my breast,
Grafting another's image on my face;
And all those tender joys were dim and shoddy
Because you steered them down a shadow stream,
Loving a stranger's body in my body
And squandering your kisses on a dream.

The Fancy-dress Ball

In February, 1919, I went to a fancy-dress ball, along with many others attempting to escape hunger and misery and the restlessness following on a lost war. I wore the same knee-length, embroidered tunic I had worn four years earlier to my first fancy-dress ball at the art school. My friend Gelen, as well as Emil and Narcissus, had been present then. This time I went alone.

Two wine-red Pierrots joined me repeatedly as I was aimlessly walking with the masked crowd in the art school's large hall, to the sound of music—the tango, the one-step, the two-step, the waltz. A tall masked man danced with me, then took me into one of the dark rooms, where he sat me on his knee and started kissing me. I pulled away from his embrace and returned by myself to the lighted room, joining the circle of walking masks for another round.

I went up to a balcony overlooking the hall, from where I noticed the two Pierrots still walking. When I came down again, one of them talked with me. We exchanged addresses. He invited me to go with him and his friend to a private home. I consented.

A tall girl with heavy straight eyebrows on a low forehead over her brown eyes came along. I found myself on a couch with men and women. Somebody stroked my leg, saying, "What taste." I had worn two pairs of silk stockings, to make my legs look less fleshy. One of the Pierrots returned from time to time, inquiring whether I wanted a drink and trying to talk to me. I was not good at it. I got up to leave. He wanted to see me home, but I refused. He executed a little dance of uncertainty at the top of the stairway as

I made my way down. I was so inexperienced I did not understand that, apart from attraction or nonattraction, he felt responsible for taking me home since he had brought me here, even though the prospects for a little sex with this strange girl were not good. I ended it by coming back up the stairs, kissing him on the lips, then turning around abruptly and descending again without one look back.

Pierrot telephoned the next day. He asked me to purchase tickets for him and another friend, as well as the girl who had accompanied him the previous night and myself. The occasion was the last fancy-dress ball of the season that same night, at the Academy of Art. I countered that I did not intend to go, having a date with a friend for a hike on this beautiful early spring day. He insisted, saying that neither he nor the others could get the tickets—I was the only one with an Academy membership card. He said resolutely that we would meet at the entrance in front of the turnstile and hung up before I could reply. He did not even ask whether I had enough money for the tickets. By chance, I had part of my monthly check from my parents, but it was a great expense for me to buy even my own ticket. As it turned out, I was never to be repaid for the four tickets.

I telephoned Lotte with whom I was to have gone hiking, got into my two pairs of green silk tights, put on my tunic, touched my lips with a lipstick, darkened my eyelashes with eyebrow pencil, and put a tiny red spot in each corner of my eyes. I could not do much with my hair, except to braid it, so I circled my head with the braids. Taking my long, gray winter coat, I boarded the streetcar, after a bite of bread, butter, and apples. On my arrival, I produced my membership card and bought four tickets.

The turnstile was at the far end of a long, high corridor, leading straight in from the outer entrance. I waited, leaning against one of the paper-garlanded iron columns. It was some time before three people, two of them familiar, approached. The girl, in a fur-collared coat, stopped ten feet from the turnstile where I was waiting, with her companion from last night, Pierrot, and another man. The unknown man knelt down, she took a shawl from her head and, folding it around his head, created a sort of turban that covered his unruly blond hair, shortened his forehead, and accentuated his glasses.

Shock hit me so hard that I felt faint. Hate surged up in me in red waves, threatening to overwhelm me. I stood staring at this stranger as he got up and walked toward me, his mouth set in melancholic determination. He wore no costume, his crumpled cutaway was shabby, his old-fashioned shoes shiny, the dark tie twisted in a heavy knot. Paulus's introduction to me was quick, the haste with which the other two acknowledge the tickets, obvious. They must have worried lest I take the hike after all.

Pierrot and the girl with the dark eyebrows in a black costume went off together. It was clear that Pierrot wanted the girl with whom the stranger had a date, and she, Pierrot. They had used and then deserted us, to reach each other. This stranger now put a limp hand through my arm and we began to walk.

The large hall had been transformed with paper by the students of the art school into a glittering, magical place. There were stands for food and drinks, but Paulus did not seem to notice. Perhaps he had no money; he looked motheaten. He suggested we sit down, so I climbed onto the back of one of the benches, which were nearly filled, and he squeezed into the last available seat. His hands started creeping up to my knees. I said, "No." He withdrew. He looked desperately tired—gleaming strong teeth behind pale lips, eyes behind thick glasses, a knobby broad nose.

He wanted to walk again. With his limp hand on my arm, it was almost unbearable. Then he started to talk. His older sister had died in childbed a very short time ago, and his younger sister had sent him here to draw him away from his pain and unhappiness at her death. His sister's name had been the same as mine, he said, pressing my arm closer. I reminded him of her—my seriousness, my intelligence, even my face. He looked into my face for the first time. He had been so close to her. We walked up and down, he talked, I listened. My heart went out to him. He had been converted into a burdened human being against a turbulent backdrop of gold and red paper garlands, in a crowd of masked people, among the strains of dance music and shouts of joy. There he stood in his shabby cutaway, beneath it a soft shirt and stiff winged collar, with a cruel mouth, a bush of hair under his turban—now askew, with thick glasses and limp hands and arms, and with poorman's shoes. Nothing fitted him. Now he seemed to me the only human being among the clowns and knights, the nymphs and dwarfs.

The music became insistent, midnight drew near, Ash Wednesday arrived. The crowd took off their masks. Everybody kissed as the lights went out. I was ready to be kissed. "No," he whispered in the darkness, "no . . . not now, when everybody is kissing." He let me go. When the lights went on Paulus smiled at me, his lips curling over his white teeth. I evaded his eyes for the first time.

"Let's go," he said, taking my arm again. His hand was not limp now. We found our friends looking satisfied and close. We all exchanged addresses—again the ritual of that time, to be sure not to become entirely lost to each other.

I insisted on going home alone. I left the three of them looking after me as I stepped down the stairs filled with embracing couples, each oblivious to all the others. The one supreme moment of exultation had arrived. They did not think of past or future in this intense moment of the divine present. I stepped over twisted legs and lazily forgetful arms. I called for my coat at the cloakroom. I took a train, waiting in the cool morning on an open railroad platform, finding myself heading in a direction opposite to my apartment, going back, waiting for connections, oblivious to everything outside of myself, aware only of my strong sense of shock, that I had fallen into a deep well, not of water but of raging fire.

When Paulus discovered that I was a virgin, as he entered me for the first time after many playful sensuous meetings, he was frightened. It meant nothing to me except for his fear at seeing drops of blood. He had conquered me long before. He was my god, my dream-fulfillment. The world had become whole. I doubted nothing, I asked nothing. With the same heart-rending intensity of my submission to Annie, I was his.

He left me at night to sleep in his apartment upstairs. When I was in his studio in the daytime, his household help would sometimes drum on the floor to summon him upstairs for telephone calls. After lovemaking, we took walks, discussing furiously. He told me about his writings. I attended his lectures—philosophy, religion, art, politics.

In the beginning, I was with him once a week for the entire night. Sometimes I stayed for breakfast the next morning, when it happened to be Sunday. We would sit in the warm summer morning on the balcony. The fragrance of linden blossoms from the trees bordering the street drifted up. He looked pale, unhealthy, and irritated. "I hate you both," he said, staring through his lenses at me and the fräulein, who retreated after having brought coffee and buns.

Later, Paulus asked me to be with him more often. I came. I got used to his falling from elation to despair and rising again to elation. He worked. I lay on the sofa, reading or pretending to read, exulting in the fact of his presence. I met his wife. I learned that she had deserted Paulus for his best friend, that their baby had died, that they were in the process of getting a divorce. On this occasion, Paulus learned that I was betrothed and would be married very soon. This seemed to upset him.

One day, the husband of his deceased sister asked me to go for a walk. We went through the Tierpark where the roses were in full bloom, their fragrance intoxicating. But when he tried to persuade me to postpone my wedding, I shook my head. When he asked, "Do you love Paul?" I answered, "Yes." When he countered, "Why then don't you wait a year or at least six months, since Paul may have his divorce by then?" I refused again. When he asked, "Why not?" I answered pensively, "I do not think I trust him."

Paulus and I walked in the Grunewald, the woods around Berlin, after this conversation. When I took off my shoes, Paulus became ecstatic about my feet. In later years, I often said that if I hadn't walked barefoot with him that day, we would never have married. That was after I had learned that his preoccupation with feet had always been extraordinary. One of his most erotic sensations—a memory from childhood—was of the mother of a friend of his who behaved unconventionally, not to say audaciously, by walking barefoot in the sand at the ocean. It seemed to have disturbed Paulus's father, who was conventional, if not rigid.

Walking together in the Grunewald—I barefoot—on a hot fragrant July day before I left, we tried to discuss my coming marriage. Rather, I said fervently, "I will come back." "When?" he wanted to know. "In a year," I said, "next year." And with that we walked home, Paulus captivated by my feet, and I mulishly determined to get married and then come back in a year or so. Paulus did not know how to kiss me.

MARRIAGE

Greiz

Nobody was more heartily welcomed into our family than Albert. My mother liked him instantly. She remarked to my uncle and aunt, who had paid special attention to me through my adolescence, that Albert had tamed me. My uncle and aunt treated him as a son. They were to disinherit me after I left him.

I fell back into the same pattern of passive feminity that I had shown to Albert before my experience with Paulus. When we met for our wedding, I was vaguely conscious of the power I had over him, yet I asked no questions when, on our last walk alone before our wedding, Albert again sank to the roadside, whimpering and moaning, doubling up as if in severe pain. I did not connect his behavior with any lovemaking between Paulus and me.

I cried passionately when my family took pictures of Albert and me—I looked like a drowned mouse. Although I was disturbed, I did not admit to myself that I came to my wedding with Albert from another man. Albert seemed to love me dearly but was altogether unaware of what was going on within me.

Before the ceremony, my older sister put the flower wreath on my hair, leaving it open in the back. One of my aunts whispered, "Her wreath is open at the back, she is not a virgin." Albert was puzzled, when at last he permitted himself to enter his wife, to discover that she was not a virgin. I maintained a blissful ignorance. He relinquished his doubts, for he could not imagine his timid, feminine childbride could have been in the arms of another man.

Albert and I settled in Greiz after a short honeymoon in Munich.

He left in the morning for school, returned for a short luncheon, and left again. I learned how to cook and clean and went on writing poetry, illustrating it, and mailing it to Paulus, with whom I had a voluminous exchange of letters.

Albert and I had sex in the morning, deliciously warm from sleep. Lying in the crook of his arm, I would tease him into making love in the afternoon, when I posed for him endlessly—in the nude, standing, lying down—his obsessed brown eyes upon me. I was his woman.

After the first weeks of submission, I surprised and angered him by coming forth with the unorthodox view that I favored the lush Rubens nudes. I defended my admiration for Rubens and the baroque, taking pleasure in Albert's anger, while slipping out of his authority. It happened at lunch with our industrialist friends in the presence of their young son. I had asked the youth, with no explanation, to receive my letters from Paulus for me, since I preferred not to have them delivered to Albert's and my mailbox. He had consented without astonishment—I had become for him the voice from the world where freedom and vice ruled.

Paulus's letters became urgent. With the same heedlessness with which he had accepted my earlier decision not to leave him and return the following year, he now wrote that he wanted to see me. With the same heedlessness, I consented. I arranged an invitation from a fictitious woman friend to visit her overnight in a town not too near Greiz; I went directly to Berlin to meet my lover. We spent the night of nights together.

Paulus's housekeeper was a thief and a whore, who must have stolen for him without his knowledge. He could not have afforded the luxuries she offered us—a lovely table set for two, a delicious meal, wine, candles, and flowers, all in readiness for us, while she disappeared for the night. To Paulus and me it was a night of adoration, of ecstatic confession, of mutual love, until the early morning, when I returned to my husband.

Now I knew what was missing in Greiz. Although I was still subdued by the sweetness of satisfied lovemaking, of friendly people, and of affectionate security, I realized that I belonged in the intellectual and emotional confusion of a pluralistic worldview. There was no point and counterpoint in Albert. Sexual satisfaction was not enough for me.

I had written poetry and painted illustrations, sending them to

[92]

Paulus. These efforts had nothing to do with the comfortable sex fulfillment Albert gave me. The poems described more complex possibilities of emotional expression, the first signs of motherliness, the cutting experience of inflicting and inflicted pain, the ecstasy of worship, the leisureliness of lovers floating on clouds. I never wrote a poem about Albert. With him there was the orderly life, morning breakfast, the kiss before he left for school, his coming home for dinner, my being drawn and painted, Sunday outings, a trip to Munich to see art in a professional, technical way. Perhaps music was our point of encounter, but even there he had such a cheerful optimism, such simple lyrical feelings.

Albert lacked animal grace. He lacked the ease of carriage and movement reminiscent of the harmony of the dance of stars, which could persuade me that beautiful motion created the music of the spheres in body as well as mind. Paulus always had such music. Others had the deliriously delightful music of the body that came through physical training. The music of the body drove me to ballet, while the music of the emotions drove me to opera. The singing human voice became to me the expression of the voice of the spheres.

I used to go alone to the opera. In Europe one could lie undisturbed on a hard bench in the upper circles among weird figures, many of whom also lay on the benches, eyes closed, oblivious of everything but the divine sounds.

Perhaps my desperate search for the man who was perfect in mind, body, and soul was the source of my continuing discontent. Perhaps I had to relinquish the myth that I was a one-man woman. My history already implied that I was not. In reckless moments I sometimes said that the combined shapes of all one's lovers would give a composite picture of the ideal lover. But why the hunger and the myth, perpetuated through all civilizations, of the one man for the one woman. Later, it seemed to me that my friend Heinrich's idea of supplementing the one man and the one woman with another couple after a period of time, when their originality had exhausted themselves for each other, was not such a bad one.

When I missed a period and realized I was pregnant, I wrote Paulus that I would leave Albert and come to him. He replied, "Yes"—no word of warning, no word of advice, nothing to show he had thought about the situation, which could not possibly produce a simple yes. I packed one or two shabby suitcases. I cried every day. I prepared Albert an especially good lunch and left it for him with a letter from me beside his plate. With the household money, I bought my ticket in the morning, at the same time taking my suitcases to the station. Just before noon I returned to the station, boarding my train for Berlin. For some reason, I put on my least flattering clothes. I did not let Paulus know the time of my arrival.

A small thin old woman opened the door of Paulus's apartment when I knocked. She wore the garb of some religious order. Paulus would soon be back from a lecture. She took me into his room, where I lay down on the couch, covering myself with a white gossamer shawl. Two persons entered the apartment. The old lady spoke in a whisper. I heard the voice of a girl, a door opening and closing, and then subdued voices. Paulus finally opened the door to the room where I still lay under my white gauze. I must have looked like a corpse. He looked flushed.

There was no time for a loving welcome. He explained that a student with whom he was supposed to work was waiting in the next room. I got up, shedding my shawl, and proceeded to the other room, intending to excuse myself for having intruded upon their time. Paulus followed me. There was a scream, a violent, "No, no!" I advanced in spite of it. Paulus had to separate a screaming, scratching young girl from a bewildered, pregnant housebreaker. I withdrew to the other room: Paulus stayed with the girl. The apartment door slammed and Paulus returned to me, offering no explanation, and I asked no questions. Much later, after a letter I had written her had been returned to me marked "Delivery refused," we became friends. She loved Paulus truly and I learned to love her for it.

I was introduced to Aunt Toni, who had taken care of Paulus's family after his mother's death. She had come now to help out after the attractive thieving housekeeper had been jailed for considerable mischief.

Toni slept in the servant's room, a tiny cubicle with bed, chair, and night table. She had a washstand in the kitchen. She never saw herself in the nude, she washed her lower parts underneath her nightgown. Toni was the kindest of all human beings, lovingly taking the confusion in Paulus's home in her stride. She showed no surprise when she found a pretty woman in the bed of one of Paulus's tenants. To survive, he rented the best rooms in his apartment. Toni simply brought tea for two. She accepted me with the same spirit. Aunt Toni was a deeply religious woman. The house was untidy and dirty—what counted to her was the virtue of "agape."

I telephoned Albert in the evening. The industrialist's wife answered. Albert was near suicide, but they were with him. She was especially disgusted with me over the misuse of her son.

Paulus's bereaved brother-in-law, Frede, who had tried to persuade me not to marry Albert, took me into his parish house in Bremen until things had settled down. He considered Paulus and me babes in the woods. He loved Paulus dearly and seemed to have a gentle affection for me. A social worker who lived in Frede's house was to become Frede's second wife soon after the death of Johanna, Paulus's sister. With her were her two children, a short blond girl with Basedowish eyes, and a dark-haired, thin, lovely boy with sparkling brown eyes, a gypsy's dark skin, and an infectious laugh. I was not much help, wrapped as I was in my own problems—and ravenously hungry. I lived with the children on the lower floors. The house was roomy and provided us all with privacy.

I wrote Albert, asking for a divorce. He came to Bremen to see me and took me to his hotel for a night. I lay asleep in his arms, but when he asked me to return to him I shook my head. He departed the next day.

Paulus came for a weekend, staying at the house. He showed me the old market place in Bremen and the famous old city hall with its vaults and wine cellar full of huge barrels.

My mother, to whom I had written, suggested that during my confinement I come to Marburg, where my sister was a nurse's apprentice at the city hospital. It must have been a relief to Frede, as well as Paulus, who was desperately poor, the country being in the throes of inflation. I left the small boy Eckart with regret. I had grown fond of him. I was to meet him again in the United States when he was shuttling between German harbors and New York harbor as a merchant mariner. By then, he had become a full-fledged Nazi and was urging anti-Semitism upon me. I can still hear his complacent voice, as he trotted beside me down 57th Street between Broadway and Fifth Avenue, "Now, let's be honest about it; let's call him 'The Jew.'" I refused to see Eckart again.

Neither my father nor my mother brought up the subject of my leaving Albert. They went on vacation. I stayed with my sister, Liesel, the nurse who would take care of the baby. I wrote letters and waited. The child refused to be born. The doctors at the clinic decided my pelvis was too narrow and introduced something that expanded like a balloon into my vagina, a painful and useless process. At last they decided to use medicine. My vision became hazy—a white eyelike dandelion seed hovered in the air over me. I was not conscious of giving birth. I produced a strapping boy. Some frightening days of puerperal fever followed, then I recovered.

A slim, dainty lady, with the face of an Egyptian princess, announced herself at the hospital. She was carrying a bouquet of flowers, bringing greetings from Paulus. She was affectionate and sympathetic; my heart went out to her. Later I learned that gossip had connected Paulus with her—their engagement had been expected. When he learned of my coming to Berlin with child, he had not known what to do. He had planned a trip with her on Pentecost. He confided in her. The story goes that she had banged on the table, exclaiming, "You are going to marry HER!"

It was thus I acquired my second husband. I have often said that if I had not walked barefooted with a foot fetishist through the Grunewald and if a girl who loved him had not told him to marry me, I would never have spent my life with Paulus. Nor was I then aware that Paulus would always move between despair and ecstasy. For my part, I had been greatly shocked by the knowledge that I was carrying Albert's child. It transformed my vague toying with the idea of leaving Albert into a decision. I could not live with Albert's child in Albert's care. I could never have felt with Albert and Albert's child the supreme delight I experienced after the birth of Paulus's and my two children.

My sister Liesel was disturbed because the baby's eyes did not follow a burning candle she held up to his face. I did not get the implication that he might not be altogether normal.

Paulus wrote urgently that he needed me. Thoughtless of rational considerations or practical consequences, I started packing. I decided to place the child in a nursery near Paulus's apartment, where I could nurse him every day. Either my parents or Albert would pay for it. My sister accompanied me to Berlin—I was still too weak to carry the heavy baby. I never wondered where the money for this adventure actually did come from. I suppose my mother helped.

The nursery looked efficient. I visited every day, as long as my milk held out. I took a room nearby and Uli came in to give me lessons in stenography, to prepare me for a secretarial job.

When I arrived at the nursery one afternoon, I found that the child had been transferred to an upper floor. He looked thin and cried nastily. I was frightened at his changed face; during his hysterical weeping, it resembled Albert's mother's face. I did not inquire into the reasons for the child's crying so desperately, but the sight of his sick-looking stool alarmed me. Someone informed Albert that the child was very ill. He took it away, by now in great frustration and anger. I had never seen the light of recognition in the baby's brown, insensitive eyes.

The child died. Albert accused me of having killed him, and was now willing to give me a divorce. I went by train to see him before burial—a long day to Greiz and back to Berlin the same black night. The dead child looked yellow and waxlike, the face still had beauty, the eyelids with the long dark lashes were closed, the little mouth looked sad, as if it had known pain. I stayed a short time. In leaving I touched the round cold forehead. Albert sent me a drawing he had made of the child's face after death. I kept it in my room for a long time, along with a photograph of the tombstone on the grave.

Paulus had been sympathetic with my sorrow. He had dreamed about my baby, while I had been worrying about his health. He had tried to comfort me with the doctor's verdict that the child had brain fever and would probably never have been quite normal. Paulus had lost his and Greti's child through a fault of the clinic. The child was allowed to remain outdoors on a balcony too long. The baby had died from pneumonia.

My divorce proceeded, Paulus was already free. I met Albert before a judge. It was over in a few minutes. When we came out of the courthouse, Albert took my arm. He seemed to have lost his anger. He invited me to lunch. I refused. We were both very sad. My presence seemed to disarm him, while I was caught in speechless surrender of myself to his image of me. Much later, when I returned to Germany after the Nazis were defeated, I visited Albert to tell him how miserable I felt for having been so awful to him. There was no talk about guilt or forgiveness. He was his old loving self. He turned to a lady friend of his and remarked, "Now you know why I have never been able to be angry with her." We spent a wonderful day together, driving in her car to the Rhine, drinking wine, eating together, and enjoying each other.

Neither the deaths of my child and Paulus's child, nor our divorces and memories of our divorced spouses ever played any role in Paulus's and my relationship. The past seemed to be over when we entered our life together. No memories.

[97]

Berlin

I was introduced to Paulus's friends as Frau Hannah, before our official marriage. My mother visited Paulus in Berlin. She sat facing him in his high-backed chair, unruly hair falling over his forehead, water-blue eyes peering through thick glasses. He was wearing his usual at-home garb, a rather shabby officer's littevka. Afterward my mother exclaimed to me in an astonished voice, "That is the boy who caused so much trouble?"

I lived in a rented room one block from Paulus's Taunustrasse apartment, which was called "the vestibule of catastrophes." If the head of the household was not in trouble, someone renting a room or visiting there was bound to be.

Uli taught me stenography. He was delighted with my new companion. Dubbed "Prince Consort" by my friends, Paulus soon established his own relationship with them.

I was introduced to Paulus's father, after due preparation. He was dignified, courteous, and friendly. He is supposed to have made a remark about the Mona Lisa with reference to me. He did not approve of the Mona Lisa, but he must have been attracted by her and by whatever he saw in me that had caused him to make the remark. He accompanied us on some trips during vacations—a fuzzy gray-and-black streaked dog with eyes mourning for affection, a gracious dinner-table personality, a teller of not unwitty stories. It was hard for me to show him affection, for I sensed the terror Paulus felt in his company. I gave it up altogether on learning that, when Paulus was to receive an honorary degree from his university, his father had demanded that his son obtain one for him before accepting the honor himself. Doubtless Paulus tried, but was obliged to accept his degree before "Little Father," as his family called him.

Later on, when Little Father visited us in Frankfurt, a long-delayed theological discussion took place. Paulus tried to evade the issue by claiming a misunderstanding. At this point I broke in, screaming at both of them that there was no misunderstanding, they were on opposite sides of the fence and they knew it and had better admit it. Paulus naturally dreaded my undercutting his intellectual arguments with emotional fervor. His father, who had a high position in the church hierarchy and was a conservative (whereas Paulus was considered a radical), kept his dignity.

Some time before his death, Paulus's father became melancholic and despondent, complaining to his daughter, "I have thought through all the problems of the world. I don't know what to think about any more."

I met Eckart and Dox, Paulus's two oldest friends. Both had had a part in freeing Paulus from parental influence. Eckart was the son of the patron of the parish Paulus's father served as minister when Paulus was a boy. He educated Paulus in modern art after Paulus returned from the war, where he had tried to teach himself through available periodicals, wading through an abyss of bad taste.

Eckart, Paulus, and I visited exhibitions of works by Nolde, Kandinsky, the Futurists, Chagall, Cézanne, Gaugin, and van Gogh. Even better, Eckart moved the two of us to tears of laughter with his devastating black humor. It shocked me to learn later that he was a Nazi with a low party number. My sister M.L., who later became very dear to him, insisted that he had feared persecution on account of his clubfoot, which he had had since birth, and that neither his pure race nor aristocratic name would save him. It was one of the shameful incongruities of a rotten period that a man like Eckart, to balance his misery over having become a traitor, compensated by having Jewish girl friends, sometimes endangering himself.

Later, in 1938, Eckart visited us in Switzerland while we were on a trip from the United States. I noticed that, being fresh from Nazi Germany, he was ill-informed in political matters. He died from a painful kidney condition, leaving my sister in unbearable grief.

Dox broke away from the church after becoming a minister. He had worked with Paulus in a parish as practicing minister. They had lectured together at youth conferences, both taking the radical side. Later on, in Berlin, Dox established a circle of young women with whom he acquainted his friends, encouraging them to get involved with one another. Huysman's *La Bas*, Baudelaire's *Flowers of Evil*, Nietzsche's *Zarathustra*, and descriptions of black masses circulated in his group.

Paulus had awaited Dox's judgment on me with great trepidation. But Dox approved, commenting that, in my elegant mannish suit and cheap but chic black-and-white cloche, I resembled a pander, that is, a male "in drag."

I took my revenge when he invited Paulus and me to his place, where he was lording it over a room full of girls. In answer to some silly challenge, I drew lines around Dox's eyes and mouth, making him look rather devilish and lizardlike. When I had first seen his photograph in Paulus's room, I had exclaimed that Dox looked evil. Paulus would never admit that Dox had indeed been evil to seduce Paulus's wife Greti while Paulus was at the front. Paulus granted Greti the divorce she requested, but Dox did not marry her.

Besides Eckart and Dox, there was a third great influence that lured Paulus away from middle-class respectability, namely, Nietzsche. One of the first books Paulus gave me was Nietzsche's *Thus Spake Zarathustra*, which broke with everything Paulus had learned from Little Father. It must have tortured the father to see his son fly away into heights and depths where he dared not follow.

The lines of the midnight song, "The world is deep and deeper than the day can read. Deep is its woe, joy deeper still than grief can be. Woe saith, 'Hence, go,' but joys want all eternity, want deep profound eternity"—these lines intoxicated me as they had intoxicated Paulus. Somehow Paulus seemed caught in his lust for pain, but I like to believe that in rare hours he found the joy that is deeper than suffering.

Paulus liked to believe that he had no enemies, whereas I preferred being confronted by people. I liked a good fight over principles. Paulus, on the other hand, would acknowledge, compare, contribute information, but he generally avoided conflict. One exception was his open letter to Emanuel Hirsch, an intimate friend from their student days who not only joined the Nazis but went so far as to apply Paulus's concept of Kairos to the Nazi movement. Hirsch had visited us in Kampen, a summer retreat, before the Nazis came to power. He was a spidery and disjointed man with a big head, wolfing his food, being disagreeable in every respect, pouring vile criticism on

Paulus, trying my patience with impossible manners, until the stroke of midnight. Then he changed into a most humble, affectionate friend, praising and embracing his pal Paulus. It disgusted me altogether. Paulus's patience with him was exemplary.

Paulus belonged to many different circles. He was only an instructor, but some of his older colleagues in the University of Berlin who recognized his abilities entertained him occasionally, breaking through the German academic hierarchy. One remarkable evening he lectured at the Kant Society, which brought him instant recognition. He invited me. From my seat, I watched him walking around, greeting friends, talking, asking questions, appearing clumsy and unsure about what he was going to say. He was certainly unimpressive—shabbily dressed and wearing strong glasses. I was anxious, fearing he might be unable to give a good lecture, but with his very first words at the podium, he was transformed. His voice rang out clearly; indecision had fled. He became the instrument of the powers of thought; *he was the word*. What he said convinced. He conquered the evening.

I attended one of his university courses on the pre-Socratics. I had read Plato, and Paulus gave me Aristotle to read. The course enchanted many of his students. It was one of Paulus's favorite subjects. (He read the fragments of Heraklitus to me at home.)

Paulus gave one lucrative course, for the fashionable circle of intellectuals in what is now West Berlin. He participated in another group that included economists, social scientists, politicians, philosphers, and people in the government. We were to find most of them again in the United States as refugees from Nazi Germany.

One of Paulus's Jewish friends was Adolf. He had been a high government official in the disarmament section during the breakdown after World War I. He was physically diminutive and had a deadly wit. I was slightly embarrassed by walking beside him in the street—I was far too tall. Adolf loved to harass Paulus and adored him because Paulus would not let his criticisms break his fighting spirit. Paulus came home exhausted after those conversations, reporting that after a long struggle with words, Adolf and the group invariably discussed the problems in Paulus's terminology.

Paulus's friend Karl Mennicke (whom we called Karolus), a member of the Socialist Party, remained in Germany and was thrown into a concentration camp. After his release, he taught a seminar in Holland. He returned to Frankfurt after the war. Karl had an engaging laugh. When he visited us when Erdmuthe was a small child, she asked me to leave her bedroom door open so she could hear his infectious outbursts.

Doris and Arnold, together with a friend of theirs from the League of Nations, were the benefactors of our whole group during the inflation following World War I, before Hitler came to power. Their gift of Swiss francs allowed Paulus and me to spend a summer in Hiddensee, where we regained our strength, living in a simple boarding house with comparatively good food prepared by a friendly, healthy Hiddensee woman. Paulus told of how he had spent a summer alone in Kampen on Sylt, subsisting on a boiled ham. During the last weeks of his sojourn, the ham became infested with maggots, but he was too poor to throw it away. He would cut the infested parts out and daily take a new risk, inspecting each slice carefully before he put it between two slices of bread.

Doris often invited us for dinner. She gave me good clothes that had belonged to her fashionably dressed sister. She talked of poetry and painting. I recall her in a long, gray silk chiffon evening gown, looking like a silvery moth. Once she gave me money, with which Paulus and I bought me a green shapeless thing of a rain hat.

Doris and Arnold entertained us at a cabaret. Whereas I was bewildered, Paulus was at ease, enjoying the lascivious as well as the farcical. Afterward I wrote a poem, "Saint in the Cabaret."

We would later meet Arnold and Doris at Yale University and again in Washington, D.C., at his Institute for Political Science. We would also visit them in their house on the tip of a Maine inlet.

Paulus considered marriage a decision of the will. He once said jokingly that he was the most faithful of all men, meaning that he always returned to his initial encounter of spiritual recognition, with a woman or a man. He visualized one's deeper self—perhaps unknown even to that person—clearing away the rubble of superficiality, often as if he had touched one with a magic wand. Friends would never forget the glory he had brought them in understanding each one's deepest being. After that initial encounter, he might easily slide down the ladder to pornography, using the women for his peculiarities.

Paulus had a feminine component that made him vulnerable to masculine women. My own masculinity was not in the sphere of sexuality.

I turned Paulus into a little god, a boy Eros. He expected me to be his goddess, taking him into loving arms whenever he emerged from the darkness of his undiscriminating sensuality. Our masks contradicted each other.

One of Paulus's marital jokes was to insist that I was his "second best." He called his first best his "cosmic reservation." A first best did not exist on earth, he said, but one must reserve a place for the great unknown One who might come, as the Messiah might come at any moment to the waiting Jews.

In Berlin I was a young woman fighting for my love life, experiencing the crowd of amorous women as one giant, quivering Medusa, the composite vagina of their desire turning into a huge jellyfish that seemed to devour me.

Paulus liked masses of people, crowds, whereas I abhorred them. He was writing *Masses and the Spirit* at the time when, on one of the hottest summer days in August, he took me to one of the freshwater beaches of the working people. I had never been swimming in a lake—our family had always spent summers on the Baltic Sea. I found myself, after a stifling train trip, among a mass of people each weighing 200 pounds or more. There were the flabby, pale and unaired, pimply skins, the neglected physiques of squalid fat mammies, flesh growing unpleasantly red under the scorching sun, men in worn undershirts, or in grotesque bathing attire, airing their heavy, smelly bodies that varied in shape and fitness or deformity according to each one's harassing job. Laughter was loud. It was difficult to find a place to sit down, so I walked around aimlessly, hating it all. Paulus, in ecstasy, stepped over their outstretched bodies.

When our mutual divorces came through, we were married. Paulus's sister Elizabeth and her husband, a minister from Bavaria, invited us to hold the ceremony at their parish near Berlin. We planned to return to Taunusstrasse the same evening. My mother came in from Marburg. She took care of the expenses. We had crabmeat and a saddle of game with all the trimmings, wine, and a fancy dessert. Elizabeth's son, Hans Jürgen, who was also our friend, tried to recite a poem in our honor, after the mocha had been handed around in small cups. He made a mistake and his grandfather corrected him, forcing him to repeat the faulty lines again and again. Hans stuttered. It was a painful moment for the wedded couple. I wore a black taffeta dress and no wreath.

On our trip home, Paulus told me that he planned to go out that same evening. Dox had arranged a final bachelor's outing for him and I was not invited. I was stunned, then infuriated. Was I to spend my first legally married night alone in my now legal home? I had hoped to transform the "vestibule of catastrophes" into a house of happiness. Above all, I was exasperated at Paulus's refusal to admit that the evening without me was meant to be an orgy. I wanted him to recognize his desire to spend our wedding night with his friends and without me. Paulus insisted that nothing untoward would take place and he left.

I took my blanket back into the maid's room from which I had just moved. I was deeply hurt, especially by Paulus's denial of the truth as I saw it. He had deflowered me, he had awakened me to an erotic reality beyond the physical satisfaction I had experienced with Albert. He had relieved me of the twisted relationship with women in which I had taken the role of a man. He had opened me to sensations of amorous ecstasy. I felt him with all my nerves, in the pores of my skin, with all physical and emotional passion. I lay through the hours of the night, shivering in cold despair, feeling extinguished in Paulus, into whom another woman's life stream was now pouring. I felt the coldness of death.

Paulus returned deeply moved by the events of the night with Dox. It had lived up to my predictions. After initial drinks, he found himself in another room alone with one of Dox's girl friends. She started making love to him, but he could not get me out of his mind. He told her about me and his problems. She remained friendly and sympathetic, and they sat talking for a long time. He came home feeling he had won a supreme victory over himself. But it was too late for me. I was ten years younger and lacked the maturity and generosity to accept him lovingly. In spite of my sexual experiences, I was an uneducated, childish being. I felt ambivalent about our marital pleasure from then on. Jealousy had sprung from the catastrophe of my wedding night—jealousy manifesting itself in rage. I was very good at outbursts of anger at the memory of myself left out in the cold. Paulus could never live it down.

I had felt no jealousy the year before when, as his sweetheart, I had stayed in his room. Then I simply handed him the safety pin or hairpin or a button part of an elegant costume and he accepted them without remark. I had even proposed to him that he make love to other women, and I had not felt a shred of curiosity or jealousy. I was engrossed in him, I felt he was engrossed in me.

Jealousy was born on my wedding night, when Paulus went with

[105]

Dox and left me alone. Or was it simply that we had made the traditional marriage vows, that we had entered upon the bourgeois state of my being a married woman by civil right and each of us had become a part of the property of the other? I became suspicious of women, asking questions, demanding "truthful" answers, torturing Paulus and myself with reports of intimacies that, had they been true intimacies, could not have been reported and described.

It took me a lifetime of suffering to distinguish between the elated, timeless moment of physical copulation and the daily striking of the clock for the hours of drudgery, separating one's life from the other in walking, talking, eating, drinking. If I had not encountered Heinrich, I might have left Paulus.

Paulus and I met Heinrich at a conference at which Heinrich spoke against Rudolf Steiner. He emphasized truthfulness, implying that Steiner had obscured some quotes in one of his books. Heinrich had been an ardent disciple of Steiner for many years.

We lunched together. He was a tall, heavyset man with a full-moon face and a high forehead under dark hair. His eyebrows, thin and wide apart, made his forehead look naked. He had dark eyes; he moved with a certain affected softness. He had sensitive tapered fingers on hairy hands. He could have been of Italian ancestry. He was a doctor of philosophy and of jurisprudence and had studied architecture. He was full of the new discipline, psychoanalysis. He professed to some practical experience himself. He had been in the Stefan George circle for a while and had written a satire about that group. When we met him he had just given up being a disciple of Rudolf Steiner. Heinrich was developing a system of ethics for the new world that was coming.

A fascinating conversation developed between Paulus and Heinrich. Heinrich had an uncanny ability to assume a feminine, listening attitude toward Paulus, and he made me feel at ease. I contributed a tale about Steiner, whom Heinrich had attacked in his lecture. I had attended one of Steiner's lectures some time before and had felt arrogantly amused at the audience, which consisted of frail-looking women and disturbed-looking men. I had watched Steiner's technique, interspersing his speech with witty stories, evoking laughter in the audience, spellbinding them again after the relaxation of participation in his humor. After the lecture he stood, one foot resting on the raised platform, talking to a goggle-eyed girl encircled by his legs. I had burst out laughing—he had seemed, for a split second, to change into a dirty red-and-gold feathered rooster, the girl into a hen.

I had often amused myself by observing the aura around the heads and bodies of my friends when I got bored with conversation and my attention wandered. I saw strong yellows, clear blues and browns, grays, mixtures of darker colors, as well as black, some whites and some olive greens. Paulus, of course, whom I watched idly while he spoke, gave off the greatest vibrations, yellow and red mixed with white, some gray, and dark, brownish black.

To Heinrich, what I confided seemed altogether natural. It was the alphabet of occultism. I heard more about Steiner, Blavatsky, and the astral plane. We talked of Jung and Freud.

Paulus was to go on to Marburg very soon, to teach theology as an assistant professor. The secretary of culture, who offered him the job, had strongly advised him to accept—he was patronizing in guiding the young and promising. He insisted that, if Paulus remained in Berlin, he would never make the grade; he should go to the provinces and then return to the capital with his reputation made.

Heinrich said he would visit us in Marburg. He had a wife and children living in Ascona in a little stone house on a hillside. We must visit with him, too.

Meanwhile, we introduced my friends to Heinrich. Uli immediately called him "the magician." Heinrich's attitude was an invitation to confide one's troubles to him. He could sit through a whole afternoon listening, drinking, eating, enjoying himself, and giving all sorts of advice, for the most part disarmingly simple. In any difficult situation he seemed to solve the riddle of the egg of Columbus. Uli introduced his lesbian group to him, among them Eve. We once talked about Italy, and Eve casually mentioned some intriguing details of the city we were discussing. Heinrich asked her when she had been there. She had not. She was only using her imagination, she explained soberly.

Eve was somewhat enamored of me and I was excited by her, without becoming the pursuer, as I had been with my previous ladyloves. It was she who played the role of the aggressor. She wore mannish shirts and suits, her chestnut hair was straight, her nose seemed to belong in an older man's face. She had well-formed small lips and a jutting chin. Eve acted like a young male, chatting endlessly about her flirtations with other women, wherein the difficulty was to make sure one was not betrayed by an abnormal young female. She talked about the bearded he-man and the silly she-woman. For Eve, a third kind of humanity seemed to exist, having a balance of male and female qualities and being equipped somewhat differently from the he-man and she-woman.

Uli and Eve sometimes arranged with their female and male partners little free evenings to which Paulus, Heinrich, and I were invited. During one of these, a long-legged lesbian aristocrat came sailing into the room on a bicycle, wearing pink leggings, her face painted, flowers in her hair, imitating a circus beauty. The kissing, drinking, and flirting were indiscriminate. I felt uncomfortable. Paulus was delighted. Uli arranged one evening for men only. Paulus would not participate, though he often talked about his latent homosexuality during his student days. Heinrich did. He came back glowing. He had made love to one of Uli's friends.

Heinrich proposed a love trip for Eve and me. The four of us went to a hotel near Berlin, where she and I occupied a room together for the night. Everything went well until Eve tried to make love to me in earnest. Until then she had only courted me, with kisses on the hand, letters, and lovely drawings of me.

While we lay in bed together, I refused the slightest liberty. Neither childish laughter nor manful decision nor yet friendly persuasion—nothing could bring me to accept her caresses.

On the following day, we returned to our harmless flirtation with nibbling kisses on ears, lips, cheeks, and hands. It seemed abundantly clear that I was no longer interested in women.

Interlude

THE MAGICIAN AND THE MOON

When the moon's delightful silver chalice
Hovers high above the verdant valley,
The Magician lifts his practiced hands,
Making it incline to where he stands.

And he draws mysterious magic rings
And a secret magic song he sings,
Till the moving moon-cup, round and sweet,
Comes to sway and tremble at his feet.

There is magic mirth in his design
As he fills the cup with hot red wine.
Thirstily the steaming cup he drains,
Pours and drinks, until the starlight wanes.

When the last, pale stars no longer show,
When the East takes on a rosy glow,
The Magician reels among the flowers,
Reels from all those moon-sweet, wine-red hours.

From his drunken fingers toward the sky
Glides the silver moon in gentle flight,
While he stands transfigured by the sight,
Fever-browed, and with his arms held high.

THE TREE POEM

Once you were a tree
Your loving twig-hands,
raised in fatherly fashion,
tender sounding
in noontime wind.

I flew through your branches,
sang in morning light,
and built my nest
in your heart.

When the weather was angry
we swayed together.
I, secure at your side,
trembled whenever you did.

But in the summer rain,
deeply, trustingly hugged
by your sheltering leaves,
I gazed sleepily
into pearls of water
falling in silver chains
round my impervious house.

HEINRICH

When you, gentle deceased,
look up to me from
the frozen ground,
I whirl my limbs in dancing still.
Sweet tastes the bread of earth,
the confusion of love.
You see me in tears?
I cry for the living—
ensnared as am I in the world—
a silver fish in a net.

TRIP TO ITALY (*Excerpts*)

August 11. The extent of the ocean is indescribable and strenuous to see. Evenings I am totally exhausted and register the movement of the ship without pleasure, the ocean being smooth like a green meadow, sometimes blue and hazy on the horizon. Today we passed England—Dover, with piers and houses clearly distinguishable in delicate colors tinged in crayon. The coastline of moderate height, yellowish-white, the sea blue, silky smooth. The first porpoise.

August 15. The dissociation from everything human and animal on board is unbelievable—no telephone, no coffee to brew, not the slightest surprise, but for the weather. On one side of the ship a pyramid emerges, beside it a block of rocks, which divide during our progress into smaller and larger rock islands. To the right, the rock islands are deep blue against the sun, with vistas. On the left, Portugal—flat, long, brownish with darker areas, presumably its forests, and with snow-white houses; gradually the higher rocky coastline comes into view. We could see the surf. Evening, the moon, brazen-faced and red after a glowing sunset. The sunset exactly between the two rock islands—an opening into the underworld. The ocean with vast cloudy horizon, which reminded me of the desolation of a desert. It was infinite in a terrifying oppressive way.

August 30. Syracuse. Drive in a car to Latomia del Paradiso, the ear of Dionysus . . . the Greek theater. I have to search for the theater, which is deeply embedded, cut from natural stone. Seen from above, it has the charming perspective of the curves of the seats adjoining the burial places; beside it, the Roman amphitheater, which is architecturally coarse in comparison with the delicate Greek lines. There is a low passage for the beasts; catacombs of San Giovanni with an old chapel. The ground plan is the Greek cross; on three sides, irregular passages with caves. Capitals with sculptured Evangelists surround the central quadrangle—heavy set, dark arches from the fifteenth century.

September 1. Girgenti. We walk in stifling heat toward the temples, the roads without shade. Slowly they come into view. We walk still more slowly around the first temple. Its one long side has no shade whatever—to the left a brilliant sea, to the right a view of the white Girgenti on a hill, the sky cloudless, the ochre stone particles of the temple glistening in the sun. Never have I experienced a more perfect perspective. The columns represent equilibrium, carrying the load without seeming overburdened, sustaining without heaviness . . . .

September 4. Palermo. High mass in the Sistine Chapel, as a priest had described it when we first visited the mosaic chapel. At nine o'clock we went and were given seating tickets. The church was decorated. On the main altar was a huge crucifix; before it, silver vases holding silver leaves; from just to the right and left, in the golden walls of the mosaic, projected silver bouquets of flowers. At right and left on the balconies were vases of asters and candles. Above the choir stalls, the main altar and its sides were covered with slim silver-light candles of different sizes in immense masses, having the effect of an enormous organ of light.

At ten o'clock, the cardinal, in red, entered in solemn state. He was surrounded by four bishops in red; and he sat on a chair at the left. Then commenced an endless ritual of taking off and putting on of vestments. The cardinal and his bishops were first in red, then white, then gold with embroidered miters; books were handed the cardinal from which he read, facing the congregation or the altar. Choir boys and bishops, everybody, in the most precious garments, bowed down. It was all magnificent, but not in the least sacred. The bishops were seated in the choir stalls and Capuchin monks leaned on the precious pulpit before which the candles shone.

It became sacred when a priest read with monotonous voice, emphasizing certain syllables. This kind of reading produced an inner shock, as if we were approaching God with fear and trembling. The magic power of times past echoed in his reading as well as in the singing of the monks, who were joined by the high voices of the boys' choir, turning the plaintive seriousness into a blissful sighing revelation. Impressive, too, was the cardinal during the transubstantiation ritual, turning bread and wine into the body and blood of the Christ at the altar, the center of which, in silver and white, presented a dark inlaid piece of eliptical marble, suggesting in a mystical way the center of the church.

September 14. Capri. A ride to the blue grotto, close to the rocks of Capri—huge ochre-colored formations, gray and black where the ocean constantly floods the stone, and some red-violet similar to the dress of the woman in Böcklin's painting, "The Breakers." A yellow or green ridge rises above the violet, and further up, the stone becomes blue or green, then by degrees black and ochre and brown, its steep slopes partly grown with palms and pine trees. The rocks at the shoreline enclose washed-out caves, where the water streams in, heaps up upon itself, and returns, puffing and hissing.

The water is clear to the bottom, green or yellowish black in shade, and pink-blue, black or black-green where the rocks are massive. There are many spectators inside the grotto. The water flowing over the rocks makes them glitter as silvery as the shrine of Santa Rosalia in Palermo.

September 16. By boat to Naples, which is dirty, hotel close to the railroad station, a section known as "il vasto" (the desert). In the museum, an obstinate fight to understand the plaster-cast cats (in Germany, I had to learn Greek sculpture from copies cast in plaster, which I abhorred). Slowly we discover the Artemis (archaic Greek), which grows more attractive the longer we look at it. The Dioscuri do not move me. Acceptable are a head of Hera, which seems a bit thin in the cheeks, a marble head of Apollo, very smooth with smile of divinity, and a Dionysus with repaired nose, and a head of Zeus as well. I am moved by working through the shapes of the faces, the way the nose, mouth, and eyes become the expression of the intended character of the gods. Apollo has the harmonious curve of the eyebrows, Zeus the brows curved downward at the bridge of his nose, which accounts for the impression of dignity. The eyes of Dionysus are nearly triangular, which results in an expression of melancholy. Very divine, the head of Zeus, with its straight nose, the expressionistic power of which I understand only now—the superhuman thoughtlessness that shows in this line, which in Dionysus becomes a heavy thoughtfulness, although never a self-reflection in our sense of intellect. These gods are still immersed in contemplation. Three torsos, especially one with the turn of his hips, arouses the feeling of the divinity of pure being. . . .

Strolling along the harbor, sunset reflecting on the ocean; beyond the gently rising Vesuvius with its irresistible line . . . illumination of water and sky . . . much pink and light blue . . . a mother-of-pearl shell on gleaming sand.

September 17. Museum. The bronzes. The big ones attract us, the small ones enchant us—the color alone, green-blue, deep saturated tones. Sometimes the eyes are painted gold. They stand, contemplating a vision of the world that we seem to be able to participate in by contemplating them.

The most beautiful of the bronzes was to us the Apollo with the golden eyes, a standing figure, slightly bent forward. He was supposed to be playing an instrument. The divine head with symmetrical curls and open golden eyes, the eye sockets sculptured to perfection.

[113]

The unintellectual, straight bone of the nose and the immediacy of the smiling, curved lips overwhelmed me. A beautiful mouth expresses a mystery of nonsecrecy, it has nothing to do with thinking, it is pure being without the intermediary of word or thought. Some of these statues appear to visualize a harmony toward which they walk through air that is clear and thin and offers no resistance of any kind to their advance . . . .

Impressive Mercury, difficult to grasp from the front, magnificent from the side—a package tightly bound together in the middle, radiating elasticity from each side, ready to move at an instant. Portrait heads of bronze, interesting ugly Greek philosophers and smooth Roman heads. Socrates is seductive in his sympathetic ugliness, his head an onion, broad in the upper parts, triangular in the lower parts of his face, his fish-mouth-shaped lips strange but impressive.

September 20. . . . In the afternoon, extensive rest, drive to San Martino, view on city and harbor. Intoxicating, the broad line of Vesuvius, which, in its slow ascent, arouses feelings of happiness similar to the well-balanced gables of the Greek temples. The city in yellow and rose. By degrees, the city lights come up, Vesuvius disappears and only the lights of the crater hang as a mysterious constellation in the still air. The ocean becomes a black hole, the houses cubic and heavy . . . in the background, lighted streets, the harbor illuminated . . . toward the hinterland the lights become smaller and shine in competition with the starlit sky. And everything grows pink in the arriving darkness. We dine on a terrace with a view of all the magnificence, we listen to the Italian street singers and watch with delight a handsome, slim waiter, who listens to the music with abandon. Music and wine, the civilized surroundings, the beautiful landscape—all give us much pleasure.

Marburg

ᛏ

Being in Marburg meant living between dusk and dawn in the twilight zone before the sunrise, after the sun of Berlin had set.

Paulus hated to leave Berlin. It was the city of Dox, who had opened the door for him to the freedom of "10,000 women's legs," as Paulus had cried out delightedly when Dox took him to his first fancy-dress ball; and of Eckart, who had opened the door of modern art. Both had guided him away from Little Father's world, instigating his complete revolt.

Berlin, for Paulus, meant anonymity and voyeurism in streets full of desirable crowds, sitting in cafés writing his papers, watching the girls go by, meeting over a sherry, being in the world. He often told me how he had stood before the houses with the big iron gates, promising himself that he would some time enter the golden gates of Berlin victoriously, partaking of all the cultural amenities, all the vice and glory, all the wines and women the metropolis had to offer.

Paulus felt an outcast in the small cobblestoned village-university community of Marburg. We did not admire the old houses with their wooden brown-painted framework showing between whitewashed clay walls and sloping roofs. We had moved from the linden-bordered Taunusstrasse in Berlin to an ugly pension with one room in the bottom of the valley where Marburg lay. The food was bad, everything seemed coarse and unbearable, including the muddled Hessian accent. We walked daily through Marburg's narrow winding streets bordered by stone walls or iron gates, behind which the fraternity houses lurked, up to the castle overlooking the open plain. The high encircling hills gave Paulus claustrophobia.

The village was in servitude to the students, chiefly to the gilded youth of the wealthier dueling fraternities. My father had belonged to one of these elegant Marburg fraternities and had managed to lure his sons in. All my brothers had fashionable cuts across their faces. My youngest brother, whose nerve at the edge of one eye had been severed, had to wear a monocle. To my younger sister it had meant invitations and status in Marburg. To my mother it had meant waiting for the *Frühschoppen*—drinking in the morning—and at night the whole rigamarole of a masculine fraternity in the upper stratas, pampered by delighted old members of the club, and endless returns to the alma mater, the student's cap over silly drunken faces, roaming the streets in a happy uproar of old fraternity songs, all lovingly protected by the still subservient villagers.

Later, on our return from Italy, the first thing we met on the train to Marburg was a group of tipsy fraternity students who pushed me rudely in the corridor between compartments. After the easy-going, smiling, charming Italians, it was a sorry comedown. I said, "Back in Germany." I hated it.

Another misfortune in Marburg was our colleagues. There was little social life for us anyway—we had no status, and professors did not entertain instructors or "foreigners" who came to their bailiwick to teach. On the few occasions when we were entertained, we met narrowness of mind, a cheap nationalism, and the utmost hostility toward anything not homegrown. I once regretted out loud that the Elizabeth church in Marburg did not have more beautiful stained-glass windows, which fact made the light within uninspiring. This was a sacrilege, the Elizabeth church was not to be criticized. We made enemies when we confessed that we would like to go to Italy. Italy was the "enemy of our country. You would not want to go into enemy country." To Paulus and me, Marburg was the enemy country.

I had my hair cut and wore modern clothes, very modestly to be sure. One day the wife of a theology professor walked past me and, turning around, eyed me with great distaste. She walked those cobblestone streets in a long, medieval dress, with braids around her head, obviously considering me an unpatriotic outcast, with which view I definitely agreed.

Paulus's main struggle was with the philosophy of Heidegger. He met some of Heidegger's doctoral students, and endless debates followed. Oddly enough, the Ordinarius Professor Heidegger and the privatdocent Adjunct Professor Tillich never met during our stay in Marburg. The gossip about what Heidigger had said in a lecture about Paulus would be carried by Heidigger's faithful underlings. Paulus would answer in his own lecture, and that would be forwarded again. In time, it resulted in Paulus's growing influence—at the end of his second term, he had a full lecture hall—but when he left for Berlin, having survived the term, he fainted in the corridor of our third-class compartment. The experience in Marburg had been grim.

In Marburg Paulus also experienced his most frightening dream. He woke up with an unearthly, terrible scream, which brought me shivering from my bed. He hurt his heel in his convulsive shock. It was hard to quiet him—he did not seem really awake for some time; covering his eyes with his hands, he moaned and wept, "Oh, Hannah'chen." Slowly he came to and told me his dream. He had gone down a street and my father had come toward him. After they met and passed, Paulus turned around, to find that my father had also turned around and was looking at him with his watery blue eyes, which had caused Paulus to shriek with terror and convulse with fright.

We had two friends among the professors—Professor v.s., to whom Paulus mentioned his wish to visit Italy and who helped him with good advice and some money, and Rudolf Otto. Both men were cosmopolitan. Rudolf Otto visited our small apartment in one of the faculty houses on the hillside, where I did my own housekeeping. He joined us in watching the percolator, the hot water spouting into its glass top and falling back until the brown liquid became strong enough, and we would have coffee and cake. I read his books. Paulus had been influenced by Otto's idea of the *mysterium tremendum*. They talked philosphy, I listened. I venerated the sky-blue-eyed white-haired, slim and youthful-looking man who talked about India, about beauty, about art. He was generous and worldly wise. We had a meal in his home, which his sister prepared. There were no status barriers. During the Nazi period he died of a fall from a tower at the top of one of his favorite mountain walks, overlooking the hilly country.

Paulus was invited to join the theological faculty at Giessen. He refused, shuddering with disgust after he had visited the place. The narrowness of the city and of the full-professors' minds, the self-important querulousness, the lack of aesthetic awareness—he abhorred them all. He was not willing to remain in the provinces much longer for the sake of his career.

The secretary of education of Saxony offered Paulus a position in philosophy of religion at the Technische Hochschule in Dresden. He was also to give one theological lecture every two weeks in Leipzig, so as not to lose his contact with the universities. Paulus agreed to this rather than remain in exile at a small university. The minister of education, who became a good friend in Dresden, professed himself highly amused at Paulus's shrewdness in stating his academic demands—this young philosopher of religion was not so impractical after all.

We went to Italy with the money from Professor v.S. and from Paulus's book, published by Ullstein. I had wanted to see Italy and Piero de la Francesca's work ever since at school when I had received fifty cents from our art history professor, who gave such rewards out of his own pocket to eager students able to guess the painter and the year of the painting from a projected slide. It had been exciting and fun. We students learned much about the Italian Renaissance; medieval art, the baroque, and the Greeks we would have to conquer for ourselves. Years later in New York, I wandered starry-eyed among the Riemenschneiders of the Metropolitan Museum and discovered Paulus's face and his hunger-emaciated body in one of the wood carvings of the master.

We left for Italy from Bremen on a freighter. Starting from Sicily, we wandered up the "boot." My knowledge of art history at that time was considerable. Paulus's historical, philosophical, theological, and geographical knowledge was fabulous. I taught him to see, he taught me the whole world. We were alone on the trip for the most part. We ate dinner in the evening—sometimes when money was scarce, one dinner for the two of us—and we always drank wine. In Rome, by strange good fortune (forgotten royalties), some extra money came into our hands. We immediately took a carriage through the park, ate decently, and bought hundreds of Alinari photographs of the works of art that had impressed us. Paulus used the material later in many of his lectures on art.

For three hot summer months, twelve weeks, we had experienced a new world. The barbarians had seen their first palm trees, their first Mediterranean blue sea (and felt its relaxation), the friendly people of Italy for the first time.

We came home thin and exhausted, but transformed and happy. I recall a felicitous event on the train to Marburg. We had taken a night train and it was chilly in the morning. Being very hungry, I greedily watched a peasant woman uncorking delicious-smelling coffee and unpacking sandwiches. She offered me some of each, which I devoured gratefully and happily. In our pockets we had our exact tram fare, and we looked like hippies.

I became pregnant and was convinced that I knew when I had conceived the child. I vomited during one of Paulus's lectures, which by then were well attended, and that put an end to my accompanying him to the university.

Our friends Friedrich and his round-faced wife, who was bedecked with necklaces and armbands and rings and a seductive manner, rented a gardener's house farther up the hill in a neglected park garden. There they lived with their two young children, a record player with all kinds of records, with books by Rilke and on Eastern wisdom. Friedrich was the son of a rich merchant in Hamburg and somewhere there was a castle bearing his name. He and his friends gave Paulus books of Rilke's poetry.

There were also two young students, Walter, the son of the Burgermeister in Bremen, and Harold, whom I called the "Wiesenprinz" because of his forget-me-not blue eyes and the growth of a silky reddish meadow of hair on his head. To me the two had sprung from Grimm's fairy tales, young, alive, spontaneous, giving Paulus comfort, helping him understand youth—good fairies in the land between dawn and dusk.

I tried to write again, I had a small room to myself downstairs. For my play I took the story from the writer of the *Tales of Hoffman*, "Klein Zaches," named Zinnober. It is the tale of a misshapen nincompoop who becomes a man of destiny through a gift from a compassionate fairy. He becomes the bearer of everything interesting or good that occurs in his presence. He seems to be the speaker at a good lecture, he seems to be the one who proposes intelligent change, he seems to look like the best of the men in any room he enters. Only "True Love" uncovers his secret, after Klein Zaches has stolen his sweetheart by means of the magic spell. The true lover finds in Klein Zaches's wig the golden hair that had caused the mischief, destroys it, and gets his sweetheart back, while Klein Zaches becomes again a nincompoop.

Heinrich visited us. Tension developed. I talked to Paulus, saying I would never have sex with Heinrich without his permission. Paulus consented but asked me not to talk about the occasions when we were intimate.

Heinrich taught me how to make love. I had been passive, expect-

[119]

ing everything from the man. Heinrich taught me his pleasure and my pleasure, he named the digestive organs and those of love, he taught me to notice the man's reactions, he followed my moods and responses with loving care. At the same time he taught me to be articulate.

My way of participating in conversation was not balanced. I would listen with great concentration until I reached the point of either agreeing or disagreeing violently, when I would make my contribution in a fiery outburst of words without logical conclusions or any attempt to understand the particulars. I poured forth my emotional utterance in the firm belief that there was no other possible solution. I had read a great deal in art and literature, I had attended concerts, visited art galleries, gone to the theater and the opera, but it took me a lifetime to express myself adequately. Paulus usually translated my utterances into some reality. Heinrich insisted on my being articulate in an orderly way. Alone with one person I expanded, bursting with questions. I was articulate when I wrote poems or plays. I might be emotional, but in my writing I had developed the ability to say what I meant.

Interlude

WOULD I HAD REMAINED UNTOUCHED

Would I had remained untouched,
Not revealed my flesh to you.
Would you had not me seduced;
Would I'd been unmoved by you,

Disinclined to listen either
To your sighs or sweet endeavor.
You would never turn your eyes,
Keeping to my heart forever.

Now your smile that overwhelms me
Makes me cringe with pain and fright—
Eyes have turned to other faces
Calling laughter and delight.

IT WAS NOT I YOUR KISSES TRIED TO FIND

It was not I your kisses tried to find
When you were bending at my knees:
A stranger's image stood before your mind.

And while I clung to you, aflame,
You took my flesh and blood on lease—
You used the fires that from my bosom came
To light your feast and fill your cup of wine.

Dresden

Dresden was gay. In Dresden I was happy. I became a mother in Dresden. I became a woman. I was taught and loved by a man I loved proudly, a man sixteen years older than I was—Dionysus, father to Athena. I was loved by my husband, who was ten years older than I was and in love with the metaphysical state of my becoming a mother. I could love Heinrich when I was happy with Paulus. It was Paulus's virtue to accept Heinrich as our companion, the virtue of all three of us to leave a veil of noncommitment over Heinrich's and my more intimate relationship. We behaved formally, showing no signs of personal affection in our daily encounters. Paulus, in suffering the triangular relationship, became a better person. Heinrich, when it came to the test, did not survive. I was my own willful self, but learning constantly.

The first great change resulting from our companionship was the new apartment. I had grown up in a conventional German house with heavy German furniture, not too cluttered. At art school I had absorbed modern trends of greater simplicity—lightness of furniture with attention to the spaces in a room. Paulus's ideal room at that time was a cave—his old room at Taunustrasse—heavy library furniture in black oak, a heavy wall hanging covering the couch with its many pillows, heavy curtains. The corner cupboard was a black semicircular piece with an opening for ashtrays and vases. It held a print of the altar by Grünewald and a woodcut by Schmidt Rotluff. There was also a color print of Nefretete, reminder of a lady friend, the one who had banged the table and said, "You marry this woman

Hannah." There was, from the time of my first appearance in Paulus's life, a weeping Magdalena wringing her hands, by a Dutch master, which had reminded him of me. I myself had never felt any empathy with the crying woman.

Heinrich had a friend named Karl at the Academy for Arts and Crafts In Dresden. He asked Karl to remodel our rented apartment, which was badly run down. I do not remember any agreement with the landlord; we probably paid the cost. I started keeping accounts in Dresden, but the overall business of living expenses remained foreign to me until we came to the United States. In Frankfurt, Paulus gave private lectures, for which he received extra pay. Whenever we planned trips, Paulus would say, "And herewith arises the question of getting hold of the cash for the trip." He would ask me how many lectures he had to give to earn the money. I would figure the price of railroad fare, hotel, food, money for wine, laundry, and guests, and something for presents to bring home. He then went off and gave his lectures, bringing the checks to me. I would return what he asked for and save the rest for the trip. The idea of saving a little something extra regularly never occurred to us.

Karl had given Heinrich one of his small paintings in a delicate style, the color of sand with pink and gray and white dabs, a bit of yellowish sky, a bit of mellow cornfield, a bit of a fence, or rather, a hint of mauve before the gray and yellow. The air between the eye and the canvas sang. I was convinced that Karl would do our rooms right. He moved in with his students from the academy. His creed was "I and my house will serve the Lord," by which he meant that with respect to color schemes he would be oblivious to practical considerations.

The result was that our friends, having seen the new apartment, brought in other friends to ask Karl to do their apartments in the same manner. A style of lightness in furniture, through the Bauhaus in Weimar, had developed with a new sense of movability. Lamps, under the creative hands of Walter Gropius and the Bauhaus, again became light-carriers (gaslight had been replaced by electric light). Women's hem lengths were shorter and hair was bobbed. Karl was in love with fluctuating light, with a breath of color seen through light. Our dining room was sand-colored with sand raw-silk curtains, a round birch table, and early Victorian chairs covered in faded brocade. The living room was pink with blue raw-silk curtains—curtains throughout the apartment were of raw silk. Heinrich cut off the legs of an octagonal table, we cut down the legs of old couches and had back cushions made to order for them—sitting on chairs was out. A small table between windows for my sewing things, and that was all, except one painting by a friend—prints were out.

Paulus's heavy oak furniture was transformed by being placed against yellow walls with sharp red curtains in his study. Wherever he lived from then on, rust red and lemon yellow remained his colors.

A friend of Paulus's gave us precious Renaissance chairs with brocade upholstery. Heinrich stated his opinion: "What you have inherited from your ancestors destroy to possess it." He cut off the heavy lion heads with great effort. We covered the brocade with red material and put the chairs in the blue-painted vestibule.

The bathroom was painted from floor to ceiling in successively stronger shades from pink to red. The pipes and electrical wires throughout the apartment were painted rust red. The bathtub was old-fashioned, the water was heated by a gas stove.

The kitchen was old-fashioned. We would probably have done better to modernize some of the bathroom fixtures or the kitchen. A Viennese lady who cooked a stew in the kitchen said later that she cried at the sight of it. I was not interested in cooking. The maid's room behind the kitchen did not disturb me. I was an art teacher. I knew about color, I was interested in everything expressing our century in literature or philosophy, I took great interest in psychoanalysis, and I read Meng's periodical on child psychology. I enjoyed my small collection of records and an inexpensive record player. I was an aesthete by education—neither politically minded nor socially aware, yet.

There was an exuberance of activity: the apartment being finished, a host of friends around, and afternoons with Heinrich, invariably, as long as he was in Dresden, playing a game of chess with Paulus. I sat by, sewing and serving sherry. Later Paulus would go to his study and Heinrich and I would talk.

I listened to Heinrich's ideas about a world order. Or we talked of poetry, or he put a record on and we danced to the music of "Celeste Aida," he whispering how I was the heroine of his dreams. Always I was wrapped in the cloak of his admiring love.

But before Heinrich came to stay longer, there was the birth of Erdmuthe.

We left Marburg in July for Kampen on Sylt, taking along my sister Liesel, the nurse, who was to stay with me for the delivery and a few weeks afterwards. We spent the summer in Kampen. We met Siegfried Jacobsohn from the *Weltbühne*, who printed one or two of my poems, Jacobs from the *Vossische Zeitung*, who gave me *Mann ohne Eigenschaften*, by Musil, and Alexander Granach, the actor, who had had his bowed legs broken and reset several times to make him presentable on stage. For one of the evenings with Siegfried Jacobsohn, we women dressed as men. I was dubbed "Schiller" because of my hooked nose, which my beautiful straight Greek nose had become when I ran into another child in the school yard, at an early age. Agonies of pain, green-blue-and-yellow discoloring—and a hook-shaped nose. Nobody in the family considered sending me to a doctor. Doctors were for measles only.

My baby was delivered in the big bedroom with the hint of olive green for wallpaper, the Venetian mirror in pink and rose, and my simple blue wardrobe with Albert's painting of Adam and Eve in Paradise, now painted silver-gray like a snow field at dusk. The baby did not want to be born; during the final minutes I must have been drugged. She looked like the Sistine Madonna's baby, worlds away, with a bush of dark hair and dark eyes, which later became gray. Paulus and I had passionate fights about the name. We chose none from our families. He wished to call her Christiane. I found the name Erdmuthe (passion or courage of the earth), which I set against Paulus's Christiane.

Frede, the husband of Paulus's deceased sister Johanna, took Paulus for a walk to protect him from my agony during the birth. Such was the custom at that time. A father did not participate in the event. That did not prevent Paulus, very soon afterward, from quoting the rhyme, "And grinning slyly, the confined father lay down with his confined wife in the childbed," an extremely difficult verse to translate, in which the man identifies with the woman, joining her in childbed.

Liesel stayed for some time after Erdmuthe's birth. She became engaged while she was there. She was an unusually beautiful woman, with a feminine temperament.

I had a quiet summer. Eve visited for some time. I walked alone in the park every day. Once, to Eve's consternation, I brought home a thin-lipped, hook-nosed stranger who had attached himself to me. He spent the night in our guest room. Eve was worried, but I did not wish to be loved. He departed the next morning early, I still chaste. After our first meeting, he returned two or three times on his travels, but he found me immovable. Paulus met him later in Holland, where he was a respectable member of society.

Paulus went to France during the university vacation, where he met his friends Eckart and Christian, the one who had given him six weeks of dubious psychoanalysis. My sister M.L. met all three of them there.

I took care of my child. I was eager to nurse her. I managed it for about three months by eating oatmeal, drinking a certain kind of beer, and resting so as not to lose the precious liquid for my child. Then I dried up.

After Eve left, I took up my water colors. Heinrich was with his family in Ronco on Lake Maggiore. Sometimes, when my paintings frightened me, I sent them to him. At the end of the summer he wrote that I should go to Elisenstrasse 7, the building facing our apartment. He had dreamed there was an apartment for him. I inquired and, sure enough, there was an inexpensive gardener's house with one big room, on the second floor, reached by an outer stairway. He returned to Dresden, living in our guest room and preparing for the winter. What he did with his room was the opposite of what he had taught us. He built a tent inside with yards and yards of cheap potato sacking, fastened in the center with a light bulb. He had a big couch with no legs, an architect's drawing board for a desk, one window that was visible, an iron stove, and, hidden somewhere behind the tent, some place to hang his clothes and something in which to wash. He must have had a kitchen corner somewhere, too, for he entertained me there every Thursday when Paulus was in Leipzig, for dinner, with flowers, food, wine, and the mood of a lovers' paradise.

While Paulus, Heinrich, and Eve were gone during the summer, I painted my own birth; I painted my father and mother copulating; I painted myself in my mother's womb, being attacked by my father, who was looking dangerous and, as someone had once told me, very drunk, so that the maid had to come to the rescue. I painted my brother at the age of six, standing and watching while his girl friend spanked my sister and me.

I painted my mother's private parts in a ceiling corner of a room as a spider, with myself as a little girl looking up at the spider in great fright. I painted my brother and sister pulling the legs off a daddy longlegs while I watched. I painted myself lying on my bed with a spider climbing onto the bed, while a sanitary napkin lay

[127]

beside me. I ended the spider series with a painting of the whole family taking a walk, each one leading a spider on a leash and looking rather gay. In one painting, I was running through spirals in terror, following my brother and sister. Another pictured a reincarnation tower, reaching with its seeds into a big spider-vagina, the female part of the mother—I was to be reborn.

Eve appeared in some water colors, casting no shadow, either dancing under water or watching me before a fire shaping a ring for her. In another, a young knight stood before a young woman lying on a sofa. I called him Stefan, a reference to Kaspar Hauser in the novel by Jakob Wasserman, *Kaspar Hauser, or the Inertia of the Heart*. It was one of the books I had lived many times—Kaspar Hauser, the child of Europe, the prince who had been stolen from his mother at a very young age, kept imprisoned without light, without companionship, without education. He was freed when he was seventeen, taken to a town, and deserted, then picked up by well-meaning people, taught to see, to speak, to write, to feel, to experience life. Intrigue followed him and he was murdered to keep the secret of the crime. The tremendous aspect of the story to me was the opening up of an animal that had been kept in a dark cellar—his sensitivity, which we humans have lost—two years of continuous wonder in discovering a world.

With the return of Paulus and Heinrich, life again became normal. With Paulus I had exchanged letters during his trip; with Heinrich I had developed a more direct approach. While he was in Dresden but not living at our apartment, I sometimes sent him a little "thought-dog," that is, I concentrated my thoughts toward him and he felt as if touched by my presence and guessed or received my message. I had painted Heinrich seated, writing at his desk, and looking down at one of my "thought-dogs," listening to his whispers. Before Heinrich left Dresden on a trip, we usually determined an hour and day when we would meet to whisper to each other. Because of my yearlong meditation, first based on a description in one of Meyrink's novels, it was easy to make myself entirely still until I became a receptacle for his message. Sending out my thought waves to him, I found him the vessel for my communications. It worked rather well. Occasionally, when either one of us could not be present at the appointed hour, an empty and unresponsive space developed. We reassured each other by letter that it had been impossible to be there, or that it had not been the right time and place to meet.

I kept Heinrich's and my extrasensory travels a secret, but usually I was not especially conscious of the possible effect of my behavior on our friends and acquaintances. It did not occur to me that my being with two men continuously would interest anyone or arouse anyone's misgivings. I asked for an invitation for Heinrich too, as often as it seemed possible, when Paulus and I were invited to a social gathering. I felt the set of rules others lived by was irrelevant. My childhood attitude—every attempt to adjust is hopeless and you might just as well follow your own convictions—must have carried me.

Heinrich's gentle moon-face shone over us for about five years, in Berlin, in Marburg, and in Dresden, except when he was away for various lengths of time. On one occasion, when he stayed with another woman, he vanished from Dresden without naming his destination. His friends inquired for him until I became impatient and asked his address from an older man of his acquaintance. On his return, we met at my house. He was miserable. He would neither touch me nor be touched. He told me about the other woman, who had usurped his private life until he could not even read a letter except when he was sitting in the bathroom. I interrupted his confession to tell him that I had once seen him with her in my imagination, making love in a certain position. He admitted it and told me the details. We both had to laugh. I felt no jealousy. He decided not to touch me for about a month. After that, we met in another city and fell upon each other in his hotel room, without the slightest remorse or jealousy.

With Paulus, I seemed unable to control my jealousy. In spite of Heinrich, I was tuned to Paulus; there was no chance for him if I was on bad terms with Paulus. Paulus and I had established the rule that, when he was on lecture tours, there would be "no questions asked," but when we came home from parties together where he seemed to have been enamored of another woman, the question was, "Did you neck?" All I wanted, I insisted, was to know the facts. Paulus dealt with sex in utmost secrecy. In later years, he would not even let himself know what he was doing. And, having necked with a girl before my very eyes, he would insist that nothing like that could ever have happened. His technique in his earlier years was to use his powers of suggestion over me.

I felt dead-tired when we had a woman guest who was obviously in love with Paulus. I would retire sleepily, leaving him alone with her. The next morning, my suspicions aroused, I might get him to admit that he had necked and petted, but it changed nothing. I had my friend, and Paulus had his many adventures. I remained jealous.

Once Heinrich placed Eve and Paulus in one room and himself with me in the next. His plan was that Eve, whose sexual pleasure I knew was with women, would flirt with Paulus while I was being made love to by Heinrich. It did not work. I could only listen to the sounds from the next room. I became more and more hysterical until at last I implored Heinrich to end the scene. I felt red rays issuing from the top of my head. It was the same sensation I had had when I stood hatless in a high valley in Sils Maria on a hot summer day, seeing the blue sky turn to red flames. Eva and Paulus were called back. They were unruffled and sympathetic. I remained jealous.

Heinrich had a ring made for me from a gold piece his grandmother had given him. He molded the wax form himself, giving it the shape of our initials—H and H. A friend poured it for him, but both initials were broken. He believed that the relationship of a man and woman, being limited, would become strained or frustrated after some time. The way out, he thought, was to share each other with another couple for whom both felt affection, compatibility, and sensuality. He rejected the usual solution of lovers, openly or in secret. He tried unsuccessfully to find a woman for Paulus. Paulus liked me, on the one hand, and the many on the other.

Heinrich was always ready to propose to his women and men friends that they try love. He once persuaded me to telephone a girl he thought was especially fitting for a young man who had asked his advice about love. I did, she came, they met, they made love, and they got married.

He was the same young man to whom Heinrich had put the question, while all three of us were riding in a taxi, "Where is the flame that unites Hannah and me?" When the young man couldn't answer, Heinrich pointed to my gloved hand and his thumb, folded into my hand under my glove. I did not feel this was indecent. I felt secure in Heinrich.

Once we had taken a train and then hiked. When we grew hungry, we found that neither of us had enough money to eat in a good restaurant. We went into one such place, nevertheless. Before ordering, Heinrich talked to the proprietor, who gave us not only a good meal but also some extra cash to get us home comfortably. Paulus was fear-ridden in unusual situations, whereas Heinrich and I reveled in them.

On our way to the opera, Heinrich once drew my attention to the restoration of the Zwinger statues. Ruined by the weather, they had been taken down and were being copied. I found the replicas badly lacking. We had long discussions about whether it might be more fruitful to let the old splendor die and have a modern architect erect a building that expressed our own post-World War I period.

I fell in love with the self-portraits of Rembrandt in the Dresden museum and wrote about them.

We befriended a mill owner, Edwin, whose wife Ida collected modern painters and their paintings. I remember their Christmas tree, reaching to the second floor in their large entrance hall beside the heavy staircase. It seemed to me then as tall as the Rockefeller Center tree seemed to me later in New York City. It was decorated with balls of all sizes and colors.

Edwin took a liking to me—I reminded him of his favorite daughter, who had died many years before—and I loved him dearly. He and I had fun one day eating trout at an inn in the Sächische Schweiz, where we had gone in his Packard, chauffeured by an ugly old Saxonian, whom Edwin refused to replace with a younger, smarter man as his wife would have liked. Edwin showed me how to bone a trout properly. We threw our unfolded napkins on the table after lunch, poking fun at the others around us who were carefully folding theirs as if they were to use them again.

We amused each other by talking about the guests seated around us at Edwin's house during formal dinners. We discussed our various travels. I must have told him about the marvel of finding the romantic blue gentians in high altitudes, for some time during my vacation I received a small package of them, which Edwin had sent from the mountains. At that time I was so spoiled by attention that it seemed natural to receive blue flowers from an old man, but on looking back, I feel the gift was as precious as the blue stone on my best Sunday ring—a friend who had the most heavenly blue eyes remembering me and wishing to be remembered. I visited him a short time before his death in the hospital. Although he was frail, his blue eyes shone like gentians. When I left, I knew we would not meet again. I cried.

Ida's fate was different. She lived through the Nazi years. Her daughter-in-law, who was a dancer, became a Nazi heroine, dancing barefoot in a silver dress, as her famous teacher Mary Wigman would dance under Hitler. Ida, who owned paintings of Klee, Kandinsky, and many internationally known modern painters, became a Nazi. A book describing her collection remains, but I do not know what happened to her paintings.

Another of our friends was Fedor, a White Russian emigrant. He was a friend of Kerenski and he wrote biographical novels. A professor in Dresden, he was ingenious, full of profound wit, and a Catholic, which gave rise to light-hearted discussion between Paulus and him about the "bag of grace" in the cellar of the Roman Catholic church that made it possible to sin with grace. Paulus would always remark that the only thing he had in his cellar was a bag of demons. Fedor's wife, Natasha, was the Russian peasant type and entirely devoted to him. She cooked Russian feasts for us all.

I lunched alone with Fedor once in Frankfurt. He kept my handkerchief, a small piece of scented lace. I did not ask for its return.

Fedor danced a waltz with me at a dinner I had given. I was inexperienced and timid about giving the dinner and forgot to boil the potatoes, so we had bread instead. That did not unbalance me as much as our waltz, which was like a rape. I refused to dance again all evening.

Fedor introduced us to the family of Prince Obolensky. The old Prince made a living by making Russian candy. We saw his beautiful, diminutive daughters kneeling in worship in their Eastern Orthodox church, the priest in full regalia—splendor revealed through the sacred, open doors during an Easter service—to the incense of burning candles and ancient church music.

Another group we were involved with was that of Mary Wigman and her students. We had lessons in gymnastics in our vestibule. Paulus refused to bend down, proclaiming it would hurt his head.

Heinrich had been offered a lectureship at Karl's Dresden Academy of Arts and Craft. He was supposed to introduce himself in his initial lecture. His theme was to be the spiritual presuppositions of arts and craft, an interesting subject on which he had much to say. But Heinrich was master of the personal only. He would sit on the low couch in the center of a small circle at our house and talk away. If the group was too large, however, he was uncomfortable and if he sensed the slightest opposition to his views he would withdraw, interpreting the lust for discussion of public matters as hostility.

Paulus, on the other hand, came alive in a discussion. He never took personally an argument on the philosophical or theological level.

Heinrich had once advised him not to lecture from fully written man-uscripts, as he always had, but instead to look the audience in the eye and speak as freely as possible. Paulus took his advice and spoke from outlines only. He gained much from the advocated method, which was entirely due to his having worked for years and years to master the subject of his lectures.

Heinrich started brooding over his assignment. He knew so much, but he had developed his style primarily in personal conversation. Paulus worried about him. We tried to persuade him to prepare an outline. We failed. The final morning, before his first lecture, Heinrich came to see us, beaming. He had discovered the right way to do it—the revelation had come to him in his morning tub. He would take an empty sheet of paper and read his lecture from it.

Since Paulus had to lecture elsewhere, I went alone to hear Hein-rich, sitting in the first row. The students comprised a small but adequate audience.

Heinrich arrived, smartly dressed in a tweed jacket and fawn-colored slacks, a sheet of typing paper in his hand. He stood away from the desk, before the audience. What we then heard was the title of the lecture, "The Spiritual Presuppositions of Arts and Craft," in endless repetition interspersed with a limited number of modifying words. Karl broke in, introducing Heinrich and saying a few encourag-ing words, (but) the lecture was considerably shortened. Heinrich did find his own method after that unfortunate beginning. He would visit the various studios and give individuals stimulating advice on their several projects.

I fell in love with another man, who had been attracted to me for some time. Heinrich took it badly, trying to destroy the new relationship by asking me to promise not to telephone him and urging the friend to promise not to see me. Nevertheless we met in the course of our social life and spent a half hour alone together.

Heinrich did not believe in the demonic as Paulus had described it in his philosophical arguments. He saw, rather, a family of nations united by good will after achieving their individuation as separate nations. He did not believe nations should melt into each other indis-criminately. Each should keep its characteristic landscape, its mythology, and its people's individuality, forming community with its neighboring states while remaining self-sufficient as a national entity. Strangely enough, he was driven to vote for early National Socialism, whereas Paulus voted Socialist and I Communist. We tried

[133]

to convince Heinrich of the fatality of the new group coming up, which only pretended to believe in idealistic national socialism.

We had innumerable discussions about the demonic. Heinrich called it nonsensical. He believed in progress and good will toward mankind and he told many stories to exemplify his view. My tranquil heart was at that time inclined toward Heinrich and his good will, although I could not quite forget my father, who had gone against his own best nature (consciously and with a perverse joy, I thought) into self-destruction. I considered him an example of a man who knew the good but did the evil, enjoying the degradation of his better self by his own evil will. When Paulus was driven and closed to reason, or when I was jealous, I felt the insanity of irrationality destroying our good will toward each other.

When Heinrich built his tent, the cave—the very opposite of the clarity of purpose he had taught Paulus and me—he fell into old patterns. When he fought in vain against my infatuation, I became a demon for him. He would close himself off from me, falling into melancholy and remorse. He wanted me to leave Paulus, which was impossible for me. He wrote a poem and a melody to go with it, which he sang for me in black despondency: "Why am I, having awakened from unsound sleep, still in your power?" He also composed a tune for a poem of mine. In writing the poem, I had had Paulus and his unfaithful fantasies in mind. Heinrich took it as my state of mind toward himself: "How many nights, when you adored me giving my holy flesh and blood into your loving hands, have you betrayed me by dreaming of another love, lying between my breasts, I longing for you."

I could no longer respond.

The solution came when Paulus was invited to become professor of philosophy at the University of Frankfurt am Main. It was a foundation chair that had been held by the Catholic philospher Max Scheler, whom all three of us had met in Crissier. Before a small, private group, who had gathered around him on the invitation of a wealthy banker, Scheler had lectured on Buddha. It had been a great experience. Shortly thereafter, he had died and Paulus was offered his chair. Heinrich was not to follow us to Frankfurt. Paulus went ahead to start his lectures and find an apartment for us.

I bought a new coat and hat with Heinrich. I slept in his arms for the last night in his tent, while our apartment was being dismantled and the furniture sent ahead to Frankfurt. I was exhausted. He was in deep sorrow and decline. He had made a last desperate attempt to draw me back into his orbit by taking my hand, trying to guide me back into former incarnations, hoping to find in me his young, long-deceased sister. I accepted his guidance but, after some time, I saw behind my closed eyes a huge bunch of lilacs in a big vase standing on the floor in a room I had just visited, where I had taken the lilacs to my infatuation. I had to laugh, at which point sanity took over and Heinrich's mysticism was drowned in a bunch of lilacs. I left.

It was a relief to arrive in Frankfurt without Heinrich, open-minded for a new life. Paulus was happy too, and we started together.

Interlude

ᴗ̈

THE DRIVE

The woman climbs into the seat beside the driver. A small suitcase rests on the rear seat next to a fur coat and a man's topcoat. "It's nice of you to take me along," says Sylvia. The man starts the car in second gear, quickly shifts into third and fourth, races through the town at 55 miles an hour, stops abruptly at red lights, speeds up when he reaches the open road. Silently—through the large windshield—Sylvia studies the beloved landscape of the car's hood, which cuts across the arc of the headlights like a slender mountaintop across a full moon. The flaring curve of the fender keeps to the right.

Sylvia observes the highway which the purring motor keeps absorbing into itself, one stretch of highway and then another—a gray stretch, a reddish one, a brown one . . . . it rolls them on a spool, devours them, excretes them again; the highway flutters away behind them as it unrolls in a curve, ragged, snakelike . . . . Villages announce their presence with signs in red and white and with warning triangles, "speed limit 25 mph" (the car leaps over a bump in the road). They fade away, are replaced by new signs "To ———," 30 or even 60 miles farther ahead.

Sylvia is hungry, she eats an orange and a piece of bread; she hands an orange and some bread to the man. They eat while he drives. The man turns on the interior light, looks at his watch, shows signs of impatience. The headlights carve out a section of the dark highway, brilliantly illuminating every stone for seconds. Sylvia

[137]

watches the stars come out, framed by the windows of the car.

She is tired, the man beside her says: "Here comes the long straight stretch." He sounds caught up in a dream. He puts his hand on Sylvia's knee, she looks up sleepily, he pushes her coat aside, lifts her skirt, puts his hand on the bare skin between girdle and stocking. Sylvia puts her hand on his, he gently raises her hand and places it on his knee, and returns to her knee. Sylvia's hand remains on the man's knee. The man revs the motor and speeds up noticeably on the straightaway. His hand burrows into Sylvia. Sylvia looks at him, her gaze no longer reaches him, he is driving, immured by the purring machine, and he is stroking her . . . or is she stroking the motor and using her power to drive with? His hand has chased all rational thought from her. Is she the bringer of speed? Is the motor the recipient of his caress—a furious caress that sends pebbles ringing against the fenders?

Sylvia tries to draw away from the man, but even as her gaze no longer reaches him, so too her voice no longer reaches him, nor the grasp of her hand as it pushes against his fondling hand. She stops resisting. The loud voice of the motor at high speed mingles with her sighing breath, car and woman moan in unison when he takes a turn in the road aggressively, without letting up on the gas, and the woman in his arm is thrown away from him without his letting go of her center of being . . . There are oncoming cars, he flicks down his brights, turns the steering wheel, signals—all with one hand.

The car sweeps through a village, lights stabbing at it from all sides, people standing in the headlights—the upper half of their bodies emerge, their faces drawn into blind grimaces. The car passes along the village street, then continues at top speed along the dark highway. Trees go by, bent like sickles, tree upon tree appear in the cone of the headlights; it almost seems like one continuous tree; speed thickens into immobility.

The woman is lying back on the seat, she opens herself as far as his hand penetrates, bends forward, bends backward, leans against him, straightens up, looks into his face . . . his mouth is coral red, fixed in a smile . . . the smile of those archaic statues whose eyes are fixed on something very far away, statues who are hastening toward something frighteningly sweet.

Once more the darkness of the highway is broken, there are swaying lanterns, it is another village. Sylvia feels as if the car were made of glass. "But you can't do that here," she says, as they move from the dark of the open road back into the reality of human habitations and faces. The man is silent, she cannot get past the sharp edge of his triumphant mouth, she holds fast to his knee and sobs obediently.

The village lies behind them, the road swings upward in a steep curve. The man slowly takes his hand from the woman, covers her knees, puts his arm around her shoulder, looks at her, kisses her lightly, releases her, grasps the steering wheel, slows down, silently and attentively follows the many curves in the road, uphill and down.

Three-quarters of an hour later the car turns into a familiar street, the man drives slowly, signals frequently, suddenly turns into a driveway, stops in front of a garage, opens both doors. The woman gets out, stands in the light and, together with him, says hello to the friends they have come all this way to visit.

Frankfurt

We went to Corsica with Heinrich. A storm swept over the Mediterranean and our little ship bounced on the waves. We sat in the lifeboats, overlooking the wind-blown waters. Seasickness hit me. One of our suitcases went overboard. We never grudged the loss. We felt something that belonged to the past had been thrown overboard, a sacrifice to the gods for our future well-being.

After an interlude in a dark, old-fashioned city apartment, where the well-meaning superintendent, who became our friend, had the heavy wooden panels painted to make the rooms light and the baroque ceiling removed, at great cost, to paint it silver, we moved to a modern apartment outside Frankfurt, where we had steam heat. The rooms were smaller. The low couches disappeared. I bought Mies van der Rohe chairs for the dining and living rooms, where I also hung lovely, expensive chintz curtains with a pattern of old French castles. A baroque table became my desk.

Instead of a house, which most professors in Frankfurt owned, we bought a car, an old open Mercedes with leather seats and a bad engine; later, a blue Opel, which bounced on the road but nevertheless carried us to our Baltic Sea vacation spot, my old Neuendorf.

We paid calls on Sunday mornings in formal dress, I in a suit, Paulus in a black coat with striped trousers. We were invited to both formal and informal affairs—I learned the difference between a "little Abendkleid" and a "big Abendkleid." I adjusted quickly with the help of some good-natured ladies who accepted us with curiosity and benevolence. Somehow it was our entrance into "society."

The city of Frankfurt was a proud ship sailing down the river under blue skies; beyond, a cloud bank was mounting. We were in the recovery period after World War I. Inflation was over; deflation was yet to come. It was a short period of well-being before the rise of the Nazi party and new unemployment. In the streets I no longer met veterans pushing carts displaying castles constructed of burnt matches, asking for money to buy shoes for their kids to attend school.

I roamed Frankfurt, visiting St. Paul's church, where emperors had been crowned (and where Paulus would receive a peace prize when he returned after the downfall of the Nazis), "The Römer," where the same emperors had been feted, the Goethe house, the old marketplace, the Zeil, and the Fressgässchen (the delicatessen-alley). I went to the Main river, had a glass of wine in a lovely tumbler, and then went into an inn in the countryside to drink hard apple cider (which was young and rather dangerous) with delicious smelly cheese.

I went to the opera often, usually alone. One of the last performances was *The Rise and Fall of the City of Mahogany,* the nihilistic, anticapitalistic pronouncement by Bertold Brecht and Kurt Weil, so much stronger and more bitter than *The Threepenny Opera.* Our friend Teddy played the *Threepenny* melodies on ecstatic evenings—after a good dinner and many good wines in the good city of Frankfurt.

Marlene Dietrich's "Falling in Love Again" and Lotte Lenya's songs from *The Threepenny Opera* were the songs of the day. When Teddy sat down at the grand piano and let go, we all listened. Somebody bent to me and whispered the words of Marlene's song; somebody said, "Put your shoulder strap back, your nude shoulder drives me insane"; somebody danced with me, everyone watching; somebody sank at my feet, insisting on putting on my overshoes for me; somebody raped me in a car. I took my revenge by being immovable and arrogantly stony when I next met him and he assumed he could make a date with me. I withdrew.

Frankfurt was lush with the Taunus Hills in the background, it was seductive and exhilarating, it was rich merchants and sophistication. Frankfurt was near Paris. It had a highly cultivated, wealthy, and largely Jewish upper class. The names of wines were whispered into your ear at festive occasions. Food was sensuous, tables gleaming with crystal and silver. Paulus learned quickly. Frankfurt was Paulus's city. Here he came into his own.

The University of Frankfurt was one of ancient renown. Paulus was now a philosopher welcomed by a host of distinguished scholars who were eager to meet him, to discuss problems within and beyond national boundaries. Whereas Dresden had been aesthetic, Frankfurt was cosmopolitan, with the great industries, especially in Höchst. Economic and sociological, technical and political realities were the themes for discussion. In Dresden we had met people through friends, and the institute where Paulus taught had been unimportant for our social life, but here we were in the midst of a university that was a grand place to take you in. The bitter apprenticeship of Marburg had been successful. In Dresden and Leipzig, Paulus had established a reputation. In Frankfurt, he could test his ideas with a distinguished group of scholars—philosophers, social scientists, economists, and psychologists.

Paulus befriended the famous brain scientist Kurt Goldstein; Max Wertheimer discussed his Gestalt theory with him; Karl Mannheim and his wife Julia were our friends; Adolf often came in from Berlin; Karl Mennicke, an old friend from the religious socialist movement, came to the city; and Max Horkheimer and his friend Fred, founders and directors of the Institute for Social Research (first in Frankfurt and then brought to the United States), often entertained us. With them the political debate became sharp and incisive. There was also the staff of younger members and friends, and the immensely talented Teddy Adorno. Erich Fromm and Herbert Marcuse of later fame were the assistants of the Institute of Social Research. Karl August Witfogel, at that time an ardent Communist, lectured and we all stood to sing the "International." I bought a record of it, while my daughter Mutie insisted on the "Horst Wessel" song. We took turns playing them.

There were also the Greek scholars—the curator, Kurt, and Reinhardt, and Walter Otto. Otto's son-in-law called to Paulus one evening after a good meal and a heated political discussion, "On the barricades we will meet again." We became friends with Prinzhorn, who had written the book on paintings of the schizophrenics. He had tried mescaline and told us about it, a harrowing experience, seeing himself looking down from the ceiling upon himself. His wife, a great beauty, later deserted him for a young Nazi.

And then, of course, helping the intellectuals in their gold and brocade evening coats, inviting them to luscious dinners and intellectual but nevertheless delicious luncheons, were the lovely and loving well-to-do businessmen's wives, called the "crêpe de Chine" by the members of the university faculty. They attended the lectures and seminars of the different dignitaries. They tried to be not only intelligent but witty and seductive as well. We found ourselves invited on a motor trip to Heidelberg, to the small Rhine villages, to drink wine and eat a hearty meal deep in one of the cool wine cellars near the big barrels. Every week a chauffeur-driven limousine would call for Paulus and return him again after a luncheon or an afternoon with one of society's charming ladies. It was the good life.

Yet, at the beginning of our life in Frankfurt, I lost my baby. The doctor had advised me to lie flat in bed for about six weeks. But a telephone call from a Berlin friend announced Heinrich's death, from diptheria. His wife had gone from Ascona to Berlin to nurse him. He had refused a doctor and tried to heal himself with homeopathy. I was convinced I had killed him by leaving him. Astrologically Taurus, the throat and neck were my sign. I believed, too, that he killed the baby within me, causing the bleeding, the fever, and the miscarriage.

Paulus took me to Italy during his spring vacation, hoping for a speedy recovery. I took one enchanting walk with Paulus on the heights of Sorrento. I bought a ceramic bunny with red spots. I fell back into bed, bleeding profusely. The ceramic bunny became a talisman against the black magic of Heinrich. Because I felt he had tried to kill me, I never could grieve over his death. I thought when I started bleeding again in Italy that it was his revenge. I called my talisman the "blood bunny." It meant to me some silly sort of magic power against the death Heinrich had wished upon me. The blood bunny took my bleeding upon itself. I then understood a poem I had written before leaving Dresden, without insight into what I had meant by it: "Somewhere in the circle lives a man or a woman/who will die my death,/who will die while I go on living."

Paulus was a hard worker and a passionate lecturer. He had a special Eros for his students in any city in the world. He broke through the authoritarian habit of the German professor, who did all the talking; he invented half-hours of discussion or answering questions, which the timid student could write out and hand him before the lecture began. He was friends with the members of his seminar, joining them after an evening of work for a glass of something. He was a brilliant speaker and in a discussion he had the ability to turn even a vague remark into a highly interesting problem worth probing.

He had left me often, flirting with other women, leaving each one of them in turn for another at the succeeding dinner party. I had to take care of the spurned one, who came to me shamelessly complaining about Paulus's faithlessness, which amused me. But on other occasions I felt left out and neglected. The security of Dresden in the protection of Heinrich was lost. I was alone. Separation from Heinrich had not brought us closer—Paulus was not close. He had a studio away from our ground-floor apartment, on the third floor under the roof. One evening he called the maid, a very attractive brunette, to bring some wine. Later, I found them standing before my bedroom in the middle of the night, talking in dark tones, she in a kimono of mine that I had given her.

I went to the Städel Museum, visiting Athena, the one with the turn in her hips, her head down. Heinrich had told me she resembled me.

I read much, I attended lectures. Paulus and I went together to dinners and entertained our friends at home. Our last resort, our travels, became crowded with friends who followed us. It was difficult to find an unoccupied beach chair in Kampen on the high sand castle Paulus had built so diligently. He was always surrounded. I retired to more secluded beaches where *my* friends could find me.

Wolfgang was in Kampen, or in Neuendorf, sharing our vacation and the old and new friends with gusto. He was Paulus's assistant, working on his doctoral thesis, when I met him. He was much younger than I, with sad eyes and a negative mouth. He needed much time and patience before he could be loving. He was altogether Heinrich's opposite. I helped him finish his dissertation. Once, after he had chased me in my black underwear for over an hour, I grew impatient and said, "Either you make love to me now or you go home." I believe he went home. When he was ready, he was king of caresses and power. We are still great friends. We meet every year when he comes to the United States from his trips to the mountains of Peru.

In Frankfurt, I drifted from Wolfgang to a handsome giant, my "blood and soil" love. He called for me in his white Mercedes. Erwin was an industrialist and had been a racing driver. I bought a special vase for the bouquets of flowers he often brought me, carefully selected from his own garden. He had daring and tenderness. We drove on icy roads and laughed when he could not get up the hill and had to slide back. We went together on hunting expeditions.

[145]

The early morning found us shivering in a tree-house, making love until the deer appeared. He drove at a racer's pace through sleeping towns, caressing me when the road was straight.

When I was leaving for the United States, Erwin drove me into the Taunus Hills for a tearful farewell. He had been physically beaten once by the Communists and to him the Nazis meant protection. In my indignation at the political defeat of Paulus and me and our friends, I suddenly cried at him through my tears, "We will be back!" He gave me a wrist watch as a souvenir.

When I did return twenty years later, he called for me in a miserable old car. He was admonished by a policeman for driving through a light, but the smiling grace of the American lady at his side turned the tide for him. We went to my hotel, where we embraced, sobbing. Twenty years had been extinguished in that one embrace.

Paulus and I usually sat together before our guests arrived, drinking a little sherry and talking. After their departure, we used to sit a while and appraise the evening. I was very conscientious in intellectual matters. I read the books of the people whom we expected—I wanted to understand the world they were bringing with them. I was proud of Paulus. I wanted him to be the center of the debate or conversation. After a short interlude of greetings, we usually settled down and the men began philosophizing or discussing world affairs. It fascinated me. This part of the evening was my world.

During those evenings when we were guests, I found Paulus the most interesting conversationalist. Of course, husbands and wives were always separated at dinner. My jealousy had quieted down. I could bear his sitting at another woman's side, but I still scanned the room in his direction, hoping for a friendly nod or an invitation to come and sit with him.

I always took good care of our house and our guests. There was a rhyme in one of my childhood fairy tales. A giant permits a girl to stay over night in his house during a big storm. She is invited to have dinner, but has to cook for the giant. Before she sits down to eat, she takes care of the cows and the cat and the dog. After the meal, the giant asks them, "Was she good to you?" The animals answered, "She has eaten with us, she has drunk with us, she has been thoughtful with everybody. We wish her a good night's sleep." I tried to be that girl.

I tried to buy nice clothes for Paulus, though there I met the strongest opposition. Paulus was not clothes-conscious and he did not know how to wear his clothes. Eve, Uli, and I, in concerted action, had gotten him out of his black coats and high winged collars into sports shirts, short underwear, long socks, and even a tweed outfit, which he wore for traveling. For his lectures—and that meant every day—he would wear only a dark business suit.

In Italy I believe we bought him a Borsalino, which he liked. I called the process of buying clothes for him "adorning" him, and I could be very insistent.

There was considerable childish interplay in our relationship, and it continued as long as I was willing to play. Paulus was often forgetful of me in company, coming back to intimacy as long as I was willing to accept him after the feast. Unfortunately, my jealousy made things more unbearable than was necessary. Only at a very late age did I find the humor to understand and to "let it be."

Paulus had bad dreams that recurred at irregular intervals. In the last year at Frankfurt, he dreamed that he was in a room other than the one he was actually sleeping in. Waking was a negative shock. This dislocation dream vanished after our emigration. He also dreamed about sheep grazing on the Potsdamer Platz, which had become a ruin with grass growing amid the total destruction of the plaza and of the adjoining streets and buildings. This dream came true when he saw the devastated city on his return the second or third year after World War II.

It must have started in the autumn of 1932. We had been in Sils Maria with Grimme, Adolf, and Karl Mannheim, climbing mountains, listening to jewels of Jewish wit, and to the men involved in the problems of politics. Our salary from the government had been cut by 10 percent.

Doris and Arnold, with their conservative friend Bergstrasser, avoided us and our crowd, until friends of theirs pressed them to arrange a meeting with the by now famous Tillich. I insisted that we postpone the invitation. I had been offended by Doris's cutting us, not taking into account that for Doris and Arnold it was a political expediency if Arnold wanted to stay in Germany.

At that time, the Communists were the antidote to the Nazis and the Socialists were in the hands of a very powerful lowbrow union whose members preferred not to have intellectuals in their midst. Karolus Mennicke was one of the few who dedicated himself to the Socialist Party as such. The Communists had the brains and the outlook.

My parents had moved to Kassel after their retirement. My mother came to visit me. I sat facing her in our heavy leather tub chair, my legs over the round arm. She started talking about Hitler in a soft, deeply stirred voice. She had fallen ill after standing for hours in the rain to see him and hear him speak in Kassel. He did not have women, he was chaste, he did not eat meat, he was a vegetarian, he did not drink liquor . . . and he would end all the trouble the fatherland had fallen into. She raved about the Socialists, the enemies of the country. I sat speechless. Did she not realize that she was in the house of a man who was a Socialist, that Hitler was our archenemy, that Paulus would be the one Hitler would wish to destroy? She preened herself in comfort, looking with friendly eyes at her daughter, obviously quite unaware of the meaning of her speech for me. I wanted to throw her out of the house, simply throw out that superstitious, infatuated dumb creature my intelligent mother had become in the hands of a half-intellectual bum. I despised her.

I was one of the few people in our neighborhood who had read Hitler. I had spoken about him to our friends, but nobody seemed willing to break through the vile language of his book to essentials. I decided to see Hitler when Erwin, who as an industrialist was being wooed by the Nazi Party, invited me to go with him and his friends to hear Hitler speak. The party must have had no money at that time—the Brown Shirts were very few and the collection boxes rattled emptily.

It was a dreary, wet autumn day. We sat close with friends from the Mercedes plant, facing the high platform. There were several speakers. The one who preceded Hitler was a very fat man. I thought him no so bad. Beside me, Erwin tried in vain to curb my vicious observations.

At last, with blaring music, came Hitler, surrounded by brown-shirted men with the swastika on their sleeves. The audience screamed, "Heil Hitler!" raising their arms in the salute. I was highly excited at seeing him and jumped up on the hard bench we had been sitting on to look. Before me, high in the air, stood what I would call, in my fairy-tale language, Klein Zaches, the parasitical nincompoop who had received the fairy gift of the capacity to attract the significance of others to himself, the mistletoe growing on a foreign tree. His voice made mincemeat of the language. I looked at his eyes. I could not find the demon. I laughed out loud. Erwin drew me down indignantly. I tried to be silent for his sake, but Hitler had failed me.

I insisted that Paulus see him. The crowd was larger than when I had gone with Erwin. With a special ticket, Paulus was guided to the platform and could see Hitler still closer. He came home shudderingly impressed by the demon in Hitler's eyes. Paulus felt the spell of the little man with the uncultured voice and the brutality of his wordy assault. He sensed great danger.

There was one Nazi among our acquaintances whom we once invited to our house against the opposition of our Jewish friends, who seemed to fear for our sanity. It was as if things were falling apart, although still politely. The lines of perspective no longer met. Kurt, our curator, was talking about the revolution of the letter carrier, of the little man who had been unsuccessful, of the small grocer who had fallen prey to the Depression and been swallowed up by successful Jewish stores. Anti-Semitism was prevalent among the beaten white-collar class. It was hard for the self-respecting *petit bourgeoisie* to hide their plight. Bitterness set in. Hitler made many promises—to the workers, to the burghers, to everyone who felt oppressed. Only some of the intelligentsia held out. Many of the university professors were pro-Nazi. It was a last triumph of reason when the attack on the university by Nazi hoodlums and a few students was unsuccessful. The university senate, fighting back, managed to insist on the punishment of the intruders. Paulus, who had been lecturing during the attack, had helped to carry battered students into a room behind his office.

In the center of the city, the Nazis and the Communists matched their wits, ending in brawls. Paulus spoke in Kassel, attacking Hitler directly.

The daughter of one of the golden-haired "Aryan" men whom I had considered a friend invited me to meet a woman their group apparently venerated as a prophetess. She was reclining on a high-legged sofa, all in black. I sat by her side, the little girl, adoringly, beside me. The black-garbed woman talked in riddles about the female and the male, about the servitude of the female. It was hideous blabber. She used her rounded fist to describe the female, and the thumb inside the fist to explain the phallic strength of the male, for which the female had to be the receptacle. I had had too many lovers and too many good friends who were more articulate on these matters than this woman. I departed.

Paulus was sometimes jokingly called "Paulus among the Jews." Most of his friends as well as the professors were Jewish. We would miss their agile intelligence and sharp critical faculties when we were without a Jewish element in society. Paulus found himself attacked by them in heated discussions. He later philosophized that the Jews were a people without space and that their critical faculties stemmed from this. Having entered space in Israel, the spice of nonattachment was weakened. They had to protect their homes.

The jeering at modern art in museums and galleries had begun earlier. Fritz, who had given me ecstasy in Kampen, guided Paulus and me through his museum. He expanded his theory that the broken images, the dark color schemes, the hard outlines, the threatening skies, the general fragmentation, the hectic mobility of the Futurists, the desertlike emptiness of the Surrealists, were prophetic signs of things to come—the painter foreshadowing the future. The crowd seemed to feel only the fragmentation, the destruction of their orderly world, in those pictures. They spit in uncomprehending rage.

At the last concert I attended in Frankfurt, Ravel's "Bolero" was played for the first time in Frankfurt. I met Baron B. pacing restlessly during the intermission. We had had some friendly encounters. He was to visit us before we had to leave, which was courageous. His wife was an ardent Nazi. He was the owner of a famous old bank. Life would be hard for him under the Nazis. Paulus met him again in 1947 on his visit to Germany from the United States. We had been guests in his palace. He and his wife had been wonderful hosts. At the concert, the Baron and I joined the majority of the audience in successfully combating the jeering of the lowbrows, who were trying to break up the music. We heard "Bolero" to the finish.

I had begun reading newspapers after Hans Simons, the owner of the *Frankfurter Zeitung,* had told me, when I asked how to learn about politics, "Read my paper."

I read a Socialist paper, too, and once took it with me to the village pond where I was watching Mutie ice skate. Some boys who looked like rowdies followed her. I had to break through their line to rescue her and take her home. Later it occurred to me that they may have singled her out because of my Socialist newspaper.

The city's mood had become feverish and restless. Parties moved faster, flirting became more outrageous, conversations flew around —"leaving the country." At the time for fancy-dress balls in early spring, we decided to hold one of our own in our apartment in the suburbs. We hadn't enough money for such a celebration, but our generous friends were delighted to help out, to send in the best wines ("no hard liquor" had been my stipulation), a butler, the necessary food, glasses, and what not. Our part was to clear out our entire ground floor, asking a friend who dabbled in painting to hang the walls with paper she had first painted with fancy-dress-ball themes and poems about the guests. The music must have come from a victrola. Erdmuthe was deposited with friends; the landlord, who lived overhead, graciously gave his permission; everybody came. It was the last fancy-dress ball we were to attend. We danced with the awareness that we danced on thin ice.

At another such ball given by Frobenius's circle, I had met an architect who was waiting for Hitler, to build—at the moment he was unemployed. We kissed. Occasionally he took the long walk to our place for a good meal. I sneaked ten marks into his pocket once, at the end of one of his visits. He was frantically in love with another girl, as I was with another man, and he kissed delightfully. We kissed again in the late morning hours of Paulus's and my fancy-dress ball. He and his love and Paulus and I sat for one sobering moment after everybody had gone. We danced a last round, kissing.

Erwin had been there too, and while we were together a woman came to me giggling, "What a wicked husband you have. You know what he proposed to me?" I was in Erwin's arms; I did not listen. I had met Paulus at a fancy-dress ball. During our last fancy-dress ball we did not ask each other questions. The world had become crowded and lonely.

The event of the *Machtergreifung* (seizure of power), as the Nazis labeled it, left us and our friends at once with the feeling of uttermost helplessness. We had been glued to the radio, listening to the election returns, when we heard the summary announcement claiming for Hitler the number of votes he needed for victory.

A student came to us the next day weeping bitterly. She could not sleep—next to her room was the Nazi torture chamber. Students decided to join the party to work from inside against Hitler. Others left quickly, as long as the way was open. An underground student organization tried to keep communications going. We had all discussed the infamous block wards, one Nazi appointed for each block who would know the inhabitants of that block intimately. Overnight, Germany had become a country of block wards. The underdog reigned, taking revenge for every arrogance that had been expressed in living or thought.

I took the streetcar to a distant section of the city where my seamstress lived. From the streetcar I saw a car drive up, two Nazis in brown shirts with swastika armbands go into a house and come out again holding a man between them, pushing him into the car. I did not leave the streetcar to see my seamstress.

The strange circumstance was that we and our friends were suddenly without the protection of the state, of the German Reich. Kurt found a way to avoid imprisonment by entering a hospital as a patient.

I met Fritz at the house of a young silversmith who was also a friend. Neither were Jewish. I had ordered a pair of heavy silver cufflinks for Erwin as a farewell present. Fritz gave me another pair for myself. I asked him whether he could burn some papers for Paulus and me. We had central heat in our little modern apartment and there was no means of burning anything. Too much flushing of the toilet to get rid of the papers would become suspicious. Fritz owned a large house with a big heating furnace and was not under suspicion. He was to remain during the Nazi period. Later, Paulus met his wealthy English wife, who had left, in England.

On April 1 there was a boycott against the Jews. People were warned against buying in Jewish shops; those who did so would be photographed. I worried a great deal about Paulus and I proposed that we leave Frankfurt for the day, driving to a village on the Rhine. We walked along the street looking for a restaurant. Before a delicatessen stood a brown-clad figure. The boycott reached the smaller places, as well as Frankfurt.

The book-burning ceremony was headed by a young minister. My "kissing cousin," who was still around, had asked us to watch from the window of one of the houses facing the famous old marketplace. The crowd was not big, but the cart filled with books were there, the fire was there, and the young minister was there, throwing books into the flames. Paulus turned away, cursing. I looked. I wanted never to forget it, steeling my heart forever against any benevolent feelings toward the "Germans."

We attended a demonstration of the Nazi party on a big field with Karl and Julia Mannheim. The crowd, a Sunday-afternoon, lower-middleclass group, was enjoying an outing under their new regime. They seemed to me a mass moved by the moon, moody and responsive.

Hans came in to talk about the Reichstag fire. We saw Max and Fred in a last intimate session at our house. From then on, I believe, everybody who could afford it and who could get away left Frankfurt.

I arranged for Mutie to stay with our friend Margot, who seemed to be safe as the wife of one of the directors of Röchling in the Ruhr. We said good-bye to the friends we could still reach.

One couple refused to leave without their parents, who refused to go, feeling they could not start a new life elsewhere. They finally did leave, after both parents had committed suicide.

Many of our political friends who insisted on staying to work in the underground were to end in concentration camps or by being killed outright.

We said farewell to a friend who poured us a glass of wine that filled the room with its fragrance. He had fetched his very best to honor us and our farewell. We drank a toast, "To overcome things to come." Our host committed suicide the following night.

I sent Paulus away. He wanted to see what the country looked like and what was happening elsewhere before he made up his mind about leaving. There had been more or less private invitations to spend six months in Holland or Switzerland, but I had made up my mind. If I was to go, I would go as far away as possible. The earthquake would rock the bordering countries far more than those on another continent. I had no inhibitions about going to the United States. My mother had come from there. My own slight differences in feelings and behavior from some German habits had shown me that her influence had carried me somewhat beyond German cultural attitudes. I was freer.

Paulus left for his trip. I prepared to put our furniture in storage. A telephone call told me to read the *Frankfurther Zeitung*—it contained some news of Paulus. Paulus, as a liberal, and eleven other professors, who were Jewish, had been dismissed. Karl had been called by the president of the university, who urged him and the others to resign from the university, to help the endangered institution. His answer had been just short of contempt, "You must throw us out." There was to be no protection at the University of Frankfurt am Main, which Paulus and his colleagues had served faithfully.

Rumors were that our house was watched. I did not see many people. Old friends did not want to meet me, if there were any still around.

Paulus was willing to leave the country when he returned from his tour. We had planned to meet in Sassnitz on Rügen, which was close to the ferry to Denmark, in case danger arose. I met him there. We sat on a balcony overlooking the ocean. He was sober in mind.

He told me about his trip and the desperation of all our friends who were not Nazis. In Dresden he was nearly caught. Ida, the friend with the collection of modern paintings, had told her masseur every word of Paulus's conversation about the burning of the Reichstag, the S.S. brutalities, the Nazis cheating in the elections, and much more. When he was returning to Ida's from a visit with our friend Robert, the Packard was mercifully halted by Ida's secretary a few blocks from the house. The Gestapo was waiting for him. The driver took him back to Robert's house. Off he went to Berlin, in the hope that the network of information did not function without loopholes—yet. Nobody followed him and he spent the rest of the time in Berlin, where it seemed easiest to hide if necessary.

We rented a small house in Sassnitz, where I did my own cooking. My sister M.L. came for a visit, as did Eckart, who carried a low Nazi party number (of which I was not yet aware). Karolus came with his new wife. When he returned home, he fell into the hands of the Nazis, but escaped later to Holland. Paulus seduced Karolus's wife. He never forgave Paulus for it.

The churches fell to Hitler. Paulus raced up and down a pier on the harbor where we took our daily walk—he was in murderous despair. A call from an American in Italy reached him, inviting him to lecture at Columbia University, Union Theological Seminary, or the University in Exile, which had just been established for the emigrant professors by Alvin Johnson. Horace Friess, a professor at Columbia, Herbert Schneider, and Reinhold Niebuhr, with his brother Richard, had found a way to call Paulus to the United States.

Horace wanted to meet Paulus halfway, in Italy. Paulus hesitated. Our ideas of distances in Europe were different from the American's. We thought it a tremendous enterprise to go to Italy for one afternoon of bargaining, even if it was for saving one's own life. Besides, Paulus had an appointment with the new Nazi secretary of education. Paulus insisted on not leaving voluntarily. I had explained carefully to him that I would never expose Erdmuthe to an education under the Nazi regime, that I knew it would be very bad to try to influence her against the regime, especially since she seemed to belong, according to the Nazi ideas about race. I had watched Erdmuthe among her friends who, unhibited by their parents' misgivings, went along with events in their childlike way.

Paulus brought Erdmuthe home from the Saar, meeting her in Berlin. We decided to return to Berlin—our voluminous mail was beginning to be suspect. Paulus met the secretary of culture. Mutie stayed with friends. I occupied a rented room opposite the parish house of Paulus's sister. On my arrival there, I saw two Brown Shirts enter a house; a woman rushed out screaming, a man between the Brown Shirts was being pulled into their official car. It was a grisly scene, a duplicate of the Frankfurt incident. I managed to have some clothes made for Paulus and Erdmuthe that were suitable for the German winter. Hers were to be much too heavy for America's over-warm rooms, and too different from the things American children wore.

Some of Paulus's friends who, despite their Jewish origin, did not realize the seriousness of the situation, wanted him to stay in Germany. Exhausting debates filled the long afternoon. It was they who intended to work with the regime. Other, much closer and older friends went underground politically. Paulus had to decide whether he could stay without endangering his own life and, even more impor-tant, the lives of his friends in the political underground. We walked the asphalt streets of the big city for hours. That night Paulus wanted to join the underground movement, to write for them. His political friends felt he was already too well known, his style was unmistakable, and he would endanger them more than he could help. He ought to get out of the country and work for them there. I felt the ground under my feet shrinking until there was none left except the bit of soil directly under my soles. We walked home on midnight streets through the thin gaslight. The verdict was, "Go."

Paulus kept his appointment with the secretary of education. I waited with Eckart in the Cafe Kranzler "Unter den Linden." Paulus arrived late, throwing down on the table three boat tickets he had bought after leaving the secretary. He described his conversation. They had wished to keep him in Germany. He had asked two ques-tions: "What about the Jews?" and "How will you deal with modern culture?" He had always proclaimed that the Nazis could not do much, but they would establish two scapegoats for the lowbrows: They would mistreat the minorities, which meant the Jews, and they would mistreat modern cultural accomplishments. After listening to Paulus, the secretary had proposed that he leave the country for two years.

I walked out of the cafe without saying a word. I flagged a cab and asked the driver, "Do you have children?" He answered, "Yes." I pressed some bills into his hand with the words, "Buy some toys

[155]

for them." I believed my husband had just been given a new lease on life. I returned to the table.

We needed passports. Paulus had not lectured for six months. The consul advised us to enter the United States under the quota, which had not been filled. I can see myself sitting with Mutie in the crowded consulate, wondering what the quota was, anyway. It sounded vulgar. But why not go under the quota? As a consequence, we did not have to go first to Canada or another country for reentry to the United States, and we were able to apply immediately for citizenship.

Before we left Berlin, I went with Paulus to the big church on Kurfürstendam. The "German Christians," the Nazi branch of the church, had taken over. Red Nazi flags with the swastika stood around the altar. We had gone up to the balcony and were looking down on the nave. Paulus started cursing, "What a devilish institution is the mass—what idolatry!" A Brown Shirt turned around, I threw Paulus's arm up in the Nazi salute; we left.

He ran down the wide street, cursing and swearing aloud. I had to laugh in all my sorrow—I was very proud of him. There he was tottering on the borderline, until the right cause arose. Then he would not budge. He would not leave of his own volition; they had to throw him out. But nobody, nobody in the world could change his spiritual and intellectual convictions, neither his father, his wife, nor a whole world in turbulence. He would leave the country and he would come back after it was all over.

His friends would say he had come back as the prodigal son came back again to his father's house. Paulus had no feeling of revenge. He returned without hostility against individuals, but he gave a speech about the anti-Semitism of the Germans that made the women in the audience weep.

I had sought refuge from the complications of a man like Paulus in my "blood and soil" relationship. I found out all too soon that the hysterics of an unintellectual man were more horrible than the hesitancy of a spiritual man. As I lay in the meadow of Rügen shrieking with laughter, reading again his book, *The Socialist Decision*. I knew why he had been thrown out—the fatherland no longer spoke his language nor thought his thoughts, and I was proud of it.

THE
UNITED
STATES

Prelude

A BALLAD OF DEATH IN EUROPE

"Here, take the list," said God. Death riffled through the pages.
"It's a very small list," he said.

"I know," said God. He was focusing on something through a telescope. "It's a perfectly ordinary list this month, but the people down there—who, as you know, get independent now and then—seem to have plans of their own." He handed Death the telescope. "Do you see the black circle around that factory down there on the right, and the one there, around that camp? It's called a work camp. And over there, around that railroad train? The black circle is my sign. It shows me who is doomed to die."

Death peered through the telescope. He quickly put it down again, saying, "Old man, I won't go down alone, you must come with me."

"How would I do that?" asked God.

"If you came along in my right eye," suggested Death, "you could come out whenever you chose."

"Why not your left eye?"

"No, no, my left eye is for seeing around corners. Come on, old man," he urged, "come on—vanish."

"And what about my reign?" asked God, as he wrapped his dark blue mantle around his knees.

"Your reign," said Death, "is finished. Make yourself small, friend. Make yourself small."

"What now?" asked God. Death did not answer. He was watching a formation of men in brown trousers, brown shirts, leather gunbelts and high boots, marching down the middle of an avenue with their right arms raised in salute.

"Actually, this road is meant for cars," commented God. "Apart from that, it reminds me of Rome. But who is that little fellow with the dark moustache?"

"Oh that one," said Death, "that one has dug up a mandrake root from under a gallows. I couldn't get him now, even if *you* wanted me to."

"And the fat one with all those garter ribbons pinned to his shirt?"

"You really must keep up to date," admonished Death. "Those are ribbons of medals; they're called 'decorations.'"

"There's one for you, among the arm-raisers," said God in a low voice.

"Not on my list," said Death.

"Not on your list?" queried God. "That is really strange. Maybe he's on the mandrake-root fellow's list." God observed the man with the moustache more closely. "Could be he carries his own list in his trouser pocket. But perhaps we can perform a tiny, larcenous miracle and steal his mandrake root and his list from him?" And God leaned expectantly from his place in Death's right eye toward Death's left eye.

"Not while you're working with me," said Death sternly. "I have my integrity."

Death sat down under a tree. God emerged from Death's right eye and sat next to him, wrapped in his dark blue mantle. Thousands of feet were marching past them—the feet of soldiers marching with the mandrake man, saluting him loudly, surrounding him protectively. Death absentmindedly took his own leg off at the knee and used it as a flute.

"It's too noisy here for me," said God after a few minutes. "You can amuse yourself with flute-playing, but I can't even think, with all these men tramping past. And where in the world are the women?"

Death screwed his leg back into place. As he stood up, God slipped into his eye again. Death wandered along.

"Do you have the list?" asked God.

"Yes, but I'm not going to fulfill it now. Something attracts me here. It must be the death." He spoke sleepily. He was no longer walking, he was floating across fields, meadows, and woods. He settled down at last in a miserable swamp and God emerged again. It grew dark. Not far away stood a railroad car.

"That car is for transporting four-legged creatures," explained God, "cows, pigs, goats—creatures they kill and eat."

"Yes," answered Death, squinting with his left eye toward the spot where God was sitting, "and who thought it up?" God took out his telescope.

"What do you need the telescope for?" Death asked rudely. "It's close enough."

"So I can see the black circle around the living things that are doomed to die," God replied.

"But," Death insisted, "you made up the list yourself, Brother, you know whose turn it is—don't you?"

Without answering, God adjusted the focus of the telescope. Death stood up, sniffed, threw out his skeleton chest, smelled the air with his fleshless nose, and all his bones rattled and began to shake and dance—with no effort on his part.

"I smell the smell of human flesh," he said in a hollow voice; it did not sound funny.

"There's the circle," said God. "A big black circle runs all around that railroad car. Somebody must have forgotten a car full of cattle. He flew toward the railroad car, his blue mantle trailing behind him. Death rattled a few more steps in place; his gyrating legs did not move him an inch beyond where he had been standing. Then he pulled his iron gloves up higher and approached the car with twisting dance steps. At the last step he hastily wrenched off his left leg and began to play furiously.

The car's sliding door moved back slowly at God's touch. Through the expanding opening fell dark-haired and light-haired children with blue lips, their arms outstretched or tightly clamped around each other's childish bodies. They fell, silent and naked, and their eyes were wide open with terror. Soundlessly as snowflakes, they fell on the dark ground through the large door. Finally—stiff and white—a nun, a silver-haired old woman, fell on top of the dead children.

Death had stopped playing. God made the sign of the Cross. He raised both hands and bowed low.

"A small miracle, God," whispered Death, "a tiny miracle!"

God bowed a second time. The children's terror-frozen mouths began to smile. Their eyes closed. Their hair became smooth. They lay as if watching lovely dreams unfold behind their eyelids.

[161]

"But we didn't know!" cried God, turning to Death. "We have made no room for them, we haven't prepared any toys for them. We couldn't send them a heavenly messenger."

He bowed for the third time. The children's corpses rose dreamily from the ground. They floated away into the night sky. For one moment they seemed to cover the moon with the transparent mass of their hair, which undulated around them like veils of cloud.

God sat down on the ground, slowly and heavily. He lowered his hands; he sat and wept.

"A little miracle," muttered Death. "You'd better not give up these tiny miracles after all. Besides," he added angrily, "they cheated me out of my job of bringing gentle death to these innocent children. What kind of death is *that?*" He played a few wild notes on his flute-leg. "From time immemorial I've known that each must die his own death—but here—this is a machine death, a mass death!" And he threw down his leg and flung himself on the ground, rattling all his bones. He howled aloud. God wept noiselessly by his side.

Men were being stopped in the street and thrown or pushed into a truck. There was scarcely enough room for them to stand. No one could have sat down. One tried to run away . . . a shot . . . he fell flat. Another was searched for weapons, he had a knife in his pocket . . . a blow . . . he fell flat.

"What have they done?" asked God, from out of Death's eye.

"Nothing," whispered Death. "They merely crossed the street corner where the truck was standing. Some sort of quota had to be filled. They will die at random, God, not because they are thieves or murderers or rapists, and not because they went to war as soldiers, but quite at random."

"That one," said God, pointing to the leader of the soldiers, who was counting the men being pushed into the truck with his whip. "That one is not destined to die."

"He is," said Death, "in two weeks."

"I can't wait that long," whispered God.

"How about a little miracle, a tiny miracle?" Death whispered back. He tore out his leg and started to play.

The man with the whip turned toward him; he opened his mouth but no sound came forth; he fell down. Forgetting the truck and their victims, the soldiers lifted up the dead man. Death pulled his long iron gloves higher. He threw a dark cloth over the driver of the truck.

One of the prisoners threw the driver out of the truck and took the driver's seat. The truck's gears shrieked as it started to move around the corner. On hearing this, the soldiers rushed toward the truck but fell, one after the other, without a sound, surrounding the corpse of their officer.

Death played a cheerful tune. It giggled, it sounded like tin cans banging against each other. "For once we've cheated Death out of death," he chuckled between flute notes. "I would love to know, though, what the Old Man in my right eye will say about this." And with his left eye he squinted toward his right, where God, wrapped in his dark blue mantle, sat motionless.

"Concentration camps," said God. "Gas chambers and scientific experiments on live human beings. They've taken death away from us, the death of the individual, the death of immortality. They've reduced life to the mere hope of an ordinary death, a death without detours, without gas chambers, without torture, without being forced to watch the death of one's child or the rape of one's wife. They have stolen death and, with it, the value of life. All that is left are death factories and mass meetings. There is no longer either individual death or individual life."

Death stared across a barbed-wire fence where prisoners were being forced to stand up straight in the mud. One of them was being whipped, the others made to watch. A guard with two German shepherds stood by, his gun at the ready.

"I'm going in there," cried Death. He was wearing a smart uniform and he, too, had two German shepherds.

"I'm coming along," exclaimed God. He climbed out of Death's right eye and settled the folds of his dark blue mantle. "By the way, where did you get these two dogs? They look so transparent."

"Oh," said Death, "I borrowed two hairs from the top of your head—your crest of anger. I'll return them later. I don't want to take away any of your holy anger."

Death stepped smartly up to the gate. The guard opened it immediately. The German shepherds pushed closer to the other two dogs.

"Well, what do you know!" said the guard cozily. "How about

[163]

a little action?" He struck the strange dogs with his whip. They leaped at him, growling. Death removed one of his iron gloves.

"Here, let me help you," he said. He touched the guard with his skeleton hand. The guard screamed in terror and fell and was torn to pieces by the dogs. His own two dogs crept backward, whining. The prisoners raised their shaved heads. Some of them recognized Death.

"Come, come!" they called. "Set us free before the new guards arrive, with their dogs and whips."

God threw the gate open. "Go," he said. But the prisoners threw themselves at Death's feet.

"Kiss us, Death, let us die gently. Fleeing means torture and death, staying means torture and death. Kill us gently."

Death removed his other iron glove. He bent down and kissed them—all except one, who said, "I want to live, let me go."

"I'll wrap you in my blue mantle," said God, "and carry you wherever you want to go."

"Carry me to Berlin," said the prisoner. "I can hide there."

God wrapped him in his blue mantle.

Suddenly Death called out behind him, "The new guards are coming—run!" God turned to see them advancing, hundreds of them, all in step, with dogs, whips, and guns.

God and Death ran, very fast. Soon they rose from the ground, with the prisoner wrapped in God's dark blue mantle.

"Don't you think," asked Death when they had reached safety, as he tossed his uniform and cap away, "that this would have been a good time for a little miracle, just a tiny miracle?"

As God descended toward Berlin to set the prisoner down, he answered, "Yes, a little miracle wouldn't have been a bad idea, but this time I really didn't think of it. . . ."

ROCKEFELLER CENTER BALLAD

A window cleaner, cleaning windows on
The thirty-sixth floor, Rockefeller Center—
His safety belt in place—mistook the path
Of concrete between rows of windows
For the avenue that was to lead him home.

[164]

And, taking off his belt—it was discovered later—
He walked, flanked right and left by windows
Glittering like opals, walked with rapid steps
Upward along the narrowing lane that seemed
To lead into the sky. Fresh breezes blew around him.

There were no trees along the road he'd taken,
But then, not many trees grow in New York.
And no red light, nor green was there. The whistles of
Police directing traffic
Shrilled far away and farther, till they faded.

He ran up the wall in giant leaps—
A joyful, winged dancer—that's the way
Two strangers saw him last, leaning near Saks
Fifth Avenue and marveling at the tower
With its magnificent array of windows.

Arriving at the eighty-seventh floor,
He veered off to the left, and left again.
Since then no one has heard from him.
His name was stricken from the register
Of Rockefeller Center window cleaners

As missing; and, as neither wife nor child
Appeared to mourn him and he was not carried
On any roster, the remembrance of
His having-been-here dwindled down to nothing,
Nor did the strangers mention him in word or writ.

STATISTICS

Sometimes an automobile is
so laden with human hatred
that death breaks out
like a corroding disease
in the motor.

Or the current of power
tears up circuits of light,
instead of serving the motion
of wheels through cable and wire.

From eyes blinded with rage,
from lips trembling with hatred,
hisses destruction of flesh
till it attacks the machine.

And we are told by statistics
that, for twelve in a thousand
who take to the highway,
death lies in wait at the wheel.

MEDITATION

See a little death wish ride by
High-hatted, the scorpion
Dancing madly, tail lifted,
Violently wishing to sting.

See the tarantula of my dislike
Stepping sideways viciously.

See the king of Death, the glorious rattler
Ready to strike, eager to sink
Poisonous teeth into the hated ones.

But do I really want to kill?
Why not throw a dish against the wall, instead,
Or toss the weeds out of a flower bed,
Or go and chop some wood, so that
Destruction keeps me warm at night?

Far better, I sit with sightless eyes,
Watching Death march by.
There they go, my death wishes:
High-hatted, the scorpion,
Viciously sidetracking tarantula,
There goes the rattler, scampering by
Powerless . . . .

HALLOWE'EN AWARENESS

Have you ever seen your skeleton
lying on a pillow, sound asleep—
delicately bone by bone
curving in a heap?

Have you ever seen your skeleton
moving elegantly in a street—
charming clatters bone by bone
walking with a leap?

Have you ever seen your skeleton
entering the mirror with a sweep—
spine and pelvis bone by bone
rattling from the deep?

New York

We arrived. Someone must have helped us with the technicalities. Erdmuthe and I danced on the ship's deck when we saw the Statue of Liberty that chilly October day. Somebody guided us into a huge, ground-floor apartment in New York. It had some furniture, a kitchen, bathrooms, and bedrooms upstairs and downstairs. A beautiful young golden-haired woman came toward me, a hot water bottle in her hands. Her accent was British. She was the wife of Reinhold Niebuhr, who had helped us come abroad.

The first thing for me was to buy a percolator for our coffee. This time it was electric. The second thing was to inquire how to set a table in the United States. I had never seen tablecloths cut into pieces. The third thing was to find wine for Paulus's daily sherry, as well as table wine, which we bought in big flasks from then on.

A maid came every day for a few hours, in the beginning; later, once or twice a week. She also shopped, until I found out that she put part of her own purchases on my bill. Besides, I also found out that one could shop either expensively or inexpensively, depending on the choice of stores.

During the first two weekends, when the help did not come in, I left the dishes unrinsed in the sink. It did not occur to me to wash them. Then I caught on. The maid, Estelle, was a lovely brown-skinned, cheerful, young Filipino woman. When we first left Erdmuthe with her for an evening, Erdmuthe said she simply could not stay with Estelle, she was too black. I suggested that she teach Estelle German. When we came home, Mutie had taught her to say *Lichtknipser* (lightswitch).

Mutie's urgent desire was to find the English word for *Popo* (fanny). We did not turn to a dictionary. I very seldom used one until much later. Paulus used one from the very first day.

Paulus had to know his city. He had wished all his life to be in the city of Berlin. Now he found himself in the metropolis of the United States, if not of the world. Reinhold Niebuhr had told us about the hubris of the skyscraper. I thought it the most democratic building in the world, with its windows of uniform size dwarfing the downtown churches. It seemed to me the house of the people, with its brash glory in glaring sunsets, its highest floors hiding in the clouds on dark days, its windows washed by a man daringly tied to first one and then another on the outside of the building, even on the highest floors. When I went downtown, I looked for a window washer at Rockefeller Center. If I saw one, it was a lucky day.

When the moon appeared in an opening between the high-rising buildings, it was another lucky day. There was the raspberry-sweet sky after a rain, there were the sharp, glaring shadows and lights of a cold windy day in fall or spring. It was a glorious city.

New York is in the same latitude as Naples, a southern and a northern city at the same time. So were the people—smiling, gaily dressed, busy but at times lazy in a way we Germans could not have imagined, a balance between extreme tension and extreme relaxation. Riverside Drive with the crowds on hot summer nights lying on newspapers on the lawn was enchanting—the music, the laughter, the spoiled kids, everybody seeming to say "Yes" to everything.

It was difficult to discover the meaning of the many yeses. When a friend in Germany would have said, "Don't call me," the friend here would say, "*I* will call *you*." It took us a year to find out that meant, "Don't call me." To say "No" seemed to hurt a person's feelings more than to tell a white lie.

And, most wonderful of all sights, there was the harbor far up the Hudson River, where the big ocean liners would dock. I took a taxi down along the river, calling out joyously at every Atlantic ship—the elegant *United States,* the French superliner, and the *Queen Mary.* The foghorns at night or in the early morning—New York. The glittering cool-hearted city, living on its nerve.

We walked over the George Washington Bridge. We visited the Cloisters. If we had thought we might be a little supercilious about the enterprise of bringing stone by numbered stone over to the United

States from France, we were mistaken. The Cloisters were lovely, they were aesthetically without blemish. The taste and the wealth of rugs, sculptures, and paintings made us exuberant. Afterward, we walked along the cliff, from which we could see the George Washington Bridge, then to the flower beds and the double-decked No. 4 bus. It would carry us down Fifth Avenue, part of the way along the Hudson, and from its top deck we could sit and look down onto the streets and their crowds. How blotched the downtown streets were from chewing gum. Everybody was chewing. At first I thought those blotches were black beetles that had been stepped on in the street.

We walked the streets for hours, in different sections, the Italian section, the Jewish section, which was in the process of being torn down but still had its pushcarts with rusty nails, old clothes, and rattling pots, broken china, and what not. We went to the Bowery, walked through Chinatown, found our way to the Fulton Fish Market, and to Greenwich Village.

We visited the museums—the Metropolitan, the Frick, the Indian, and the Museum of Natural History, which in later years I visited often to look at the rocks and the collection of Tibetan art.

The event, however, was the Museum of Modern Art. There we returned to a "home town" we thought we had left behind, to Cezanne, van Gogh, and many works dear to us, in a beautiful, appropriate setting. The museums' technique of display in the United States seemed so much more advanced than in Europe. There was space enough, there were informative, guiding remarks at the entrance to each room for the many who came without knowledge to get acquainted with the masters, noting the time and the place and the development in the history of art. The Museum of Modern Art was the first place that made us feel entirely at home.

We felt at home, too, at the opera house and in the theaters, though in the theater the language barrier severely restricted understanding.

Paulus had to learn English. Two students for whom I made breakfast in the early morning, when Paulus had, as he put it, a fog in his head, tried to teach him. He was used to sleeping late. When the president of the seminary suggested that he go to chapel as everyone else did every morning, he is supposed to have answered in sheer horror, "But that is before midnight."

I had a student teach me, in return for German lessons. We read

The New Yorker together. I was concerned about the jokes I did not understand, especially those with huge women and little men. I took my student to *Rosenkavalier*. We sat high up in the family circle, but we enjoyed it because it was a superb performance.

We had one rather ghostly party on the roof of Union Seminary. Though it may have been fun for our guests and we enjoyed preparing for it, it was a vain attempt to reproduce the gay atmosphere of Frankfurt. It had the same ghostly quality as our first Christmas party with émigrés, when Paulus thought he could ask his guests to wear tuxedoes—the response was negative.

We had wished to bring together our American friends and the many German friends who had come in from Germany. We had received permission to use a closed roof garden, we had arranged paintings of our friends on the gray cement walls, we had set tables with place cards, rather than follow the usual way here of selecting one's partner before sitting down or simply standing around in cocktail-party fashion. We made the setting more like that of a café in Europe. Paulus had written a verse for every single guest, but when the time came to recite them he was rather high. Everything was somewhat disarrayed, and the spirit of the game was lost.

Suddenly we lived among a whole block full of neighbors—three elevators' worth above and below us, and every elevator passenger was supposed to make a cheerful remark. When we were asked, "How are you?" as a matter of politeness, Paulus would, in all barbarian naïveté, answer at length about the state of his misery, until the elevator stopped and the poor native, who had meant nothing more or less than, "Good day," fled.

We detested neighbors. We had left a neighbor-infested house in Frankfurt for a small house in the suburbs. While in Berlin, we had never inquired about the dwellers next door. Now we had a six-floor house full of neighbors. The deliverance came when an American friend disclosed to me that Union was not exactly a house full of neighbors but, rather, groups of scattered friends, and those who were not close friends one could treat without unnecessary responsiveness. The secret of social behavior seemed to be the concept of having one's privacy. Nobody tried to come painfully close. Whereas the Germans exhibited the soul, Americans asked only a friendly sociability. They were willing to help, but maintained reserve with respect to personal feelings. To me this was salvation; to some German friends it meant coolness. So it was only a block of people after all, with the exception that Union Theological Seminary ethics required the pretense of neighborliness. We had so much to learn.

We started to enjoy our refrigerator, I learned to shop, we became more articulate in conversation, admiring the patience of our hosts, who seemed amused at the blue streak of imaginary English I produced at their parties.

A friendly American took us to see *Hamlet*, the Shakespearean play that meant most to Paulus (I preferred *Macbeth*). We could not react the way Paulus would have liked after the play—we were exhausted by hearing English exclusively for an entire evening.

Other American friends took us to see Mae West in *My Little Chickadee*. I burst out laughing about twenty years later, having caught on only then to her comical performance.

We saw *Four Saints in Three Acts* by Gertrude Stein, and of course we went to see a burlesque show and took our educated friends along.

I continued my education without Paulus but with the help of Mutie—going to movies, reading her school books, learning her children's rhymes ("I never saw a purple cow. . . ."), reading *Winnie the Pooh*, and giving a birthday party for her, when I stood in the middle of the room with kids stampeding around me, overlooking me—screaming, running, hopping, childish dwarfs, being busy just by being noisy and running. Estelle and I must have grabbed them one by one as they rushed past us, to get them to the table for cake and juices. It was an exhausting experience.

I had not yet learned the art of distracting kids by constantly offering something new to hold their short span of attention and keep them from senseless destruction. It seemed to me the essence of the American educational system was to distract, whereas the German had been head-on collision, confrontation for the sake of order. I learned later as a camp counselor that the goal was not to enforce order; the goal was to teach children to make their own order, to arrive at some orderly procedure out of their own vitality. I had much to learn.

There was another difference. German children were brought up with fairy tales in a world of the imagination—witches, heroes, magicians—and more or less cruel children's books such as *Struwelpeter*, in which thumbs were cut off to punish the disobedient. It was a world of punishment, cruelty, utterly unreal sweetness, magic rescue from disaster, and of course extensive games of war. It was

[*173*]

a long time before I came upon the American equivalent, the comics, which I found hard to read. They took me into a visual country of picture language.

As a child I had considered it punishment to help with household chores. American children seemed to enjoy the house and its chores. It was their playground. There seemed very little spitefulness. They were not consistent, they were easily distracted, and they were generally amiable. The root of the American creed was the "Yes." This new mythos, as we experienced it, gave an audacity to every single person. He could become the president of the United States, he could go from poverty to riches, he could cross the color line. He had a chance, and, it followed quite naturally, he would give the other fellow a chance. The country was multiracial and it had learned to say "Yes" to a multitude of languages and customs. If a child ate with bad manners according to European standards, he could be said to be following the Chinese custom of belching after a successful meal. Criticism was expressed positively.

There was the "What can I do for you?", a helpful question. It was one of those attitudes that might be in earnest—one had to find out.

We would have to accept the new mythos of a new country, leaving the old mythos and the old country behind. The railroad songs, the cowboy songs, the Negro jazz, which Adorno had exploited and explained so carefully, all would be guidelines. There were no tales of Jorinde and Joringel, no sagas of emperors and kings. There were no castles along the immense rivers, there were no quaint alleys—streetcars were a sensation in San Francisco. Otherwise, the United States was a country of cars. Highways were not for walking.

A stock response when one told of something either sad or joyous was: "Yes, I can imagine how you feel." Set against the German unwillingness to use empathy, it was quite a proposition. When someone was down, everyone wanted to help, hoping to be offered help in turn when he was down. The generosity in tips—the small change rolling around—had to do with the feeling: "We are in the same boat." When I took sick, my neighbor's chicken soup appeared. It was such a disarming gesture. People would be willing to help in almost any difficulty. When another good cause came along, they would be helpful there. One received help, then was on his own again.

Every morning after Mutie had gone to school and Paulus to his office or his work, I tried to read *The New York Times* and cried. I listened to Frank Singeiser over the radio. Sometimes I understood what I read, sometimes I did not understand what I heard.

We missed so much in the new country. We would never understand the subtleties of the American joke, which was visual as in *The New Yorker,* or its uses for making a point in after-dinner speeches. We were used to the clumsy, logical German way of hammering home a point. It was not easy to follow the swift flight of an escaping remark.

We were, in the beginning, halfway between here and abroad. I tried to write letters across the ocean but the water did not carry loving thought. I remembered old stories in which the persecuted left a body of water between himself and the enemy. We had put a large body of water between our enemies and ourselves; we were safe. But we could no longer convey our good wishes to our friends on the other side. No yearning helped. We had left.

Paulus was eager to find out about the red-light districts in New York. Wherever we had been, Paulus had first walked around and then guided me to the "whore" streets. Heinrich, with whom we had both walked in search of humanity, used to sniff, explaining mischievously that one could smell pleasant fragrances of liquor, dried powder, and semen issuing from that district, which seemed to belong to the real face of a city. Not that either of them had ever used such a place. Paulus had never engaged in sex with whores. He and I had sat and talked in a brothel in Paris. When we once met Karl and Julia, we had walked for what seemed hours in search of an indecent locale where certain sex practices were shown. The men were afraid of getting into trouble, afraid of paying too much money. At last, we women grew impatient, demanding action, and the place was found. I remember that we looked from a gallery down into the depth of an artificial lake (a niche under glass) where two girls were floating around and pretending to make love with each other. A dildo was used. I had preferred the family brothel Paulus had guided me to, where father, mother, and children sat between nudes. One of the nudes came to our table, where we placed a silver coin. She turned around and took it with her sphincter muscle. It was hers then.

In Marseille, we had gone in the early afternoon through the red-light streets, whores standing in the doorways trying to lure us into dark entrances. In the middle of the street, a girl took Paulus's hat, the expensive big Borsalino, our pride. He was bewildered. The street screamed with silent laughter. I jumped, turning back I tore the hat from her hand, and we ran. It must have been a story told in the district for a long time.

In Paris, Paulus took me to a street that had what looked at first like the window displays in one of the big Fifth Avenue department stores. But the dummies in different outfits were human beings. I was intrigued. This was the dream street of male desire and female submission. Here was the simply dressed girl looking like a neighbor or the sleeping beauty in pink veils; here was the girl with high boots and a whip or the lady in violet velvet; here was the girl begging for punishment. It was a window into hidden truth.

In New York, we could not find any red-light district. We learned only vaguely about call girls in hotels. What men did outside of marriage was kept hidden. Sex seemed a strange word here. It implied copulation without imagination. Where were the dreams accompanying sex, the sleeping beauty, the riderin, the submissive woman, the proud queen whose instep would be kissed? Sex implied a cold bed and satisfying a physiological need only.

We found some sort of consolation in Harlem. Somebody must have taken us to Small's Paradise, where one went up a steep staircase, watched by an old pockmarked Negro, whose muddy uniform with gold braid we feared a little. Later we would shake hands with him. Inside the dark, long room, we sat facing clouds that drifted behind an orchestra of Negroes, who played noisily and shrilly. It was as if we had entered a tropical forest with parrots screaming, dark faces peering out of the jungle, falsetto voices, and brilliant colors. A Negro danced with me, a Negress with Paulus. We did not know the rhythm so we stopped dancing, but we sat there and felt good among the emotional outbursts in color, voice, and smells, which we had missed so much—at Union, nobody smelled of anything. We felt relaxed at Small's and returned there with our friends, grateful voyeurs, taking in the primeval charm of the hearty men and swaying women. We considered it an aesthetic show. We did not think at all in economic, political, or social terms.

Once we dared to go to a show in a basement where there were mostly Negroes. In the dancing space at the center of the room occasional performances were given. A nude Negress painted gold, having danced with a Negro twice her size, leaned her body against a post and masturbated with violent snakelike movements, while her former partner and another girl unmistakably performed the acts of intimate sex. It did not seem vulgar or fleshy. It was filled with the natural vivacity of these beautiful black people.

People at the seminary did not think our adventures such a good idea. They had misgivings about our dancing with Negroes. Later, others objected to our aesthetic attitude concerning Negroes. Paulus and I had talked about the black image from primeval times on, the dark people being considered the least aristocratic . . . in psychic circumstances, the black or dark one always the devil . . . the black soul against the white soul . . . black as a magic color expressing evil or dark, underground powers . . . in fairy tales, the black princess, submerged under water, reappearing as white and no longer evil.

Much later I was asked to participate in a meeting on Negro problems. The seminary president's wife proposed inviting some Negro women to Riverside Church, perhaps for afternoon tea. I broke in rudely, saying that I could not see any remedy as long as the housing problem was not solved. Sitting together would solve nothing. One of the women said she always addressed Negro servants as Mr. or Mrs.

Harlem was an involved American concern. Paulus and I had not thought about it. To us, it had been just another part of the city, where people huddled together with others of their own race, customs, language, and likings. We had seen the Jewish section, the Italian, the Chinese, and the German at 86th Street. We thought the Negroes were especially polite and thoughtful. In the subway once, when I was unsure whether I was on the right train, I asked a Negro man. He gave me directions and disappeared, but when I came to my station, he reappeared, showing me the way. I thought then, not that he was protecting himself from being accused of talking to a white woman, but simply that he was being thoughtful.

An inkling of the difficulties of the Negroes came to us when we met a white German girl from Hamburg who had followed a Negro friend from Germany to the United States. He was the light-skinned son of a socialist Negro woman. He could have crossed the color line, but for his political creed. We went with him to Times Square, wishing to take him to dinner at some relatively inexpensive restaurant. People began following us. The young man informed us that he would not be admitted to the restaurant. Our Negro porter

[177]

at the seminary, when we told him we were expecting him to come to our apartment, did not like the idea of one of his black brothers being our guest. He and his German girl were out of money and we gave them a basket of food. They tried to find a room where they could live together, but the Negroes resented the white woman, the whites resented the black man. The unhappy story came to an end when the girl returned to Germany.

I saw movies about Negroes, no longer the Shirley Temple kind with the tapdancing black minstrel. In one, a Negro crossed the color line by going to another state and pretending to be white. He was found out, the community rebelled, and then they accepted him. In another, a Negro girl who could have passed for white came back to her Negro community to help her black brothers and sisters. World War II was to change the spirit of the Negro. Martin Luther King was a lodestone, racial rebellion coming with intercontinental communication.

The jet was the guilty one. The world could have no more secrets. We would hold our ears against the news from interstellar communications. Every spot in the world where anything unusual was happening would be our neighborhood. Our friends would reach across continents and our foes would be next door. There was guerrilla warfare and the search for peace all around the globe.

We celebrated Christmas with a Christmas tree and wax candles. Whereas my father had made a Christmas tree for children, my husband's tree was an aesthetic tree, a work of rigorous meditation and a mark of his personal spirit. It was bought after careful choice among several trees, carted home, put up a week or so before Christmas. The door to the Christmas room was closed in the evenings before Christmas Eve, while the tree was being decorated with great circumstance. Paulus resented any hand on it but his own. I would sit with him, drinking wine and writing Christmas greetings, while he weighed the branches down with apples on strings, then rounded its shape by cutting off unwieldly branches. If a branch were missing, he would try to insert a piece of branch brought along with the tree, bending and molding until it had the shape he intended. He always perferred silver or gold balls, if we allowed him his choice. Sometimes I fought for color and then he carefully inserted a strong red, sometimes a deep blue, or even green or pink. Sometimes he permitted silver icicles floating down from the branches. For him, however, it was always an earnest task. I asked him once to let Mutie decorate the tree that year and Rene the next. But it was impossible for anyone except Paulus to decorate a Christmas tree in our house. If Mutie did an interesting job, during the night Paulus worked over the tree, leaving nothing of her intentions. It had become Paulus's tree again.

Our Christmas tree pleasure after Paulus's death declined rapidly. Teddy decorated the tree in East Hampton once or twice. The third time, he could not come in before Christmas. I could no longer shop for a heavy tree. I bought an artificial pine, which was fairly tall and looked rather like a tree, though it had no fragrance. Somehow it served the purpose—we did not have to spread out our gifts on an empty floor, but it had become a piece of convenient merchandise. The Christmas tree had died with Paulus.

Horace's wife, Ruth, was the daughter of the founder of the School of Ethical Culture. She let me participate in a sex-education class there. I was stunned by the attitude of the others in the class, who were courageously breaking through the secretiveness of sex relations, expressing without hesitation what seemed most intimate and hidden.

Ruth and Horace and Carol and Herbert, their intimate friends at Columbia University, took us in their car to Ruth's house in the Adirondacks on Thanksgiving Day. They gave us the most precious thing one can share among friends, a weekend at their country house. We walked through virgin forests on hardly recognizable paths, between newly fallen trees with rotting trunks felled in earlier storms. Horace and Herbert manned two canoes as the Indians had used them, paddling us across a lake. The wind was fierce. I was scared to death. They had to carry the canoes across a spit of land to another part of the lake, then paddle on to the house.

Ruth and Horace later invited us to Martha's Vineyard after our trip through the Thousand Islands to acquaint us with one of the loveliest vacation lands for intellectuals weary of too much civilization. They were staying in a barn, where we slept on mattresses spread out under the roof.

Occasionally I was allowed to wash the dishes, Ruth cooked, Horace shopped, and we contributed to the household. After a week or so we found a one-room house some way from the barn. They showed us where to shop and came with their car to help out. They secured an Indian woman for us, who came in her car to clean and probably to shop. It is only now that I can imagine the harrassment we must have imposed upon them with our presence and the affection that went into the numerous details and sacrifices they made to help us in every respect.

Once we attended an evening in a barn where their friends were gathering. Someone started singing and I heard for the first time the song about the Mississippi, "Old Man River," who just keeps rolling along. The melancholy of the big river, the sense of wide open spaces in other songs, caught my imagination. I cried. I felt a part of it all. And I bought a victrola so we could hear songs like "Swanee River" at home.

Mutie lost her bathing suit on the beach. Friends said it was not polite to let the kids run around in the nude. Not even the kids? I was shocked. And the expression was not "naked" but "in the nude." I swallowed my arrogance. It was another country and another custom.

Our one-room cottage on a hill away from the ocean was surrounded by fields of meager, dry grasses crossed by walls of stone, which the farmers had collected from their lands. On top of a hill overlooking the ocean and the inlets of the bay, Paulus found his place to work after a morning swim in the sea—open ocean, white sand, with a rock here and there, tied in by the grassy dunes. He had tried in the beginning to build a sand castle as he had in Germany, but his new American friends stared uncomprehendingly and finally gently explained that there was no private property on the beach. Sand castles or deep holes playfully built were flattened out before leaving the beach, so that others would not stumble over or into them. In the land of private property there was no place on a public beach that one could playfully claim as one's own. The country belonged to the people.

I asked Horace to translate the "Jabberwocky" from *Alice in Wonderland* for me.

In the little green house I photographed Erdmuthe through the windowpane, looking mysterious like a Mona Lisa. Somewhere, somehow, we acquired a cat, which followed us every day to the sandy edge of the grassy path leading to our beach. We had once taken her to the ocean but she was so bewildered and unhappy there that after that she stayed home, waiting for us, hidden in the sharp fronds of the dune grass.

We learned about poison ivy and wild grapes, American lizards and the dangers of poisonous spiders, about colibris, the yellow and blue flowers, and the lovely dark-pink dog roses.

I painted water colors of the landscape stretching out wide to the horizon-blue water between green and sandy tongues of land. I took photos of Mutie with a yellow strawflower wreath in her white-blond hair and had her take photos of Paulus and me to send to friends in Germany. The American summer was ripe and hot; we looked tan and healthy.

During one hot after-luncheon rest, we conceived Rene. I was not supposed to have any more children, at least without an operation, but I can still feel the relaxed Pan-hour (Erdmuthe out somewhere with a friend) and my sense that this would be a child. I had the same feeling when we conceived Erdmuthe in a small dark room under the roof with a gilded ceiling. There were the glory and the satisfaction, the intimacy and closeness, and the pure relaxation of love.

Soon after we had emigrated, we started asking people to join us for Christmas. People were lonely on Christmas Eve, especially Germans, Jewish or not. We had all shared the Christmas tree and Christmas Eve in the old country.

Friends sent their emigrating friends to Paulus as the head of Selfhelp for German Émigrés. At first he brought everybody to our house for a meal, but after a while it became too much, in amount of people as well as of money. Of course they were all poor—doctors who had to take a special examination here, philosophers, economists, psychologists, the intellectual elite of Germany, businessmen, bankers. They had not been as lucky as we were in coming in on the quota, nor were they able to continue in their professions.

My sister sent a few of her doctor friends to our house. Our old friends from Frankfurt had come, Kurt and Eva, Max and Maidon, Fred and Erich, and the younger members of the institute. It grew to a stream of emigrants, knocking on Paulus's office door, meeting at our apartment, where Selfhelp was founded. Many of the old friends were responsible for the founding, but Paulus was obliged to carry the burden as president in the first years.

Christmas, the most intimate family and children's feast, became a representative enterprise devoted to our Jewish émigré friends, to our Jewish American friends, and to other friends as well. After a few years, they considered our Christmas their domain and it was difficult to change the evening for the friends so our children could have a few intimate hours with their parents on Christmas Eve. Paulus's life had changed. From a privte citizen, he had become a representative of his émigré brothers, of his political views, of his gift for making friends in the new country, and of his theological views. It was easier for a student in trouble to see him than for one of his children or his wife. Home life was irritating.

As for my relationship with the wives of the seminary faculty, it was resolved when they finally found a niche for me in their minds. On my ladies-of-the-faculty evening, I asked a German woman who was a psychologist to talk about psychology, probably the psychology of children. Somehow by the end of that evening the other ladies had decided I was the artistic type, which set me apart from their ethical endeavors, and so I had found my place in their imaginations.

Mutie went to boarding school, for which the president of Union had provided a scholarship. When we first took her to the school in a modest little corduroy suit, with Rene, fat and blond and angelic trotting along beside her, Paulus with his beautiful "wasp" face, and I tall and blond and not too badly dressed, the head of the boarding school breathed an audible sigh of relief. Rene put a maple seed pod on his nose, which made him look all the more cuddly and rosy. This New England lady then said outright, "Oh, I am so relieved," took Rene's hand, and showed us over the entire school grounds. I suppose emigrés to her meant Polish Jews sitting on potato bags, clad in rags.

Despite her welcome, Mutie had a hard time, but I never regretted her having attended one of the best schools in the country, learning the manners and the arrogance of the rich American families. It amused her that one of her classmates was a British girl who had some high aristocratic title. It did not amuse Mutie that, just when we had managed to buy her a lovely suit, the skirt was stolen, and it was quite clear that one of the wealthy girls had taken it.

I rented one of our rooms, so I would have a little money of my own for clothes and an occasional theater ticket. I remember coming back from one of our extensive trips during the summer and screaming to Paulus, with windows open onto the seminary court-yard, that I simply had to have money for one pair of shoes, one suit, and one winter coat for Rene's return to school. From then on, Paulus tried to curtail his endless free lectures and other free obligations. He would ask for a fee, which was very hard on him. He hated to be the one who seemed in need. Beyond the door of his house, he was the glorious lecturer and helper, but within that house he was the poor man with a shabby salary and a tremendous number of obligations, in accord with his importance; the man who found it more than difficult to supply his family, however poorly, with clothes and food and their other necessities, not to mention the pleasures of a movie or a play. It was at this time that I often went downtown and stood in line for a single theater ticket. Mutie and Rene had to go it alone, or if Mutie sometimes invited a friend, I would get two tickets, but we could almost never go to the theater together.

Slowly the ability to choose clothes of good quality came to us. In the beginning, they had all looked alike. In Germany there had been few ready-made clothes. I had patronized a shop in Luxembourg, where the clothes were expensive but suitable to our social needs. I had also had a seamstress who cut clothes on my body—she was an artist—and another who altered a few things every year and did the mending. Here, we were delighted by ready-made clothes.

Buying a coat was an enterprise. I once bought a fur coat the seams of which soon split. It was with wild outcries and hysterics, produced at the store, that I managed to get another one without losing too much money. I can see myself, haggard and pale, badly dressed and full of fierce resentment, cornering the floorwalker and bursting into the supervisor's office to replace that coat.

Paulus and I were on bad terms. His lady friend lived across the street from us. He spent his evenings with her, came home tipsy, and then grew angry if I waited up for him. He was to contract trichinosis from imported German sausage he ate at her apartment. He helped her get a job at the seminary. He asked me to invite her to one of our big Christmas parties. I was polite, but she left early. I decided I would not torture myself by inviting her again.

She died of cancer. When I first learned that she had cancer, I sat down at her feet once during a social gathering at Union in a gesture of empathy at her unhappy fate.

One day Paulus sent me his friend Adolf, to go over our budget. He seemed to feel I was not efficient enough. I had learned the hard way and could show Adolf my books. After a long study of them, he said hesitantly that I might spend a bit more on food. Paulus's wine budget at that time was comparatively bigger. We had so little money and yet we felt that friends and the theater and going downtown belonged to life. When Reinhold Niebuhr had proposed that

[183]

all faculty salaries be cut for some reason, I wrote to the seminary president that a cup of coffee between lectures, a play now and then, traveling, and such good things of life belonged to life and I was not willing to wait for the rewards in heaven, even if my husband was one of the ministers of God.

Only at Harvard did things get better. The salary was better and the fee for lectures became successively better. We were able to live a modestly comfortable life there.

When Paulus's lady friend was buried, I was in East Hampton, fiercely cleaning out the basement of our house, exorcising evil. Some of Paulus's friends accompanied him to the funeral, people who were rather surprised later when I was unwilling to confide in them or accept them lovingly after they had fulfilled their commitment to my husband's friend. When I asked Paulus about the children of his lady friend, he broke into sobs—they had hated him.

I will not write about our children. I promised them not to talk about their problems and our life together. At any rate, we were very close and much time went into their care. At times I accepted jobs so they could go to camp. I believed the American camp was one of the molders of democracy. Later, they attended boarding school and were both well known for their abilities. I felt in this instance, too, that the good American school would give them entrance to American life.

One other dream was fulfilled in the United States: Heinrich's dream of the threesome and the foursome. Even after our failure in Frankfurt to achieve a foursome with Paulus and his friends, which had left me alone with the two beloved people without Paulus, I had not forgotten that dream. Paulus was not to be one of the four. In New York he moved farther and farther away from me in our personal life.

While Paulus spent much time on lecture tours, I developed my own relationships with friends and lovers. I met one woman who was one of the many loves of a friend of mine. We talked and acted out the dream of a foursome—two couples. Sometimes there were three of us. In the 1970s it would not have meant much; Woodstock and the communes had happened by then and wife-swapping had become common. But at that time it was still something of a liberation. It meant more than a quick copulation. It was a break with the whole concept of monogamy, it was the new concept of participation without losing one's identity, of becoming more and not less in a foursome. One no longer lived inside a picture frame, pressed flat on a single plane, one moved out into thinking not in opposites but as a group. Fulfilling my vision of a human couple in copulation—not heard through a door to the paternal bedroom, secretive and dangerous, but acted out by close friends, who would embrace you and whom you would embrace without loss of personality but clear-eyed and loving—this removed the curse of neurotic jealousy from me. It was participation, not extinction.

Heinrich had insisted that two couples, loving, would go back behind the experience of being the children of parents, would, so to speak, carry out an act of love with their parents. After that, you could go back even further, behind the parents of your parents, which would be an eightsome, and so on—a play of the imagination that made me feel as if I were running through a dark tunnel from station to station, where waiting couples welcomed me and passed me on to the next stop, further back in time.

During our last years in Cambridge, the drug question came up. Our young friends were immersed in it; they believed that with drugs they could come nearer to God. Paulus and I had gone through many ecstatic experiences and demonic letdowns and we both felt that drugs provided a shortcut without the personality development that must accompany such experiences to make them fruitful. There might be danger of confusion. Moreover, yoga training made me feel rather indifferent to the chemical production of ecstasy—ecstasy occurred with the practice of yoga.

I took marijuana to oblige my son. I found that smoking it influenced my visual experience, producing both a gay, ecstatic enchantment and a sense of being threatened. When I looked at palm trees, they became crystaline in the most seductive colors, taking on the quality of sunlit jewels. On the other hand, a chair at the end of the sitting room seemed to take on a threatening attitude; it seemed to move toward me. The next day, my son smashed a door window with that chair. Marijuana gave me a sensual experience without creativity—color, taste, well-being, ill-feeling, but nothing especially creative or enlightening. It might be a marvelous drug for a dictator who wanted to keep his subjects' realistic aggressions within a dream-like, sensual state of inactivity.

LSD, which I took only once and under proper guidance, seems to me to produce a far sharper response, with surprising insights

[185]

into real experience. I found it especially enlightening to look at people, getting some sense that their deeper selves had opened up to me. I also found myself threatened by my familiar old spider phobia—in my normal consciousness, less urgently than it had seemed to be under the influence of LSD. I managed to slip away from it during the LSD session, but I can believe that a repetition of the drug could have brought me closer to the darker fears of my life. Nevertheless, I maintain that images produced under the influence of LSD are not very different from certain stages in meditative procedures.

Paulus went regularly to lectures and performances at the New School for Social Research—the university of exiles. Many scholars from abroad had assembled there by this time. Sometimes we met at our homes for dinner, but the splendor had gone out of it. Instead, we would meet for luncheon in inexpensive Broadway restaurants, or after dinner in our apartments.

Some of our professional friends moved to the suburbs so as to have good public schools for their children. The first cars among the émigrés emerged.

Robert and his new wife Elsa, who had been the Swedish ambassador's daughter in Russia and had done much for the relief of German prisoners of war in and after World War I, turned up in Cambridge, and visited us in New York.

A beautiful light came into our lives in the person of Trude, who had been an exchange student and then married the son of a wealthy family. She arrived in evening clothes when we first met, looking fashionable and being very sweet. She was soon to be included in President Roosevelt's circle. Even sooner she was to divorce her husband and marry a Jewish intellectual who was a favorite of Mrs. Roosevelt. Later she took an official job and once in a while thereafter her name or that of her husband, who wrote a column for the *New York Post,* would be in the papers. It gave us a breath of a nontheological atmosphere.

When Paulus, Adolf, and another scholar were invited to a luncheon with President Roosevelt, it was Trude's friendship with Mrs. Roosevelt and the President that brought about the invitation.

Paulus and I were once invited to the Roosevelts' country home. Paulus went, while I remained weeping in our dark kitchen, cleaning house—I was covered from head to foot with poison ivy from smoke

[186]

from a fire in which we had burned some poison ivy along with cut greens.

Despite all our activity, we émigrés were a homeless bunch, reading *The New York Times*, sometimes grasping the news, sometimes misunderstanding, learning about the further plight of the Jews in Germany, crying bitterly every morning with shame and anger about the fatherland, pretending, in letters to our friends still there, that everything was all right.

During our first summer in the United States, Trude and her husband invited us to one of the Thousand Islands in the St. Lawrence River near Canada. Paulus was asked to invite another couple who were also émigrés, and he chose Hanna and Gerhard, whom I felt we hardly knew. They took their children. Erdmuthe and I joined them somewhat later, because she suddenly contracted a serious infection. Paulus wrote me he was missing me, describing the situation, and mentioning that he had developed a friendship with Hanna.

On the day I arrived, after lunch and a quick game of pingpong with Gerhard, we went to find Paulus and Hanna. We found them together on the lawn. Gerhard told me later that he had once found them on the roof, Hanna in the nude. I refused to let Paulus speak to me alone about his "friendship" with her. I had had so much experience with his denying every fact until he made me believe him and not my own eyes, and I was sick of being betrayed. After dinner, when the children were in bed, Paulus, our friends, and I sat in the beautiful library of the house and began to talk. He could not evade the facts with which I faced him. He threw himself on the floor, screaming and kicking, because this time there was no way out. When we were alone, as usual he was contrite and full of regret. I kept my pride. I stayed. I felt protected by Gerhard, who was gentle and reserved toward me.

Two years later, Gerhard became my friend.

Paulus had to explore his new country. He first went by bus and train to California, making stops here and there and coming home filled with enthusiasm. He had to show us everything. And he did. We borrowed money on our insurance policy and off we went.

It was tremendous. We took two trips together when Rene was small. Later I went with my daughter and son-in-law and the grandchildren.

We had come from a country so highly cultivated that even along the train embankments one saw small potato fields or vegetable gardens. The forests were well cared for with no underbrush; everything was under close scrutiny; fallen trees were immediately removed—as a matter of fact, I don't remember ever having seen a dying tree that was not already marked for cutting down.

There was not much open space or shoreline in our country. Relatively, the Baltic Sea and the North Sea were puddles. Here we went from ocean to ocean, across deserts, mountains, plains, and high plateaus, crossing majestic rivers, passing around lakes the size of a sea, stopping at canyons whose deep gorges we had never even known existed, wandering in the petrified forest between age-old trees lying like fallen columns of Greek temples. I wrote, "In Europe you look at man-made ruins, here you find the grandeur of ruins before mankind came into being." The trees, so huge that you had to walk far back from the trunks to see where they ended in the sky, seemed as tall as those in the fairy tales about large forests in my home country. The ferns were so tall I felt myself back in my childhood, when I had sat among ferns imagining that they sheltered me like trees. The tarantula was as fierce-looking as the dream spider of my early years; it was big enough for my imagination. I could lose my fear in the face of reality.

The Indians seemed to be roaming the desert even yet. On the high plateaus they came with the sandstorm across the desert, in my imagination. We saw them in reality at their powwows, as we experienced cowboys in small villages, sitting on their heels or, at the rodeo, riding steers, lassoing the young bulls, and riding ahead of Mutie and Rene, when we stayed for a few weeks in one place and let the children ride Western saddle. A cowboy lifted each of them onto a horse, placed the reins in their hands, and rode ahead into the wilderness, singing.

We also saw the Pacific near the orange groves and along the coast of Carmel, where we went up to the Big Sur.

We came back feeling it was our country. We could still see the grizzly bears feeding across a ditch, the brown bears meeting us on the roads in the park, the ranger on top of a mountain at the fire watch, saying, "You want to see something?" and proudly showing a young tarantula in a bottle, his way of being generous—everyone across the country had been generous and open with us.

Memory of the old landscapes paled before the Mesa Verde with

[188]

its Indian skyscrapers cut into a cliff, the oldest mud house in the United States in Taos, Old Faithful, the taste of Death Valley—sand on your tongue—the empty distances between towns and cities, the loneliness of the desert, and the two oceans.

Paulus and I had different ways of expressing our displeasure. I would burst into a rage. I could rave beautifully, unexpectedly pouring streams of abuse on my poor adversary; on occasion my wrath was totally inappropriate. I seemed to accumulate large amounts of criticism, holding it all back until, suddenly and at the wrong moment, I would explode in a tremendous temper tantrum, pouring out all I had held back over months and months. Probably most of what I said was correct, but the time and place were entirely wrong. Afterward I would have a sheepish sense of relief at having liberated my feelings. It was hard to remember why I had been so harsh. I was forgiving and could be the first to extend a loving hand. I believed one should not go to sleep in anger, and I probably kept to that for my own sake.

Paulus had a different approach. He got rid of his negative feelings toward the world and another person by being negative—dribbling negation—all the time. That caused me to become fiercely positive, fighting his negation of the world with my optimism. He had a way of arguing that became what I called "logistic" after a while. It meant that he was no longer referring to the subject of our argument, but was involved in the process of seemingly logical deprecations of problems. These, of course, meant nothing to me, since I was mainly occupied with the emotion of the argument, and I would break rudely through all his logical attempts to prove his point, which by now had lost all point to me. In some instances, when this went too much against his grain, he might throw a desperate temper tantrum. I would stand by, cold as a fish on ice.

Somehow parallel to our different ways of expressing wrath was our predilection for either pornography or detective stories. I was shocked and troubled when I found out about Paulus's inclination to pornography. He would cover a pornographic book with an acceptable book during his rest hour. He hid his inclination from me for many years; I discovered it by chance one day in the United States. I cried and was so troubled about the deformation of the human image, as I saw it, that I talked to a friend, a psychoanalyst, who must have helped me gently to understand the motives behind reading pornography. I tried, then, to give Paulus pornography, which of course did not work, since the main appeal was its being kept secret from me. But he used me to order books for him, and of course his many lady friends took pleasure in it. To them it was a welcome basis for conversation.

It was much later when I suspected that my equivalent to his pornography was my relief through detective stories. Agatha Christie was one of the writers whose books I could read in one night, meanwhile forgetting all my personal troubles. I still consider her books *The Murder of Roger Ackroyd* and *Endless Night* stories that go to the heart of the human encounter.

When we left Germany for the United States, I promised myself to try again to save our marriage. But it did not have a chance. Paulus, after Rene's birth, became more estranged than ever from the family. Nevertheless, he did not want a divorce. When all his arguments and entreaties failed, he threw himself on the floor, his limbs flailing. He sent his friends to me, imploring me not to divorce him, saying that it would ruin his career. Paulus considered marriage a decision of the will. I could not see it that way.

I was tired and overweight, depressed, and not very pleasant to live with at the time. A violent attack of fever broke me completely. I lay in bed, raving that the hatred I felt within me would destroy me. I felt poisoned by my hate against Paulus. When the fever left me, with the help of strong medicines, I was so weak that my daughter, who was studying drama, proposed to take me to her gymnastic teacher, whom her drama coach had recommended to her, to loosen her up. I went.

I found an old woman with books about the wisdom of Asia, with knowledge of the spiritual and physical aspects of the dancer's body. She taught, and had been taught by, great artists, being a great artist herself. From then on I went to Ellen regularly, sometimes with Mutie. My figure stretched, my body became articulate again, my emotional being developed the positive. One of her words of wisdom was, "Do not arouse opposition." I had been prone to do that for the last unhappy years of my life with Paulus.

After two years of healing exercises with Ellen, I went on to a yogi, having become intrigued by breathing exercises. Our friend Friedrich had given me a book many years before, remarking that it was all I needed. It concerned many dimensions of yoga. My yogi was strictly Hatha Yoga. After participation for a short time in a class with several others, I took individual lessons. The yogi was good to me and did not make me pay more than I could afford. In eight years of concentrated study at home and with him, I learned to his satisfaction all the movements but one. He taught me breathing. He would light a candle and I would meditate. He was light as a feather. His closeness was bodiless when he corrected my position with gentle, unearthly hand. I invited him with his lady friend to East Hampton, where he took a chilly bath in the ocean. He gave a demonstration at Union Seminary. I tried to introduce Ellen there, too, and Paulus did take some lessons with her. She was delighted with his bounciness. But Union was not quite the right place for physical exercises. The ladies of the faculty felt so overburdened with spiritual or physical homework that they did not appreciate either Ellen or the yogi.

To me, yoga was the great liberation. I had studied over the years, read books, and now I was approaching meditation. My emotional life disentangled itself without special effort. I remember watching my emotional rages walk by in ceremonial procession. I overcame my flashes of clairvoyance. I learned to ask for knowledge but to disregard information that came to me through my sensibility—when I felt it was not my part to know more than the friend or my husband would confide to me.

This was hard in my relationship to my children. It was common family knowledge that I had known about my daughter's sickness from a distance; that I telephoned Rene's boarding school during a conference there to decide about some mischief on his part; that I saw my son camping under a net on an ocean beach (which was so at the time); that I saw him fighting for life under water when he had suffered sunstroke and had a dangerously high fever. I also refused to react to my knowledge of my husband's adventures, unless he told me of them himself.

I had to separate myself from all mediumistic situations. I had to gain control of myself. Slowly I came to feel moments of being in harmony. In one way, perhaps, I went against the rules in accomplishing my purpose. I did not have one special "guide." There was Friedrich to show me the books, there was Ellen to prepare me, there was the yogi, and perhaps Heinrich had a part in it, but, when I started the strange enterprise of getting hold of myself, I went it alone.

Later, I met with two Zen masters. When I told one of them

my troubles with clairvoyance and love, he said gently, "One can *live* it, too." In turn, when my psychoanalytical friend told me about experiences with her patients, I said the same words to her. I had gone beyond psychology to meditation. "One can live it, too" may be my password.

Finally, a German master who had studied in Japan gave me great insight and help. I am grateful to them all, for yoga finally calmed my emotional turbulence, which had emerged from my own soul and disturbed my relationship with others.

Interlude

LANDSCAPE

Was there an outcry from Pan in the garden?
A dancer, soaring behind the gate of winter's park?
Was there a statue of stone leaning on laurel?
Winter closes in again. Snow on the ground.
An old woman brushes in passing,
Brushes, caressing the white marble,
Buried torso of immortal youth.

AGING

Can you stop time
for me?
Can you hurry the sand in the glass
for yourself?
Can you grow years older in days?
Shall I beseech the hours not to race,
turn back the clock hands, make myself younger?
Who wants to live in reverse like an
overwound toy? Life must be lived
undisguised. Quite without tricks.

OUTSIDE OF TIME

Outside of Time
Where tall trees grow,
Where ferns stand high
Water falls low,
We stand in childlike wonder
You and I.

Outside of Time
Where the ocean rolls
On coral reef,
The pink shell glows,
We meet in childlike enchantment
You and I.

BALLAD OF THE TRUE NONLOVE

When I first met my true nonlove
I fell at his feet, asking
To sacrifice myself for his well-being.

When my true nonlove complained
He could not cross the chasm between us,
I threw myself down and bridged it.

When, furthermore, my true nonlove saw
Glass walls rising to divide us,
I broke the panes and went to meet him.

When my true nonlove intended
To leave, I suffered such anguish
He took me in his arms in no time.

When I asked my true nonlove to stay,
He declined nevertheless;
He intended to remain my true nonlove.

RIVER OF MY TEARS

River of my tears, welling up (as always).
"Give me a smile, Sad One," you said,
"I am leaving.
(standing on the far side of the door,
mounting your white horse of dreams
before hotel room number so and so)
Give me a smile, Desperate One:
Be a white cat purring for me,
Proud One. Give me a smile,
I am leaving."

BEFORE THE MIRROR

It is time I seek to understand, not emotion.
In Venus mirror my reflection does not age—
Still, there is that little something,
Sand, falling through narrow funnel;
Falling and falling, ticking time away.

I must have had the perfect shape at thirty,
Swing of my thighs moving lazily,
Gloved hand clasped around man's thumb.
(Those lovers, calling on me, teaching me
my share of intoxication, filling my mouth
with wine, while you were not yet there. . . .)

Saturn, clipping my beauty as a sculptor
Chips a block, "don't make my face so haggard."
My hands had no veins before—the smell of Death—
The fullness of my neck declines, brows sink.
My foot's high instep . . . Don't go on chipping,
Give me one more night . . . No answer . . . Chip and tick.

Harvard

Harvard seemed the deliverance from all evil. I was rid of the loving psychologist who would telephone most urgently to see Paulus, promising him a good cognac when he came, and being very surprised when I asked her how she would like it if I were to invite her husband for cognac as urgently as she was inviting mine. I was rid of the whole German community, which had occupied my husband unto exhaustion. He was on the Council for a Democratic Germany, founded at a time when we had still hoped that a spontaneous uprising would occur in our old country. Later, the council went on to prepare guidance for Germany after the war was over. He had been president of Self-Help, the organization for German émigrés and later for émigrés from other European countries as well.

I had met Bertolt Brecht when the council was on the verge of breaking apart. Paulus would not agree to having the Communists take it over. Brecht arrived late, and although a millionaire, he was shabbily dressed in an old military coat. I admired his cunning, but Paulus felt obliged to spar with him.

Many of the émigrés returned after the war, to the East Zone or the West. One of the more ridiculous events was the departure of Dorothy Thompson's secretary for a triumphant return to the East.

Paulus was sixty-nine years old in 1955 when he left New York for Harvard. He had lectured in Germany, during his three-month summer vacations, every other year since the end of the second war. I had spent one vacation in Germany and Mutie and Rene had been there another year. Paulus was invited to return for good, but he did not want to go. He did not want to leave what he had built up in twenty years of hard work in the United States. His loyalty was here.

Harvard was solid. Harvard had no status. Harvard did not need status. It was self-contained.

The circle we were privileged to enter at that time consisted of people who, in the eyes of the world, had arrived. In their own eyes, they were shaping the world, either by being called to Washington by the government or by writing books, lecturing, and discussing matters of worldwide import, each in his own field. Frankfurt, when we had been there, crossed the borders of Germany to the rest of Europe. Harvard had wiped out national borders. It was serving the world with all its means of techniques and intellect.

The religion department of the university had been built up by the recently named new president to serve the same international community, and Paulus had been selected, not because of his theological virtues as a member of one denomination, but as a man who reached out to those in all denominations, and even to those outside the churches altogether. He was asked to join the Harvard faculty as a University Professor. Besides being a great honor and acknowledgement, that title meant that he could lecture in all faculties of the university. He was to be invited by the faculties of medicine, philosophy, and psychology, to lecture and to participate in discussions.

Paulus and I were both happy to be back in a university atmosphere. There, theological terminology was no longer necessary. Meeting great men and talking with them was such a spiritual luxury. To feel natural again, without arrogance or inhibition, was the precious gift from Harvard to Paulus and me.

At the time of his move to Harvard, Paulus was interviewed by *Time* magazine. Paulus was sandwiched between Marilyn Monroe and a boxer hero in *Time*. Rene said that it wasn't his intellect that had put him there, it was his charisma—people loved him. That was true. Paulus was both loved and venerated, and he carried it off with dignity and without vanity. When I mentioned his being "a well-known man now," he sighed a little. From outside it looked glorious, but from within it was consistent hard work as well as a spectacular lack of privacy. Not that he did not enjoy walking every morning through the Yard to his office, where he was met by his secretary and his assistant. For the first time he had sufficient help with his tremendous mail from the world over, and he had help with lectures and seminars. But what he enjoyed most were the sessions of his doctoral candidates in our apartment.

He made some speeches that aroused considerable attention, one of them at a *Time* celebration. Luce liked him, and the younger staff enthusiastically agreed with him when he made his address not an occasion for praise but for questions. To me it was such a happy, mad rush. Many of those who had been on *Time*'s cover before were there. I enjoyed the diversity of the guests. How we gaped at them—famous comedians, actors, politicians, diplomats, artists—so many particles of a whole world. I was inclined to exclaim (echoing Paulus's "10,000 women's legs!"), "10,000 variations of the human race!" Everybody had a wonderful time, with dignity and without arrogance. Among 10,000 kings, there was no need to show off.

For a short time, late in his career, Paulus was offered top money for lecturing. He loved to travel and to lecture and it was difficult to hold him back.

I was happy to explore the campus, the first beautiful campus we had inhabited. The Harvard campus included Cambridge and Harvard Square. The Common belonged to it, and so did the Charles River. Students sunned themselves on the banks of the river, the rowers exercised on the river, and every day I walked to the river from our apartment. Sometimes I went into Boston, exploring old streets, wandering with amazement among the shabby-looking shoppers on the main street, or walking to the swan boat for a ride on the lake for five or ten cents. The museum was somewhat outside the city. I discovered the Gardner Museum and was amused at the variety of tastes and displays in the old private residence.

We even attended a few concerts, but Paulus was no longer good at listening to music in a public concert hall and I did not especially like the programs. I went to lectures instead, hearing a series of political lectures by George Kennan, sitting at the feet of Aldous Huxley, attending Paulus's lectures once in a while.

I never missed the autumn colors, making a tour alone, and each year I was intoxicated anew by the glory of New England. My mother had often told me about the burning red maples in her country, adding always that in Germany we did not have such fire in fall.

At Harvard I felt accepted. Paulus needed me and cherished my being there. He talked as in the early days about my beautiful, "great" face. I cherished him and felt the old joy in seeing him coming and going, growing a little more tired, a little slimmer, carrying on valiantly.

We were both invited to Japan. He was ill the night before we were to leave. His doctor, who knew him well, advised going. So we did, and it was glorious as always traveling with him. The Japanese thought he had "Buddha ears" (the elongated ears of the master). They made little jokes about friends from the United States who rushed about instead of looking. Paulus liked to listen and to look, he liked to understand, he took his time. We were shown many beautiful things with great patience on the part of our hosts. We cherished every hour in Japan and learned to love the Japanese people. Our entering an Eastern culture was a great stimulant to Paulus's thinking.

We made another trip, to Egypt and to Israel. Paulus and I had been invited to Israel, but I pleaded for Egypt. We visited both. I have a photograph of Paulus emerging from the grave of the kings. He was sick in Egypt and again in Israel, where by marvelous chance he found a German doctor who knew his name and helped him. As a consequence, Paulus was able to continue the trip, which was so important to him.

At Harvard, Paulus introduced me to the son of one of his friends, a Nazi's dream of racial purity, with reddish hair, a pale mouth, the hooked nose of a medieval knight on a sarcophagus, and the tortured expression of a figure from Breughel's vision of hell. I stood facing his straight, slim body with the proud neck, hesitating before I put out my hand for his formal hand kiss. He bent his head low. I experienced the same profound shock I had when I saw my husband for the first time as he knelt at the feet of another woman. Then, it had been the shock of "hate without knowledge." Now, it was the shock, just as profound, of "love without knowledge," the fervent wish to see the anguished face melt in a smile, to free him from the dreadful past as a German who had been condemned to live in a Nazi-ruled country, to make him free from imposed inhibitions. I had a single impulse: to fall at his feet, to love him, to cherish him out of sickness into life.

The white knight, my androgyne, had returned from my adolescence, but he was no longer inside of me as a part of my own dream self; rather, he stood facing me, the messenger from my home country, where he had been a hero. With him, the German language came back, pure in diction, and the fate of the German people beyond my political hostility reached out to me.

We saw each other often, I called for him, I rebuked him, I called him back. He came, he never left me, he returned at my call. How many masks we removed from each other's faces in our loving struggle for survival, always finding a new face and a new delight, experiencing greater depth of individuality. We had shared a similar landscape as children, unknown to each other. We had had a similar fate in growing up in similar home towns. Our social strata had been the same. In him, I came back to my own country. We were children of the same neighborhood, leaning across the hedge between two small-town gardens, saying to each other, "Come on, let's do things together."

I had learned at last to reach out in compassion without greed.

We shared the pleasures of intellectual, aesthetic, and emotional intercourse. We did not share any sexual life. It would have seemed incestuous to me, whether because of the great difference in our ages or because he looked so like my brothers, who had all perished in the course of World War II. We most certainly had those golden moments when the friend seems to become the glorification of all that makes life worth living, but some demon or angel always cut through our reaching out for bodily fulfillment, either from my side or his. Curiously enough, I felt so much a one-man's-woman from then on that I never permitted another hand to touch me in any more than an affectionate greeting.

In one of the worst snowstorms of the year, Paulus's plane circled over Washington. It was at last able to land and, many hours later, he was able to proceed to Washington, where I awaited him in our friend's office. The storm had been catastrophic, but nothing had been able to dampen our enthusiasm over the invitation from the future president, Jack Kennedy, to join 250 intellectuals as guests at his inauguration.

First, Paulus had declined—he was to be on a lecture tour. But the pleasure of his friends in his invitation drew his attention to the event as a historical one, which I would have hated to miss. So we were there, I standing for hours facing the platform in a cold wind, seeing the President and his wife. Paulus was still luckier.

He was seated somewhat closer than I was, but we all seemed to feel a new enthusiasm, a wonderful expectation of things to be fulfilled.

When President Kennedy was assassinated, I was arriving in Munich. My German friend met me inside the gates of the train. When he told me, I felt faint with shock. I sat all evening at his house and cried without restraint, while he tried to find out the particulars of the President's death. It was, in some inexplicable way, as if a part of one's own self had been amputated, as if one's own most personal hope for the well-being of a nation had been ruthlessly cut down. Those who loved Kennedy, for whom he bore an image of new life, would never get over their pain at the destruction of a noble man before he had fulfilled his task. The loss of his as yet unspoken words hurt most of all.

It was harvest time for Paulus and me. Whatever had been alive in our relationship in our young days had stayed alive after sex had reached its dénouement. I felt compassion for Paulus, I could enjoy him again, loving his noble aging face, listening to him on social evenings. Paulus and I indulged in a new, secret marriage pact. He gave me a heavy gold ring made after our own design. We felt close again in these years of our advancing age, when he felt sheltered in my new understanding of him.

He was getting a little hard of hearing, and I could help him in that. He was also forgetful of events, but when given a key word, he would remember and go on. He had to write down the names of the philosophers he wanted to discuss in his lectures and, to his disgust, he could no longer remember his friends' telephone numbers. He was still eager for his mail. In East Hampton, until the very last day, he insisted on getting out of the car to go into the post office and retrieve it himself—by this time I thought it was his right to keep his secrets.

We had again met Herbert Marcuse and his wife. He was a professor at Brandeis and we had good evenings together with Susan Sontag, then married to a friend of the Marcuses. I liked Herbert and I enjoyed hearing discussions between Paulus and him, which were always vivid, and often rough on his side. He was fond of Paulus and would telephone, saying, "I am already longing to see you again." His wife took me to a peace demonstration, during which Erich Fromm spoke and Joan Baez sang. Eggs were thrown at Fromm. I thought the whole thing uninspiring—I did not go for peace demonstrations. Fortunately, Paulus was not a pacifist.

The Marcuses came to dinner at our house after Kennedy's election and we women had a sharp argument about loyalty to the United States, which had taken us in as émigrés and from which we had received every advantage and help. She was now glorying in tearing down the influence of that government. The two men sat by while we raved. We separated in anger; even Paulus could not see her side. To me it seemed nothing but a bleak lust for destruction. Herbert and I embraced and kissed. Paulus and he were very sad. Paulus wrote to them, excluding me, and trying to make up.

One of the most delightful events in our Harvard life was the appearance of two people, George and Joan, an architect and his wife. In matters of intellect and in understanding Paulus's writings, Joan was no dilettante. Paulus and I both marveled at her beauty and intelligence. We both delighted in her glamour and her naturalness. She had studied Paulus's thought and was not only a glamorous woman but a very good student of his works, a connoisseur in art, and a vivid and enchanting personality. She had had infantile paralysis and recovered.

George showed us some of the houses he had built for others; moreover, he and Joan often invited us to the house he had remodeled from an old mansion into a most delightful living space for his wife, himself, and their children. It had Greeklike proportions, lying among trees on a hill with a sloping lawn and a lake at the foot of the slope. It breathed beauty and relaxation. In the spring, when we visited them for Easter, Joan indulged Paulus's childlike pleasure of hunting Easter eggs.

Paulus was never to know of their move to a penthouse nor to see the "White House," as I called it, a clear strong melody reconstructed from an old house under Maine skies, on the tip of an inlet facing the open ocean. George gave up architecture. He would not design one of the new prefabricated houses that could be put up anywhere without individual consideration. He started painting and found the same melody—the expression of his personality in color and line—as he had in his architecture. He is incorruptible with a truly independent Yankee spirit.

Interlude

THE CHILDREN OF ZEUS   *A Comedy in Three Acts*

The "Children of Zeus" are three daughters of Zeus by three different mortal women who were themselves the progeny of Zeus and mortals. Each of the daughters has a singular birthmark: Taura, daughter of Zeus and Europa, has cow's ears; Ledinah, of Zeus and Leda, has swan's feet; and Daninah, of Zeus and Danae, has a completely hairless body.

All three have half-human and half-divine friends: Taurus, a centaur, half-horse; Nereus, a triton, half-fish; and Bocksbein, a satyr, half-goat. Each daughter also has a human suitor and as the play opens the girls all want to be mortal, forgoing their immortality to marry their mortal suitors. They are in rebellion against being "misfits," as they call themselves, and are concealing their birthmarks from the three mortals.

The girls live high in the mountains in three different areas of a cave separated by hangings. They receive dinner each night from their centaur, satyr, and triton. These three often sport on the rocks above the cave, which has a large vent through which they converse with, tease, proffer gifts to, and make music for the daughters of Zeus.

The mortal suitors discover the girls' odd traits (with the slapstick help of the satyr, centaur, and triton) when they call bearing gifts, two of which cause difficulties—earrings for Taura, sandals for Ledinah.

There is considerable light-hearted horseplay, and the comedy begins its dénouement with Daninah marrying her mortal and Ledinah deciding to accept her mortal suitor's invitation to be his "hidden wife."

Taura remains in her own part of the cave after Ledinah has bidden her good-bye.

TAURA. [*Jumps up and rushes to the sculpture of Zeus and Europa. Removing the curtain, she throws herself down before the sculpture.*] Father and God, I have spoken many prayers before your image. You have never listened to me, nor given me a sign for an answer. My hour of decision has arrived and I will curse you in all the heavens if you do not respond to me. What right have you, Father of the Gods, to play love with a mortal woman, to override her human and your divine origins, to let a child be born who is a misfit in either world —the world of the gods and the human world? Poor help is immortality, if I crave to love like a human being; poor help is a human heart, if you give me at the same time the sign of beasts—my silken ears. Answer, my Father, answer me, Zeus! [*She remains on her knees, beating the floor with her hands.*]

VOICE OF ZEUS. Here I am, daughter of Europa and Zeus, what is your wish?

TAURA. Take them away, take away my ears, Zeus, I want to be human!

VOICE OF ZEUS. Daughter of Europa, thine ears are the sign of the descent of a great power, and not a misfit. I created you without seeing, driven down into the pool of creation by your mother, the beautiful woman. I did not remember you until you called me today, loudly enough to create another whirlpool of thought power that I could not resist. I cannot take the sign of the god from you, the sign of the power of nature. But I can put a spell over your friend, who is now on the way to you, to make him forget all his worries about your "misshapen ears," as he calls them, so you will be well received by everybody. Your children will be human without blemish. You will become mortal like your husband.

TAURA. And the other side of my nature, "divine nature," as you call it, being in the circle of the seasons, taking a wild fling with my friend the Centaur in divine abandon?

VOICE OF ZEUS. Should you live with the Centaur, you would be a part of the play of nature, immortal like the seasons and the storms. Daughter of Zeus, listen well to my last words to you. Tell me, or better tell yourself, what do you imagine your children will look like, when you envision them coming out of time toward you? Which seems the sweeter to you, the sting of Centaur, woven into the coming of Spring, into the falling of Autumn or copulation with the rich merchant, the builder of ships to cross the ocean—silks, bedspreads, necklaces, and all . . . . [*His voice trails off.*]

TAURA. [*Deeply moved.*] Wait, Father Zeus, wait! [*She stays on her knees.*]

LEDINAH. [*Getting up slowly, going to the bas-relief of Leda with the swan.*] I will take you along, Mother and Father—Zeus, great god of mischief and protection.

[*Ledinah remains with bowed head, moving her lips in silent prayer. ANTONIO enters, followed by slaves carrying a litter. He lifts LEDINAH in. They leave silently, followed by slaves carrying the relief and a trunk with LEDINAH's clothes. TAURA stands up and walks into LEDINAH's part of the cave. NEREUS, the triton, pops out of the well.*]

NEREUS. Gone she is! What else could she do, loving him so much? But I am so much the lonelier for it.

TAURA. [*Lightly.*] Gone she is, Nereus. I will be the last one to leave, or I may never leave. I will inherit Ledinah's part of the cave, if you let me and try ability on her loom.

NEREUS. [*With dignity.*] I will be very happy to see you around, Taura. I like a sniff of the other world once in a while—the world of two legs, or four, instead of fishtails and fins. You don't know how bored one gets with one's little world, bored to death with the whole lot . . . .

TAURA. [*Lightly.*] You are an in-between, too, like Daninah, like Ledinah, and me. But the other two gave up their lifepower for death and the human atmosphere, for the warmth of the valley. They have forgone the proud loneliness of an earth power living within the whirling seasons. The mortals down there live against the seasons, in houses protected by fire against the cold, by a roof against the rains, in precious furs and weavings against their nakedness.

NEREUS. [*Smiling.*] You have all that, too. Here is a cave against the winds, built by nature if not by you, I admit. Your fire is still burning in the open and blackening you. How often have you complained about it! And how about your own clothes, woven into colorful and intricate patterns?

TAURA. [*Smiling back.*] But up here it is only the necessities, down there it is the gadget.

NEREUS. [*With a friendly tone.*] Why not a gadget? The creator of the world created innumerable gadgets, shaped tiny cells into the most complicated functioning parts of bodies, of the cosmic world, are according to his whim. Fins of so many shapes, wings of so many sizes, crystals of so many forms. He is dreaming while he creates, putting his divine hands, which are neither burned by fire nor shattered by rock, into the bubbling bowels of the earth, throwing out handfuls of beasts and birds, plants of such different growings, trees and crystals, all of his own playful imagination. Why should he care to know what creates itself, born out of his lust for creation? Everything is a bridge to another shore, an in-between—the rock wants to be grass, the grass wants to be bird or fish, the fish or bird wants to be mammal, the mammal wants to be human, the human wants to be like the gods.

TAURA. [*Bowing her head.*] And I wanted to give up my privilege as an in-between of god and men.

NEREUS. The world of the half-gods—the powers of nature, and the world of the humans—protection and affection—do not mix well, my daughter. You are still a storm and a fire on the back of the Centaur, sweeping over the plains. Climbing high in the mountains, you are part of the immortal power of nature. You can still create storms, from which the mortals try to protect themselves in the valley. That is the difference, not the gadget.

TAURA. What will become of me if I reject my paunchy mortal Centurio?

NEREUS. You will have children, for you crave to become a mother. You will have children like Centaur or like yourself—four-legged or two-legged. Or you might bear a child resembling Centaur, but with a longing for the human world and the safety of the valley, and that would mean tragedy.

TAURA. And if I go down into the valley as a hetaera for Centurio's sake?

NEREUS. You will have a house and slaves and female pupils to teach the arts, singing and dancing, weaving and making love. You will be worshipped by the young men of Delphi, who will come to you for entertainment, wisdom, and lust—everything they do not get at home. Your paunchy human friend, married well, will visit you once a month while his wife is not able to receive him.

TAURA. And up here?

NEREUS. Up here, you will always be yourself—alone, but not lonesome, your own center of life, your own immortal swing.

[*208*]

TAURA. And if I tire of myself?

NEREUS. You will go to the top of a mountain and call Death. He will come in the eternal darkness of a whirlwind, which is stronger than you and will tear you into particles, or in a lightning that will burn you to ashes, in a wave that will dissolve you into pearls of water, falling as a rainbow into the sun.

TAURA. And Taurus?

NEREUS. He might stand beside you, proud and silent, for a fleeting moment while you bend down to drink, seeking you in his own time, evading you at times, suddenly throwing his powerful shadow over you while you rest in the meadow, chewing your divine ear, kissing you with the gentleness of a breeze in summer, overpowering you with the force of the wild spring. He will be like a storm, too, not like the warming fire of the hearth. He will be burning or cold. He will lack human affection.

TAURA. [*Smiling.*] But he has faithfully brought food and has prepared it, for the last five years and he has never asked anything in return.

NEREUS. [*Sadly.*] And so have I.

TAURA. [*Lovingly, gratefully.*] And so you have, Nereus.

NEREUS. Then it cannot be so bad.

TAURA. It will not be too bad.

NEREUS. [*Getting ready to return into the well.*] You breathe in, you breathe out, you dive, you come up again. Yours is the choice, fledgling of the gods, backward or forward, into time or out of time. It is your decision. [*He dives under.*]

BOCKSBEIN. [*Rushing in.*] Taura, your human boyfriend! [*He races through the room, races out, and jumps to the roof. He takes out his flute, playing the three themes again, soon staying with the Centaur theme. TAURUS appears on the roof. He has a wreath of wildflowers around his neck and one in his hand. Music and voices. CENTURIO enters, followed by a red litter and many slaves with torches. TAURA walks to the sculpture of Europa and Zeus, which is unveiled. She has noticed Taurus on the roof. CENTURIO signals the human music to silence. Suddenly, from outside on the roof comes the neighing of a horse and the wild theme of Taurus played by BOCKSBEIN, who is jumping up and down in a frenzy. The neighing is answered by the braying of a donkey, the barking of dogs, the humming of insects, and the shrill cry of birds, mixed with all the powerful noises of nature, the howling of winds and the falling of rain. TAURA listens, she laughs, she makes a mocking bow before CENTURIO, slowly and proudly*] *removing her shawl from her ears, shaking her head so her ears become visible.* CENTAUR *throws one wreath down to her, she catches it and puts it over her head on her shoulders.*]

TAURA. Taurus, half-brother of the gods, take me to you tonight.
[TAURUS, *climbing down to her, takes her in his arms in confusion. Curtain.*]

GRACE CATHEDRAL

Under the tutelage
Of his powerful radiation,
Lights began to emerge
Like candles caught in a wind
Or like will-o'-the-wisps.

But there was no doubt
Where the heart was to be,
Under ridiculous hats
And poutingly painted mouths.

Over middle-aged paunches
Of well-behaved gentlemen,
A lightness occurred
That steadily grew
Under his golden-mouthed music.

And his emanations,
Shielding them like a roof,
Made lights grow brighter
And more reliable, as if
They would burn on—
Even after Church.

SAN FRANCISCO HOTEL LOBBY

Thoughts are not being sought after,
Thoughts are in search of—

Swarming like hummingbirds
To be called into the stream of
An outgoing breath,
Pronouncing words.

They might hide coyly in a glass
Of bourbon, hoping to be whisked
Into language by surprise.

They are inclined to dissolve after
Three bourbons without water,
Getting a bit fuzzy at the edges.

Having soaked too long in
Hard liquor, they flutter in
The speaker's mouth
Like torn wings of butterflies.

HIS FAME IS FOLLOWING HIM

His fame is following him,
A train of brocade.
When he enters their room
When he speaks his thoughts,
He is opening a jewel case
Of moon-shiny pearls,
Rubies of the heart and
Diamonds of the spirit.
People gasp at his wealth;
They have faith in his words,
Faith that will heal.

[211]

Chicago

꙳

Chicago was an inland city, the great lake actually a landlocked sea. The sky could be high over the city or smeared with fog. A vicious storm could turn on in a minute. Tornadoes had raced through the city. In ten minutes, the city could be invaded by a howling windstorm, a screeching icestorm, or a blabbering rainstorm. The people had to be hardy to survive. Their heavy-hipped ladies and broad-backed men populated the hearty velvet-and-gold-decorated steak restaurants done up in the old French brothel style.

The opera was mediocre, the theater nil, but more mediocre still were the uncomprehending crowds at the opera. The city's life was not aesthetically interesting, but everybody was warm and *gemütlich*, too *gemütlich* for me. I preferred the bristling and nervous, artifical crowd of New York.

What I did like were the barbaric, round-towered, high-rise apartment buildings over the canal along the Loop. They were a genuine expression of a strong coarseness in a city with wide avenues in its center, with out-of-town crowds like those in Boston, a middlebrow city with a few secret hideouts for those who could afford horses and children and farms outside the city limits—hearty, patriotic, and rich.

I remember one rich man who earnestly wanted to know about Paulus and his books. What should he read? He talked about the seizing of spiritual values as if he could get hold of some useful merchandise. Nothing, I said, he did not have to read anything. He was surprised. Didn't I want to sell?

I learned to love the high dome of the sky, those soft cotton-ball clouds, the air so different from the cobalt blue skirting an ocean. The softness, the accumulating heat, the breeze turning ferocious, the black thunderheads. Paulus liked to look at it from our eleventh-floor window. I shuddered and closed the curtains.

The sky and the lake in Chicago made me think about the Indian before the white man came. In my imagination, Chicago was only a fata morgana, overlooking the wild vast prairie—Indians peering out of the high grass, buffalo herds tramping through dream-streets, and poisoned arrows pointing at you out of the thickets. Somehow Chicago seemed never to have left the prairie.

Paulus had one particular boon during his lifetime. Living in a university community, he would find the best doctors who, very often without charge, would help him understandingly. This was especially so in Cambridge, where a German doctor gave him treatment for all sorts of ailments that come with old age. When I had a gallbladder operation, which came upon me rather suddenly, I had not seen a doctor and had described the many signs of my illness as nothing but discomforts, but I was well cared for. Paulus, at the same time, had an exploratory operation to test a lump on his neck. After the doctors decided it would not affect his health, we forgot about it.

One discomfort that might not be dangerous but could not be overlooked was his recurring gout. It seemed ridiculous but it was painful. Fortunately, modern medicine had its preventive means.

He found a wonderful doctor in Japan, who proved to be German, and whom we first called on after a bout of drinking at a bar, where Paulus, in the best of spirits, drank between twenty and thirty of the thimble-sized glasses of delicious warm saki. The result was a feeling of great benevolence and an incapacity for getting up. We were with friends from the American embassy, who carried him home and sent the doctor. The next morning, I believe, while Paulus was still in bed, our host came in, pale and disturbed. He tried to explain to me that the notice in the paper, which announced Paulus's cancellation of one of his classes, had been misspelled. In the complicated Japanese characters, the error in the paper stated that he had died. It was easy to come to Paulus as a living member of the human community with the bad news of his death. We were arⁿused and made a joke of it, to the great relief of the misspelling newspaper reporter, who came and apologized profusely.

The best doctor, perhaps, was the Israeli doctor in Tel Aviv, who treated Paulus when he came back from a car trip to Lake Genezareth, fatigued by pain and having suffered terribly on the road. He was a savior with the best of medicines on hand, which enabled Paulus to go on with the trip.

In Egypt the rescue came through our Arabian guide, a charming and good-natured man who simply had us rest at one of the barracks near the graves of kings and scholars, where we sat in the shade and drank hot tea, to recover from the effort of walking up and down steps and threading our way through the serpentine pathways among the graves.

In Chicago, Paulus was under the constant supervision of a doctor. He was a good patient, willing to do everything prescribed. He always seemed to be happy to fall sick, which entitled him to lie down and relax from his strenuous life. He was by now an old man, still traveling extensively in spite of his fatigue. At one time it had been the money he had had to make to keep up our standard of living, which was rather expensive when we rented hotel apartments in Cambridge and Chicago, that kept him traveling. Now it was the momentum. Paulus had decided not to buy a house or install us in an apartment. We sent the little furniture worth keeping to our house in East Hampton, the books to his Harvard, and later his Chicago, office.

I did not mind a bit being without presentable living quarters. Our initial sloppiness stood me in good stead. I had by now developed the philosophy that surroundings do not count that much. It was wonderful to live in a well-chosen setting that expressed one's personal taste, but I had found that as long as we were with friends, whether in a shabby or an elegant place, there would be no failure of communication. We created the atmosphere, wherever; luxury of self-expression was nice but not necessary for friendship. I no longer felt miserable at the thought of myself crossing some hideous blue and red pattern on a cheap rug in a rather run-down hotel apartment. It amused me when our Chicago hotel started to deck itself out in turquoise and velvet. Such incongruity no longer sickened me.

Chicago University was on a three-term system, and during our three years there we spent one term in two successive years in Santa Barbara, California. For the rest of the time we were in our Chicago hotel apartment with three large rooms, kitchen, and two baths. The ample living room had a view on the lake.

Paulus, in his old age, had a most exact schedule. He left home at nine. At first he walked to the university but very soon he took taxis, which were easy to get. The friendly old black porter with the personable face, with whom we all chatted while waiting for a taxi, would call one from a nearby stand that catered to Negro drivers. They were not always very good drivers or very well informed of the city's geography.

I lived in taxis—the city was too dangerous for an old lady like me. I met the gamut of drivers. The most courteous and intelligent proved to be Moslems. They believed in politeness, wanted their kids to be educated, and were pleasant. The veterans were good, too. They had some discipline and were articulate and easy to chat with. Then came the horde of the uneducated. They drove like mad, they were afraid to ask a policeman for directions, they started raving about revolution and made you feel threatened. Because they might even be high or drunk, it was often an adventure, either getting home safely or keeping an appointment in town.

I became interested in the race question, which at that time had become urgent. The Chicagoans were very proud of their mixed housing projects. The theological department of the university seemed to be one big nursery for black problems—every single wife a social worker by her own choosing. I admired these people greatly, but I had to make my own decision and I decided against becoming a social worker. I was just not made for it. My approach to human problems was to face the person next to me and either find communication possible or depart. Our way of being generous was to invite our friends and students, helping our children or a cause, which was personal. The idea of giving a Care package as a Christmas present, to blacks or whites, instead of a personal present, somehow enraged me. I thought it was escaping the personal relationship and considered it in no way humanitarian. The love and thought that went into selecting a present for a particular beloved person seemed to get lost in this approach. The personal, to me, was what counted. And it has remained so.

The personal relationships, the friends Paulus brought into our house or who took us into their with warmth, these were the consolation for being in this unkempt city. One could not go out—even the natives admitted that—without being in danger of being robbed.

After our first year in Chicago, Negroes sometimes loitered at the lake near our hotel, where Paulus and I used to walk together and where I very often went alone. It was inadvisable to walk in seemingly empty streets. You had best watch out who came toward you or who followed you in a nearly deserted street. I learned my lesson. Once a group of Negro youths coming toward me bumped into me intentionally. When I turned around, enraged and ready to scream at them, I met with such a sneering readiness to return and club me that I walked on, glad to escape. Another time, again on 57th Street between our hotel and the university, meeting my eye with hateful persistence, was one of two ragged Negroes standing on the curb with a shovel and another instrument they might have used to harm me. I stared back into his eyes, meeting him head-on with pride and arrogance. But I breathed easier after I escaped his glaring declaration of revulsion at my being.

Nevertheless, one early afternoon I walked to one of the most frightening Negro sections; I wanted to see for myself. I was stopped by a uniformed guard before a heavily walled office building from whom I asked directions. "You better hide your pocketbook," he said. "Put your money in your skirt pocket. I'm watching the telephone girls, who will come out in a minute now, and they will be robbed if they don't look out. These people will drive by on bicycles and snatch your purse. They'll crowd you to the curb. You'd better go home." I did, but one morning I got up courage again and walked with a package to mail to the nearest Negro section on the South Side. There were many young people loafing in the street. I went into the post office and sent my package off. People were polite, I was not molested. I asked here and there for street directions. No trouble. But the atmosphere in Chicago seemed very different from that in New York's Harlem. In New York there was a settlement of people who had lived there all their lives. Here it looked haphazard, with people drifting in, homeless, seeking opportunities but lost in a gray merciless city. The farm population, who would receive unemployment checks from the city by coming into the city's orbit, were responsible for the different mood. Harlem in the days I knew it had respectability. The streets I visited in Chicago had none.

I returned to the hotel and to Paulus and our friends, who cared for the city and for us, too. Never have I felt more warmth than through the friendship of the Chicago people. The casualness and generosity of Jerry, the dean of the divinity school, made Paulus's life very happy in Chicago. He was a former assistant and an old friend from New York. Now he had become a helper in all the complicated affairs of state in Paulus' life. He was able to advise Paulus which of the seventy-five invitations for lectures Paulus had received were fruitful as far as the audience was concerned and, too, which of them would bring money. He would come to the apartment by himself and the two men would sit with a bottle of wine and chat. I heard their laughter across the room. Paulus would laugh with Jerry, and Jerry confided to me that he had never felt Paulus was much older than himself. They felt like pals.

Paulus's genius for friendship would accompany him to his very grave. He was sick more often now—heart and digestion. Sometimes he had to rest for a day or two. The doctor gave him the stimulants old age required to make him feel well and able to attend to his duties.

He still traveled much. Santa Barbara was one of the places. To me, it was paradise—palms and the ocean, with mountains in the background. Paulus was asked to give the main address for one of the large sessions of the Pacem in Terris conference arranged by Hutchins, who lived in Santa Barbara, and his Center for the Study of Democratic Institutions. I heard Hutchins lecture, and we had supper with him at the wonderful old hotel by the ocean. We visited him at his newly built country house and later were shocked to hear it had burned down entirely during one of those fierce West Coast forest fires. He and his wife had been so happy in it.

I attended Paulus's seminars and found the young students delightfully open-minded and direct. Mackenzie Brown based a book on the seminar.

The beauty of the campus, which was still in the process of being built; the daily trip to the university from our motel on the ocean; the endless diet of crabs and shrimp, which we bought, fresh from the sea and ready to eat, in one of the shops famous for seafood; the cool sun which heated up during the never-ending days of good weather—it all came together in one enchanting routine. I was happy in Santa Barbara.

A walk along the beach under the regal old palm trees or a drive to the small zoo with its peacocks, one among them glittering white, was enough for me. Or I went up to the park in the hills above the city, past the monastery from which the monks came for Paulus's lectures, also attended by Catholic nuns who sat like pigeons in a row on a telephone cable, listeining with reverence. The park was always beautiful with cactus of all sorts in bloom, a ravine that smelled of trees, and unusual flowers. We went there with our son and his wife, with my German friend, with our Far East expert who lectured in San Francisco—they all visited with us there. The harbor before our motel with its pier was a daily walk. Another was up the hill overlooking the harbor, to which I had discovered a neglected path.

Paulus could have gone to Santa Barbara as a full professor with a good salary, but he preferred to take an engagement in New York. One of our friends had offered him a political-philosophical chair at his New School for Social Research, an evening college for New Yorkers, which he meant to build up. Paulus, at the end of his life, was drawn back to the metropolis. The golden gates of Berlin, mirrored in New York, called again. He accepted.

He would have had, for the first time in his life, a luxurious salary, a hotel apartment downtown, and a return to New York. I tried in vain to lure him to Santa Barbara. It would have been so much more leisurely than New York, where he would have had to live by his nerves. In Santa Barbara we could have lived more through our vegetative systems. Paulus wanted New York.

He became very ill the day after a successful lecture, a short time after our return to Chicago from summering in East Hampton. He was in the hospital for ten days. He died peacefully while I was with him.

"Today is dying day," he had said. "Today you must not leave me at all." "But the nurse is here," I said, taking his hand and pressing my cheek to it. "I will be back as soon as possible." Slipping out quickly, while he lay breathing heavily under the oxygen tent, eyes closed, I passed by the desk, muttering to the nurse there, "I will be back soon," casting a glance at the machine that wrote down every heartbeat of my husband's in room 315, next to the nurse's desk, to make possible the best surveillance. At the slightest change in the chart, a nurse or doctor rushed into the room to ascertain the patient's state. A gentleman in a dark suit was watching the zigzags of the chart. "My, but that is an irregular heartbeat," he said. The doctor at the desk was silent. I walked to the elevator, then out into the street. It was a lovely day. I searched in my purse—no more money—I'd better go to the bank. It was late but the outside window was open. I cashed a check, walked through the still sunlit, warm streets to the hotel lobby . . . mail . . . the doorman, mercifully not asking how the "doctor" was. I threw my coat off, the nice old colored maid had waited for me and opened the door to the hotel apartment. It was her way of showing her affection. A quick drink, lemon and the eternal Cinzano . . . something to eat . . . "You better" . . . a hamburger and sliced tomato, a cup of coffee.

We always had had a cocktail before meals. For luncheon Paulus preferred a sweet Madeira or Marsala or even sherry. Then lately, after he came home from his office—earlier these days than usual—we had both had a Cin and if he was on time we watched Walter Cronkite and Eric Sevareid on television. But that had been only those last ten days after we had come back from the country and before he had to enter the hospital.

I phoned New York. A bewildered grandson answered, mother was not there, he had just come in from school. I explained that Grandfather was ill and Mammy was supposed to come as soon as possible by plane. . . . Phoned the son, in California. He would take the afternoon plane from San Francisco, which would bring him in early in the morning. He would go to the hotel and inquire and then to the hospital if necessary. I had telephoned yesterday when, all of a sudden, the change in him had worried me so much, but the doctor had refused to commit himself. "Listen," I had said to my son, crying for the first time, "I think he is going to die, his voice has changed so much and his breath has a rattle."

The next morning when I arrived at the hospital, the doctor had confirmed my uneasy feelings. "A sudden turn for the worse, and his digestive tract seems to have failed entirely." Better telephone the two children. The doctor went with me to his own office. When I came back to the sickroom, glancing at the chart I saw the beat was erratic. "There she is," he said. The nurse said smilingly, "He wants you, you are a better nurse than I." "You have more experience," I said, smiling back and helping to lift him; he wanted to sit up. I settled down in a chair, his face against the light. He extended a limp hand, I folded my own around it. His breath—he had been under oxygen again since yesterday—still came heavily, though less so than in the morning. "My lips are trembling," he said. I looked at his lips, they were white and quivering. "Let them," I said easily. I was looking at the time, our daughter might come in any minute now. "Listen," I said, "it might be that Mutie will visit with us. She wanted very much to come last week but the doctor said it would be better—" He interrupted me with an expression of deep shock. "Oh no," he said, "that is the end." His breath came faster, more laboriously. I went out, telling the nurse, who wagged her head sorrowfully, that it obviously was not a good idea to have told him. But when we both went back into the room, he seemed to have forgotten. He lay quietly with closed eyes, but even now he seemed to have some consciousness of his state, saying, "I live mostly in dreams now."

There had been that half-hour here and there when he was able to talk about his experience of visualizing his own dissolution, his very physical decomposition. "Everything is slipping away under my feet," he had said, "in these hours of emptiness of time," and he had described the river of time, symbol of the depleted, emptied-out time, and he had, curiously enough, nominated his night nurse, a nondescript, elderly colored woman, as the magician to hold the time line in order. "This straight line had no content, it just went on and on and on." He had had terrifying imaginings in the afternoons, so that, after the first two days when he was mostly unconscious, and always very surprised when I had to leave because he felt he had not spoken to me at all, I came in the morning, left for lunch, and cambe back in the afternoon.

He said, "Let men not tempt the gods . . . let men not attempt to see what the gods cover with night and horror. . . ." The horror was "being handed over to the indistinct fearfulness . . ." "That this 'All' is over already and still comes back," he said, "so you are delivered to the vast ocean of the impenetrable depth—possibilities, anxieties, imaginings—and this is not the metamorphosis of my own anxieties, imaginings, as the doctors tried to convince me. . . ." (The doctor tried to tell him that he had not entered another world, that his fears were transformed into pictures.)

After the first night in the hospital (his second day), he was very excited when I came in, hardly able to speak, suffering pain, his voice a whisper, slipping off again and again, but always insisting on telling me his dream. I learned later that, in the evening hours of his first night at the clinic, his heart had failed. In the afternoon I managed to write down the dream: "I awoke and found myself in a situation which was very uncanny. One of my thoughts was, I have died. I see a man who is very interesting and who has in a certain way very sympathetic features. He says to me, 'You know what happened?' Then, 'You know what happened to Hannah?' I asked, 'Did she die?' He answers, 'Yes. Somebody perished on a trip.' My first thought, 'Is it Rene?' 'Yes.'. . . ."

I tried to tell him that when those frightening images came back he should let them float by, even if his own image was involved.

That was the way the trained yogi looked at the thought-processes of his own imaginary thinking: the knower watches the thought-images glide by. The next day, he said he had imagined all his dead friends from the last ten years, and then all the dead of all the wars he knew about. Since he had a historical knowledge of many wars, there were many war dead. He said, "The underground of the war alone [he meant simply the earth] . . . this word alone, all that happens on the soil of the landscape. The victor wins and with it everything is forgotten that happened." He talked about the dying in wars, "One sees the enormous problems of the bodies and how refined the body is when it is taken as an organism [in the hospital], and how brutal it is when it is all cut into pieces [by cannons]."

I asked him how he solved all the horrors of the war, how he could survive the many war dead. I later came across a quote from Milarepa, the Tibetan saint, which seemed to be exactly the way he had expressed himself: "If you realize the Voidness, Compassion will arise within your hearts." He talked about a period of losing all differentiation between himself and others and out of it a great understanding coming to him. No longer was there any distinction between friend or foe. There was no otherness. To me, this referred to his incapacity to hate, his need to stay on the "borderline," and, even by taking sides, to try to resolve through understanding.

He said, "I am in another condition than usual, less active, more dreaming." He rejected with horror the idea of throwing a flower into the vacuum (the void) of the empty stream of time. It had to remain a void.

He wanted to know what happens to his centered self after death; there would be no memory of his person as a person. I tried to tell him that his thought-images would be there, that his thoughts, having changed the substance of our cosmos, would enter the circle of the spiritual powers, which created the images of the world. He spoke about the Tibetan Book of the Dead. "Go after the clear light," I said, "the clear light will guide you, not any self-centered immortality." We talked about the Buddha powers which have the same spiritual unity—if you look through a many-faceted crystal you seem to see many Buddha images, but if you forgo the crystal, there is one Buddha spirit and as much as you are the spirit you will be joined with it. He said, "And what will you do?" Giving up any comfort of denying that I would be alone soon, I said, "I will go to our little house."

The doctor came in, bending over him because Paulus could not speak very loudly any more. He wanted to tell the doctor that he had canceled all his meals after having labored conscientiously with the dietary nurse for every meal for the weekend. "All my hard work," he whispered triumphantly, "all my work in vain. I am eating nothing at all . . . absolute asceticism." The doctor laughed outright. He looked at me. I laughed too, and he said, "Nobody has ever told me this way that he is not going to eat."

"My poor Hannachen," he said at the beginning of his stay at the hospital. He cried, "I was very base to you, forgive me." I could not see him cry. I was glad I had experienced forgiveness as something very rare and precious and I was glad to give him what he wanted me to give and I was glad I could say to him that I had liked his face from the first day to the last, that I never doubted his spiritual power, and that in my heart some sort of benign smile, not cynical laughter, had come through for him, and that this feeling of the absurdity of life and love had carried our last years together.

Today was dying day and there he was, wasting away in his hospital bed, which was rolled up or let down according to his whim. I could sit with him and stretch out my hand to him and tell him that he was always profound enough for me, that he broke through the thin ice of a superficial consciousness and that that was the way we had lived together.

I read letters to him, and some of them he was able to grasp —among the last ones, a booklet with medical jokes and a colored postcard from his grandson. There were yellow roses from Mary and our son Rene, one of the first bouquets to arrive and blooming to the end. He was surrounded by flowers. And then there was the little white soap-cat that grew imitation white fur. The afternoon nurse always had to show it to him and he worried about one of the whiskers, which did not seem to grow properly.

It was at the end that he suddenly wanted to get up. He wanted to walk, to sit and dangle his feet, the only physical act he had wanted to perform for two days in the hospital. The nurse, who was around all the time now, left to ask the doctor. When she came back, his urge had left him; he just wanted to sit up. We cranked the bed up and held him, and then it happened—one gasping breath, the oxygen gurgled in his mouth, which was open. I held his hand. I told the nurse, "Hold his hand." She was standing on the other side of the bed. She grasped his other hand in her delicate small brown one. Another gurgling, moaning, failing sound. The nurse said, "You'd better leave now, it will be too hard on you." I shook my head, I held his hand, all of a sudden he let go, his body pranced as if in ecstasy, his bowels let go and his hand let go, he fell back, his mouth was open, his face became yellowish, his forehead came forward like a lotus flower in blossom. A doctor came in. The nurse led me to a chair near the window. He looked at his eyes. "Do you have a flashlight?" Somebody brought one, and he shined it into his eyes. He closed the eyelids with a professional, gentle gesture. He refrained from pulling the sheet over his face. He turned to me. "She may stay for a little while," he said. I said, "Yes." Someone came in and took the oxygen out. The head doctor came in. He held my hand until it hurt. He said, "Whenever you are ready, we are waiting outside." The nurse said, "I have a few more things to do here." I said, "You have seen this so often." "Yes," she said, "but with some patients it is different." I said, "We'd better take his things out." Somebody came in with a paper bag.

I had not brought anything to the hospital since he had been ill, except his Bibles—a small Greek New Testament, a German Bible, which had been his from his first year of life, and an English version. I had hoped to read from the Bible to him when he became restless, if he wished me to, but he had only touched the Greek version with his frail hand. He did not wish to see the other Bibles or to have the Bible read to him. I was glad. He belonged to the world, to the cosmos, not to one book.

The nurse put everything in the paper bag. I left the small white soap pussycat, which was fuzzy but had bald spots where the nurse had touched it, the endless flowers, which had arrived continuously, even at the last. I threw away his shaving kit—old and ragged, but nothing in the world could have induced him to buy a new one. I threw away his combs and brushes, his slippers. Someone came from the hall to let me know there were two women friends outside. I shook my head—no time to see anybody. I was alone with his body. He looked yellowish now, very much at peace and beautiful. I touched his poor hand, it was still warm and soft. I touched his gleaming forehead. The nurse came in with a doctor; she touched his hair as she went out. I touched his hair, his forehead. The nurse and I embraced and kissed. . . . Outside, the doctor with the bag and the head doctor were both waiting for me. We went downstairs. We walked to the head doctor's car. The young doctor put the bag in the car and shook hands with me. The head doctor drove me to the hotel. I told him, "Don't get out." I bent my face over his hand and departed.

The black porter took my bag, I walked into the lobby, to the elevator. The bellboy captain went up with me, carrying my bag. He asked, "How is the doctor?" I said, "He just died." He was silent. He opened the door of my apartment, I fumbled for a tip, he shook my hand and said, "I am very sorry." I found later that the porters, the bellboys, the drug store and grocery clerks were all easy to talk to. Theirs was the simple death without television, radio, or newspaper announcements. They knew death was for everybody.

My withered Negro maid with half her teeth gone was the dearest and most comforting soul. "I know how it is," she said. She was there to open the door for me, to spare me from digging into my purse for my key and being seen. She knew, too, that I wanted to get rid of all the small things that reminded me—the socks, the underwear, the old suitcases, which were too many now. She did not question me. If I were silent, it was good. If I talked to her, she responded through her missing teeth.

The telephone operators, eight elderly women who had never seen us, responded without fuss. They shut the telephone off for me and took messages. They opened it again and let calls through, either in his room or mine, and always graciously and cheerfully. I went later, greeted them and thanked them. The bellboy captain and the bellboys sent the telegrams up by the dozens, not one by one to be tipped each time. They pushed letters under the door instead of ringing. They tried to help. The people at the desk let me go through the lobby without looking at me, the elevator girls granted me the privacy of my grief, not to mention the manager, who reduced my bill as a sign of his sympathy. Those were the people who did not count as mourners. He had not given them anything but his daily presence. They had served him, calling his taxi when he came out, carrying his bags, and saying, when he departed, "He was a good man, he was a real boss, he was always kind to us."

The other friends, the intellectuals who had to get their own satisfactory sorrow out of it, came later. They had to insist they were there and to cry on our shoulders. One member of the family finally said, in mock horror, "I don't want her to cry on my neck anymore. After all, she should be comforting me." There were the ones who were natural and loving; the ones who were demanding their share of sorrow; the ones who wanted to participate in our grief, whatever the means, who were angered by our attempted isolation; there were the heads of state, the heads of universities, who wanted the widow to come right over to their memorial services as an added attraction. There was the friend and employer who knew what was needed, who took over to protect us from publicity, who provided money, who loaned his bureau and his secretaries to help with all the pressing demands that arise at the death of a distinguished man. There was the private secretary who did what she had to do (and there was a great deal) with a smile, without pursuing her own sorrow. There were baskets of fruit and cookies and candy and chocolate . . . there were flowers . . . there were timid utterances of strangers. Grief is a manifold experience.

And there was the gentleman from the crematorium office, reserved, but cheerful and easy to deal with when we drove out together—my daughter, my son, and I—to see his body (they had both arrived too late to see him at the hospital). We talked about our driver's son and his school and the neighborhood. When we decided to see his body once more, after his brain had been given to medical research, the cremation representative had said in confidence to my daughter, "I think he will look good." He had asked for a suit and a shirt and socks. The crematorium sent a car for us. We walked through the entrance hall, where a woman sat like a wax figure behind a desk, into the room with the casket. My daughter looked at his face over the shirt collar, the familiar suit and necktie. His hands and face had shrunk, he was painted excessively, but nothing could mar the dignity of the forehead. The mouth was painted in a sweetish smiling curve. The hands, my daughter and I touched them as we were leaving, were still there. My son stood by silently. We walked out, I went over and shook hands with the woman at the desk. Then we turned to each other: "He is not there."

That was why we had gone. He was not there, he was in our community as a family, the most precious experience in our sorrow—the daughter frail and unknowing when she had arrived, the son, arriving early in the morning after having heard over the radio, having been prepared. These two, for eight days, helped gloriously and unselfishly with all their youthful power and stamina to protect their mother and her interests. They laughed and cried and dared to talk about their father as he appeared to them, and at the same time pronounced him a great man who had made his imprint on the face of his culture and on the world. Trust and communication reigned for eight immortal days.

I did not then talk about our leaving our country house, about our last *Rundgang zu zwein* (walk together). I had often cited a line from a German poet while we were walking around the meadow on our property, a path cut into the tall grasses for a comfortable stroll. He used to say, "I want my *Rundgang zu zwein*." While he was in the hospital, to comfort him, I cited the verse: "Pass over in silence that which is not given to us anymore, promise to be happy, if nothing else is permitted us but a walk together." He cried. He said, sobbing, "And this will not be ours anymore either." Then I knew he grasped that act that he was dying and we said when it happened I would tell his sister, I would be good and understanding to his many friends.

I did not then tell about his last lecture and his last party and the tap, tap, tap, the next morning on the wall of my bedroom. We lived wall-to-wall in large comfortable rooms. Each had its own bath, his room had a desk to write on. In those last days I had often seen him sitting in a chair in one corner of his room, saying, when I asked, "Are you asleep or awake?", "I am thinking." He looked lost. He said he sometimes needed one hour for one sentence.

That evening before the lecture, he had to take one pill. He discovered, to his consternation, that he had misnumbered the pages of his manuscript. "You don't know what it would have meant," he said. He looked exhausted after the lecture, but he insisted on going to a gathering with his friends, professional people who had attended the lecture. Later, in the hospital, he told me that during the lecture he had had some sort of premonition (of sickness, or that it was the last one, he did not say). After lecturing he liked to relax among friends in festive rooms—with intelligent men and pretty women, with wine or whiskey, and with good conversation.

He sat in the kitchen before a small table, drinking and eating little tidbits I brought him. He drank and talked, he did not get up much, but he was happy, he moved about the room occasionally, greeting friends here and there. When he wanted at last to go home, we sat down again with a young friend near the door, he facing him while I joined the women at his feet. At the end, I invited the young couple to come the following afternoon for a chat. Friends brought us home. We were happy and relaxed and good and tired.

I must have fallen asleep right away and I must have heard something before the knock, three times, tap tap tap (disorganized dreams, nightmares in the other room). I awoke immediately. I knew at once. I put my housecoat over my nightgown—they matched, hotel attire—and walked through the narrow hall into his room. He stood between the two beds, moaning. He was desperate, he had taken five pills, they had not helped. I remembered the doctor saying to me, when he had tried to warn my husband and then spoke to me privately, "And then one day the pills may not work anymore." I wanted to call the doctor right away, but he did not let me. Every attempt of mine ended with an agonized cry of his. He sank down on his knees, doubling up in pain. At last he was ready to let me call the doctor. I did not have the private phone number. I found it, which took time, while he was moaning and crying out in a horrible, muffled voice that seemed to come from the bowels of the earth. The doctor was there. "No more pills," he said. "I'll have an ambulance sent." Then waiting, pain, crying out. I took him in my arms, I held my hand against his back. "The only thing that helps," he sobbed, falling down on his knees again and moaning. I went to my room, phoned the lobby that an ambulance was coming, room 308, and managed to get into a dress, snatch up my purse, my fur coat and cap, and to comb my hair, all accompanied by the sobs of his dark unearthly voice. I returned to his room.

At last, the ambulance—two men, motherly, concerned, putting a blanket around him (I had managed to get socks on his feet), putting him on the stretcher. He was crying out in pain all the time. Down the elevator, through a back exit into the ambulance. I sat with him. The streets were quiet. "We will be there in a minute." The emergency entrance . . . the head doctor with two assistants . . . a booth ready for him . . . oxygen (he sobbing with pain), an injection, a tape-recording of his heart . . . I sitting on a chair outside the open booth, curtains drawn back. I got up and walked to him—he wanted me—then stood where the helping nurse was standing as she moved aside. "You can stand here," she said. A room upstairs . . . pain pain pain . . . another morphine shot, oxygen. They put him into bed, changed his nightclothes for a white hospital gown. I take the crumpled pajamas, the socks. Vomiting, retching mercilessly . . . . pain pain pain. They move his bed to another room next to the desk so the staff can keep him under close surveillance. A machine is brought in, then put out by the desk . . . wires connect with his body, oxygen, the machine, and intravenous fluid. Somebody brings me the cup of coffee I had asked for. I sit and wait. It must be eleven in the morning. The question of nurses. The doctor proposes an afternoon and a night nurse and that I be there in the morning. In that way, they could give him all the care he needs. The doctor leaves. I sit with him. He seems to be unconscious most of the time, asking for me at intervals. I leave to get a few things.

I don't remember whether I walked home or took a taxi. I ate something, telephoned my daughter and my son, got some of his things. Before I left the phone I called the secretary, who would call the dean and cancel engagements. In a few minutes the dean called me. Later the calls of friends, letters, telegrams. It spread like wildfire over the newspapers, magazines, the radio, television. Friends fell victim to calls for information. The shoemaker, who had always put his name on my soles for repair, asked, "Is that you?" The grocer, the druggist, "Was that you?" Letters, letters, telephone calls. Letters from Europe (he had canceled a trip there and sent a stenciled letter, adding a personal word to each of those to whom it was sent), these were the answers . . . private . . . intimate. The secretary tells me, "Don't get sick. Now you are important." And right away flowers, flowers, flowers, in the house and in the hospital.

When did it start? It was already bad when we left our country place for his university, but he was always so cheerful in between attacks. He had had to take pills more often that summer, and the trip back to the mid-West was not without incidents. But perhaps it started with his beloved record player, which in the last weeks of our stay in East Hampton did not want to play anymore. Perhaps it went on with the death of our housekeeper, who met with an accident while returning with her husband from a vacation, or with the death of a very old friend, or with the dying of another companion of his philosophical and theological struggles. Someone close to him was always dying and he took it hard, as if he himself were part of every death. Or was it when I could not find the way to the house to which we were invited, and he had to take a pill . . . or when we walked along the beach and he turned around, instead of accompanying me to the jetty, returning much sooner than usual . . . or when he became less able to answer his letters and complete his tasks and I had to help him? Between times, he was slow about doing things, he still got the mail and the paper, crossing the main street, which always worried me because he walked so much more slowly than the passing cars expected human beings to walk across a busy street. For those ten days in the university city, when he tried to take a walk, he called it "inching and benching," walking a few steps and sitting down a few minutes, but he felt unable to climb the steps of the bridge across the highway to reach the lakefront. Or the drive to the mid-West, when we had to stop once for a pill in the morning. Afterward everything was all right, a smooth, fast drive. He liked to look at his watch, saying, "One mile a minute," when we were on a sixty-mile-an-hour road, or "One and a third miles a minute," when we were on a seventy-miles-an-hour highway. He liked to drive with me, sitting beside me dreaming, snoozing, doing nothing, watching the world fly by, looking at the sky, observing the weather . . . cheerful. We had a good meal, cocktails and wine, and went to our room not too early.

There the trouble started. He had cramp after cramp and insisted he hadn't enough pills left to quiet them. He walked up and down in the motel room, he ached with pain, he tried to lie down, to sit with pillows. I asked him for the prescription bottle from which he had taken the pills, putting them into the silver snuffbox I had given him for carrying pills. He did not look among his medicines, he insisted he had taken the pills from the druggist's hands and put them directly into the snuffbox. He had no prescription. I telephoned the desk, asking for a doctor. At the doctor's office I talked to a nurse, who looked down her nose at me—on Thursday it would be very unlikely that I would get hold of a doctor, they all went out on Thursday. I got the name of a druggist, telephoning twice. First he was not unfriendly, but he had to have the prescription. The second time, he was simply rude, saying I would have to go to a hospital, which was about fifty miles away. Yes, he saw the seriousness of the situation. I hung up. I pretended to be less worried than I actually was. More calls would not help. I proposed a sleeping pill, one or two, to my husband, and that, miraculously, helped. He fell asleep, he slept soundly until morning. We found there were enough pills for an emergency on the road. We arrived in good time, had lunch at the bar in the hotel. His secretary arrived with mail . . . an appointment with the doctor. On the following day, I unpacked his things, my things, and he unpacked his medicine chest. He came to me, confessing he had found a liberal number of pills that he had forgotten (this after we had wangled another bottle of pills out of the druggist who had the prescription). At that, I cried, without letting him see me. The incredible tension of bringing him home safely and discovering now that all his suffering and all my frantic efforts had been unnecessary. Neither the rude druggist nor the unfeeling, snooty nurse (who was supposed to be a helper) need have entered our lives. I tried to expunge them from my memory as quickly as possible.

And, of course, I then remembered that I always had to find things for him, that he always refused to find what he needed—he came in despair and I went and found "it." His secretary told me the same story. He was convinced before he looked for something that it was not there, and at one point she made a bet with him that she knew it was in its place.

During the last ten days before he went to the hospital, the attacks came in the morning . . . three pills a morning . . . today only one or two. The doctor had given him a medicine that helped him over the night (the cramps had started at night, too). On his advice we had canceled the European trip. Now he could not even draw the curtains for me. He used to draw the curtains in the living room, which were many and rather heavy. He opened the windows, put the heat on, and came into my room to open the curtains for me, to put the heat on there, and to talk for a minute. He had slept well or not so well; he had had a dream that he wanted to tell me. Now he could not draw the curtains anymore. For his records, which used to be on one of the shelves over his head in one of the coat closets, I found a quick solution. I put them on a table within easy reach in the closet (the closets were like small rooms, they were so large), so there was no trouble, he could manage.

Came the day when he could not take his bath without trouble. He must not lock his door anymore. I went in once and there he stood beside the tub, feeling ill. Or I went into his room (usually we left each other alone in the morning and during working hours). He stood there with a strange, faraway look on his face . . . no, it was nothing, he had just taken a pill.

He conducted two seminars and gave one lecture. He felt happy to teach . . . nothing happened there. With all the foreknowledge and all his fatigue, I still felt he had so much future before him . . . his spirit was still ready to take on new tasks, ready to learn, ready to give. . . .

As to the extended publicity that accompanied his death, a remark in one letter made my spine tingle with the sense of history. It was a letter to my son-in-law from a friend who was an editor of United Press International, which said:

"I thought you might be interested in seeing how UPI covered Paul's death, so here is the file. As I said in our conversation, Chicago (HX) broke into another story in the middle of a sentence to send the bulletin. This happens only in moments of history, because editors become angry when a break-in occurs before the end of a paragraph."

Interlude

LAST DAYS IN EAST HAMPTON

I

His eyes, estranged from seeing,
Viewed the splendor of late Summer,
First-falling fruit and earlier sunset
As if watching through a gray glass
(All things so far away).

His mouth a wondrous wound, speechless,
No longer finding words for this vision
He had so often tried to convey,
Unconscious of its silent depth.

II

Like a vulture in a sycamore
By the wayside in Yucatan,
Death was hovering
Wherever he went.

[233]

Even in the apple tree of his back yard,
Hanging low with red-cheeked fruit—
Even there
Death announced himself.

III

After he left,
his house deteriorated with him.
Every grain of wood
opened its pores, evaporating his being.
Even the red curtain,
having become aware of its redness
under his searching eye,
faded in shabbiness;
Walls became spotted
like hands, speckled with circular death;
Wine glasses wailed—
having resounded so gaily
when he lifted them to his friends;
Even the Electrola,
voice of his nightly vigil,
broke when his grasp was not there.

TO P. T.

Spring has come. You will not see it.
Having become ashes, nourishing Spring.
Would you could see through the eye
Of sky-blue violet,
Cluster of lilac
And appleblossom.
How you loved walking under
Denuded trees last Autumn,
Red-cheeked fruit circling gray trunks
In superabundance,
Just before the white hand of Winter
Summoned you . . . . . .

East Hampton

East Hampton was dream country. Paulus came back to me in East Hampton. The children felt at home in East Hampton. They left and came back again after adolescence. Their children grew up during vacation time in East Hampton. East Hampton was leisure to them, leisure and the ocean, and hospitality for themselves and their friends. East Hampton to me was my grandmother's house, only I had become the grandmother, taking care, spoiling, and permitting my children to help me after my strength declined.

East Hampton was the seasons, the scanty prespring with the ocean droning, the overwhelmingly sweet young summer, the hot, humid August, the quick and cool September. It was Indian summer with red gleaming woods. I drove through copper and wine-red leaves to the blue bay. I drove to Montauk, the road lined with autumn-colored bushes and berries, men and women picking beach plums for their jellies. It was the desert, the wandering dunes with skeletons of gray-and-white bleached tree trunks being buried in waves of white sand, relentlessly coming in year by year, killing the slender green-leafed young trees.

East Hampton was the hurricane, throwing waves far beyond the usual shoreline, undermining houses, eroding dunes. The people on the dunes had to evacuate, the old trees bent like blades of grass. There must not be a movable chair outside, it might break against the house in the ferocious dance of the winds. The morning after the hurricane was cool and blue and clear and clean, aromatic trees and a fallen trunk crowding the fragrant lawn, fresh as the first day after creation.

East Hampton was the people of East Hampton. The elderly gentleman with manners of an aristocrat who was an agent to rent me a house. He drove me around in his beautiful car—it was lilac time in the spring. He showed me green-hedged cottages on well-kept lawns. He showed me the golf course. When I left I had a bunch of lilacs he had picked for me. We rented an apartment in a former horse stable. It still smelled a bit like one, but it was clean and neat. It had a decaying garage, a spot of green in front, and a tree. Paulus wrote under the tree every morning. I went shopping on a bicycle. Once I came back on foot and the postwoman took me in her car, muttering something about a Christian soul had to lend a helping hand. It did not occur to me that I could be the object of her pity. I did not think at that time that I was pitiable, carrying two heavy paper bags of groceries for more than twenty minutes. It did not occur to me to have the order delivered. One store did deliver, but it was supposed to be fiercely expensive.

The old man and woman who owned our place were neighborly. The old man collected the garbage. He showed us once where he took it. After we had bought a car, we took our refuse to the dump ourselves and my daughter dubbed the inarticulate emigrant from some eastern country the king of the garbage. He told tales of the stray cats and dogs and of the people who reclaimed things from the dump that others had discarded there. We thought that was very interesting. We had conversations with the king of the garbage. He told us how he built his refuse heap into land safe enough to walk on. He would stand on the slope overlooking his garbage empire. One year when we came back, he was not there anymore. In another year, a new dump had been built, the old one was closed. It was then I decided to assume the expense of a refuse collector. Some years later we removed the two zinc trashcans from the side of the house to a wooden shed behind the garage. We lined plastic garbage pails with plastic bags before we put in the refuse. It saved time and stayed cleaner. We had grown up with the garbage.

We had rented in East Hampton after Paulus had first motored down the New Jersey coast and along the Long Island coast with friends. He looked for open ocean, I wished for green trees and protection from the sand, the glaring sun, and the steady coastal wind.

We had rented two or three times. The Japanese surrender came while we were there. In East Hampton the atom bomb seemed incomprehensible to me. The following year we rented a small gardener's house with the ceiling falling down in one room, with a faulty heating system, with a huge kitchen, and an old iron stove. And then we bought our own house.

East Hampton was friends, Paul and Marga, and their children, a congenial group of intellectuals whom we would not have met in the city, Max and Edna, the group of architects, the art critic, the new painters and sculptors . . . people in small houses and big houses, with shabby cars, with limousines. Somehow it was a democratic community. Hospitality was extended on the lawn, near the bay, with an orchestra and buffets served by maids and a bartender for the drinks, or roasting weenies out in the yard, or setting a table on the grass for a luncheon served by maids. It was gracious and informal. Once in a while when the host's house was outside the village, a benevolent policeman would direct the traffic. Cars would roll up on sandy byways away from the main street. It would smell of honeysuckle and roses. The fences between properties at that time were merely rough-hewn split rails or privet hedges trimmed neatly, more often low than high. The country was open to everybody's gaze, the opposite of the high Italian stone walls surrounding each house and taking the ocean beaches from the people. The ocean here belonged to the people, the white, wide sandy beaches were clean, the bay beaches were seamed with shells and seaweed. We could collect the small, transparent yellow and pink bowlike shells to put into a glass jar or shallow dish at home, or try to find the ones with tiny holes in them for making necklaces. We found a horse-shoe crab. Once we watched two horseshoe crabs mating in the bay. We took a tiny, golden-brown horseshoe-crab shell home, and I sent one to my mother in Germany. The antiquity of the shape of the creature was overwhelming.

East Hampton was the gardener who taught us how to clear our field. We had asked him to clear our property of honeysuckle and poison ivy but found it would be too expensive. So we took the two brothers for two days only. They observed that we could do it ourselves and showed us how. The plumber informed us about the repair needs of our run-down heating system, without ever thinking about taking advantage of the ignorant emigrants. The plumber's son was a college graduate. We felt honored to be talked to. We were shy and uninformed. People helped. There were two house painters, who had since died; the one painted our rooms a vivid

[237]

blue during the winter months, the other became a friend. We visited him at home and talked with him at the beach where he kept his fishing boat, when time permitted. He was ocean-possessed, as we all were. In the beginning we walked to the beach, in later years we had a car.

Paulus complained that East Hampton people did not love their ocean—he never saw them walk to the beach. We discovered that almost every citizen took a quick trip to the beach in his car some time every day, just to see how the ocean was doing. In a storm or in the lull within a hurricane, the cars would roll to the beach, the people would stand watching, returning to their homes when the storm returned to finish its cycle, careful to avoid trees and live wires on the road.

East Hampton was Christmastide, when the citizens planted pines before their houses and lined the main street with Christmas trees gleaming with blue and red and white lights. Christmas was for everybody. Christmas was not confined to the privacy of homes. The village became the open house of the Christian message.

People started to say "Hello" to us after five years. Now the men had grown older, but they still greeted me, they permitted me to shop with my tear-stained face and my unsmiling misery after my husband's death without showing any sign that they saw my misery, which I could not help carrying into the streets. The post office people, with whom I had much to do at the time, corrected my mistakes, gave me advice, were friendly but never pitying. Once in a while one might make an appreciative remark about my husband. After two years, or three, I learned to smile, to take part again, to show that I knew we were together. They left my peace undisturbed, even when I did not participate in the many small ways I could have helped. They trusted me to my privacy, giving me all the personal friendliness I was able to accept.

East Hampton was Mr. Schaefer, the owner of the small taxi fleet (how many cars in the beginning, one or two?) who spoke German and was so good to us. I still believe he gave us the "native" rate, because everybody knew we were not rich but loved the town and wanted to stay on.

Later, I drove with his sons in their Cadillac to Kennedy airport on my trip to foreign countries. We talked about their families and mine, they were friends.

Still later, East Hampton changed. The crowds came in. I had become a regular and I could say to the shopkeepers without feeling I was intruding, "A few weeks now and it will be Labor Day and we will have peace again."

East Hampton was my cocktail party, five years after my husband's death. I had lived in near seclusion, but I wanted once to thank these friends who had received us in our time, who had come to our house. We had enjoyed each other mutually. I invited them after five years and they came, out of friendship, out of loyalty, or because they understood that I wanted to give a sign of gratefulness for the pleasure they had all given Paulus, making East Hampton full and rich and reverberating with the life he enjoyed.

And now that East Hampton has changed with the crowds coming in, it has tried to provide more than commonplace pleasure. There are the two theaters during the summer, where plays, avant-garde theater, and unusual movies are offered. There are, of course, all the affairs for benefits, including Sophie of Saks and meeting Mrs. Martin Luther King, and Women's Lib. There are many exhibitions of art, and there are the ladies of the village, who take care of the trees and put on the village fair, and there are other occasions. I do not mention the churches and their activities. I never go to church and the East Hampton people take even that in a benevolent spirit. Everyone lives his own life, and they have accorded me the freedom to live mine.

The chauffeur had driven up the driveway in a fitting black Cadillac (black for mourning). He had stopped at the turning circle at the back entrance. He brought my fifteen pieces of luggage up the two-times-seven steps of the small staircase leading from the kitchen entrance to the upper bedrooms. I had given Paulus's clothes-hanger suitcase to my son-in-law. His other suitcases and bags I had left at the hotel. I brought my two clothes-hanger suitcases, four or five compartment suitcases, shoe bag, toilet case, a typewriter, a diplomat's case, and my coats. I gave Schaefer the fare from Kennedy airport and a substantial tip. I felt dizzy from the two hours' drive and the journey in the jet—Chicago to New York.

I walked around the yard. The day had been bright, the golden maples were still in leaf, the apples, which nobody had gathered during the month of our absence, lay rotting in circles around the tree trunks. Brownish, crumpled leaves lay in the wind-protected spot between the house and the privet hedge. The evergreens stood

[239]

along the split-rail fence. I walked the spaces between the trees on the lawn—the winter-naked weeping beeches, the Japanese maple, and the birch, no two of them making a straight line with any third tree. We had taken great care to plant in curves and circles.

I went into the little house with its spacious living room, with its dining-room corner, and the many bookcases filled with our books flanking the red-brick fireplace. Everything was present, proportions unchanged. I thought about Paulus's anxiety lest the trees fail to reach the height he desired before he died. I had said, "But the main thing is that they are there. It does not matter whether we see them." Now they were there and he was not. The house was there, the house in which we had lived together, transforming it by living in it until it fitted us like a skin.

It had been such a sordid small place when we had bought it. It had been bought for such a sordid reason, on my insistence. Our marriage had been broken into small pieces by the relentless assault of the many women—not only his sweetheart who functioned as his secretary and who had lived across the street from us in New York, but the émigré friends, newcomers, students, socialites, wives of friends. I had tried to get away. I had taken an extra course so I could teach in this country, to earn my own money. But how could I get away from a man whose life I had lived, whose children I had borne, whose thoughts I could guess, who was as close to me as my own heartbeat? I had been exhausted by my own inability to love this man right, been disgusted ever so often by his childish attempts to pretend he loved only me. Only after a bottle of wine at midnight, alone with me, did he confide, admit, reassure, and talk about his infidelity as his predicament, adding that, if I were to remind him the next morning about our conversation, he would remember nothing.

I had answered, "All right. I will stay, but you have to give me a place where I can be alone and protected." He never protected me, he always protected the other woman. It took me years to realize that the hostility of the other woman toward me was just as painful to her as my hostility and sorrow were to me.

Then, when I met the man I had loved at first sight, without knowledge, just as I had hated Paulus at first sight, without knowledge of his being, a change took place in me. I laughed at the tinkling chain of his houris, baring their navels and their breasts, their fannies and their feet, dancing for him as I had danced for him, too. He could not leave them even as he could not give me up, he could not discard a single one of them. When he went back to Germany after many years of absence, there they were, surrounding him with aging sagging breasts, with fattened navels, flat feet, thin hair, and wasted faces, imposing on him, serving him, never letting him go.

When I had demanded that he buy me a place where I could be by myself, I had no longer any need for his kind of love. I was nothing but a piece of bleeding, tortured womanhood seeking my peace from the seesaw of suffering and hate.

And then the miracle happened. The house drew him, he came and stayed, selecting the room, after torturous indecision, that suited him best, remaining envious of our rooms after he had had first choice. His first deed around the house was gingerly making a small path of stone slabs from the front steps across the lawn, while I was furiously working around the fence to free the property of poison ivy.

I returned to the house—the sun was going down—walking upstairs to open the desk he had kept locked.

I used to find small notes, short letters, all sorts of signs from his lady friends. I had even written a few sentences about his need to be discovered by his wife, while remaining secretive. Later, I had found the pornographic letter under his blotter, left there when he departed for a lecture trip one early morning. I had been so troubled I had shown it to a psychologist friend. He had advised me to burn it. I did not. It seemed to me that this was one sign of his real life, the expression of his needs, which I could no longer share with him, the overstraining of an intellect to live with the demon. It had seemed to me in my later days that the demonic was something you could dissolve in meditation.

I unlocked the drawers. All the girls' photos fell out, letters and poems, passionate appeal and disgust. Beside the drawers, which were supposed to contain his spiritual harvest, the books he had written and the unpublished manuscripts all lay in unprotected confusion. I was tempted to place between the sacred pages of his highly esteemed lifework those obscene signs of the real life that he had transformed into the gold of abstraction—King Midas of the spirit.

I could have found the pages of the sermon he had written while his daughter was very ill. He had not taken her in his arms and healed her with love. Being close to her had aroused fear in him. He had to transform her into the magic of words for all the world to hear. I could find his fear of his son in those pages, his anxiety that his son would outgrow him, like the trees, after his death. His fear of death, his lust for life were there, his feelings of inadequacy, the triumph of the forces that grasped him in ecstatic power, when his face was lit by desire, searching out another victim of his ever-hungry need to be worshiped, to possess and to be possessed. It was all in his books, human beings pressed like butterflies, whole landscapes of oceans, trees, blades of grass, and mountains, pressed between the pages of these often-discussed volumes.

Streaming out of the open drawers, I saw the many-colored flow of emotions he had aroused and that had aroused him—the red of passion, the sharp poisonous yellow of competition, the black of despair, the blue of devotion, and even the white of innocence he had not been able to destroy; the glorious eternal feminine capacity to love, to shelter, to protect, and to offer with devotion, even to survive the onslaught of the greedy male; seeking shelter, deserting shelter, coming back to shelter, embracing, torturing, making suffer, giving happiness, changing the life-feelings of all these women. Whether they cursed him or loved him, he had pushed the knowledge about the *mysterium tremendum* a little beyond their narrower concept of life, love, and the powers of enchantment and destruction.

Where did I come in? I had shared it, hated it, loved it, rebuked it. I had fought for survival, being submerged, serving him, being aware when I was pressed between the leaves of the folder, cursing him for turning me into an abstraction. Every morning I was willing and glad to live again; every evening I felt shoved beneath a heap of stones.

I went and listened to his lectures and sat at his feet with shining eyes, just as the others had, soaking in the power of his spiritual being, forgetting about the biological aspects of abstraction.

So where did I come in? We shared a combination of individual knowledge, enthusiasm, and power of living. Perhaps our moment came in our travels together. I was not only the listener for his geographical, historical, and philosophical-theological knowledge. I had studied art, I could show him lines, composition, color, technique, and the intuition of my own enthusiasm. My mediumistic ability was involved. I could sense the flavor of past centuries, I could make the poems of the great and the faces of the kings come alive for him. We both used our love for life to explore the manifestations of civilization wherever we turned in our mutual travel. There was never any disturbance then, for the feminine did not appear on two earthly legs; the lure was cosmic. We were both at home there.

I lit the fireplace and sat for two days burning the great man's past, as he had wished me to do. The fire did something to me. I would go on living. It freed me from his past. The unraveling of my grief would be slow and painful. I would be numb with sorrow, feeling the loss of his presence. I would not remember him on my travels to India so soon after his death. It would be impossible for me to talk to people who had known him well. I would offend our mutual good friends by refusing to see them. A few of our friends would break through my isolation. After two years I might be able to talk to a friend, with effort.

I decided to look at my own life and try to come to an awareness of what I had lived. I insisted that I could go back to the time and the place of any experience in my life and find it there untarnished, living it again as it was, remembering its sweetness and sorrow. This I have tried to do.

Postlude

DREAMS

"This will be a sellout!" cried the old woman as she entered the shop.

The proprietor, moustached and with a reddish, pointed, and scraggly beard, wearing an old-fashioned pince-nez on his narrow nose, did not look amused. He buttoned his dirty old gray jacket, patched at the elbows, with the one remaining button. His baggy trousers fell over the tops of his unpolished shoes. Putting his bony, brown-flecked hands into his jacket pockets, he said, "So." It sounded more like a nasty "so what" than a simple inquiry.

The old woman paid no attention to his mood. She looked gay in her long, multicolored gown, topped by a red scarf that hid her old-woman's neck. Her red shoes sparkled.

"Time to celebrate," she said, "I want my dreams back."

"That depends," replied the old man, "on how much you are willing to pay."

"Oh," she answered, rattling some change in an invisible pocket of her gown, "you can hear it."

"So, out with it." The proprietor pointed the way into the inner recesses of the basement store, a long, dark, narrow room.

"Give us some light," said the old woman.

The proprietor turned on a switch, and racks of puppets sprang to view. They were suspended by the long rods at the backs of their necks. Some were mobile, with swaying hands and feet, arms and legs. Others were dolls without movable joints. Above and behind the racks, on the wall, was painted a backdrop of a tree, a garden, a house, a room.

"There they are!" exclaimed the old woman. She took a deep breath and smiled broadly with her big, old mouth. "All my dreams!"

"Those you haven't forgotten," said the old man. He sounded sarcastic. "How many there were that you did not even know about."

"They no longer count," she retorted. "Only what is visible and remembered counts."

"Now you pay for them," said the proprietor.

"I paid for them before," said the old woman, "and I will pay for them again."

"There," she said, "look at me, the fat baby. I weighed about ten pounds and almost tore my mother apart."

"That makes you happy," said the proprietor.

"Birth is an enchanting assault," said the old woman.

"You had your assault in your mother's womb," said the old man. "Do you remember?"

The old woman grabbed the baby puppet with her right hand and seized the fetus puppet with her left. The proprietor pointed to the scene on the wall behind the place on the rack where the two puppets had hung. The old woman put on her glasses.

"For that," she said, "I need my long-distance glasses." "My father," she added, pointing to an overly tall, thin, red-haired nude man with a pointed beard. He had his hand on the throat of a tiny black-haired woman, who lay in bed and was trying to push him away. Her body was swollen in advanced pregnancy. The old woman stared at the picture. "That's why I wanted so much to be raped, instead of loved gently," she observed.

"Take the puppets," said the old man shortly. "Two for a quarter."

The old woman threw them into a big, square basket with a lid, which the proprietor had opened and pushed toward her. She took a quarter from the pocket of her gown.

"Here," she said. The proprietor nodded.

"You always did like to pay your debts. Do you still want to buy back all your dreams?"

"All that I remember," she said firmly, "and the reality within them, too. Here is a reality. Look, my father is delivering me. He looks loving and joyful."

"Yes," agreed the proprietor. "He's unwinding the umbilical cord from around your neck before it strangles you."

The old woman followed his gaze to the next scene on the wall—a baby carriage in front of green curtains.

"It's my parents' bedroom," she whispered.

The child in the carriage was watching the father urinate.

"Nice," she said.

"Here is a photo of you with your sister and brother. They are frail, you are sturdy. Your mouth is wide. As your father used to say, 'If she did not have ears, her mouth would go all around her head when she smiles.' Your eyes are big glass marbles flecked with gray, green, and blue. They roll from one corner to the other. You have an insatiable lust for life—the third child, born in Taurus. How stubborn, unruly, unbending, and proud you are. You throw terrific temper tantrums when your sisters and brothers do not give in to your demands. You run in circles with a butcher knife, screaming that you will kill yourself, because you feel injured by the others. You destroy a favorite toy because you think the toy-giver has wronged you."

The old man took a child's sewing machine from the rack. "Remember?" he asked. "Isn't this the one your sister gave you that you destroyed?"

"You give me realities instead of dreams," the old woman said tartly. "I wanted my dreams."

He took a woman puppet off a hook. "Here is your mother," he said, "and there is your dream mother," pointing, "the mother spider, hanging in the ceiling corner, larger than life." A tiny child was standing fear-stricken under the spider, looking up. "What about it?" he asked. "What about the spider?"

"I remember distinctly," said the old woman smartly, "the last time I had anything to do with spiders. I sat on a stone bench near the ocean. Behind me were spiderwebs with spiders in them. I did not even brush them off the bench. I forgot them as I watched the blue sea."

"Sold, then," said the old man, "along with a whole lot of other spider paintings—backdrops we have not even displayed. But what about the small spiders sitting on your arm—the danger signs

[247]

announcing that your lover or your husband was busy with other women?"

"I can handle them now," said the old woman. "I met the girls who had given me spider dreams. I sought them out."

The old man pointed to several toy spiders, lying on his hand. "Settled," he said, forcefully throwing the handful into the basket. "There are a lot of childhood things left. What about your religious spree, your obsession to help?"

The old woman took down the next puppet, a pale, thin child with wide eyes. "This is the one," she said, "who went to church twice every Sunday while her daddy preached; who lay under his desk on the fur rug and cried bitterly throughout one dark Good Friday afternoon, mourning the death of the Savior, Jesus Christ."

"A whole afternoon! But later on you said good-bye to all of Christianity."

"No wonder," retorted the old woman, "with a huge father-god who towered over me in the pulpit and a theologian for a husband."

"Ah, yes, but you used to write biblical poems."

"When I was an art student, you mean," said the old woman. "That was aesthetic and those from my childhood were antediluvian religious memories."

"And how about Buddha, Shakti and Shakta, Yin and Yang, meditation?" the old man asked.

"That was yoga. That was antireligion," she said.

The old man threw a couple of puppets into the basket—a godlike image of Christ on the cross and a Christ giving blessing. "Do you remember that one?" he asked.

The old woman stared at the scene on the wall that had been disclosed when the religious puppets were moved.

"Do I know it! The curse of a lifetime. 'Take my hands and guide me until my blessed end, eternally. I don't want to walk alone, not one step. Take me along, wherever you walk, step by step.' Translate that into a model for marriage behavior!"

"You must have suffered," said the old man. "but, oh, how your husbands must have suffered through you!"

"So much for the candy-sweet Jesus." Taking down another, he said "How we have here the helpmate. Is she from your Christ-loving cycle? At one time you wanted to help anyone who came your way, to improve and save, and feel healed through healing others."

"Hardly!" she exclaimed. "I gave up holding the Savior's hand to be with the ugly, rejected little hunchback who takes care of a family of deserted children. The story ended in a torrent of helpfulness. Perhaps that is why I never liked to mend my clothes—I did not want to become a hunchback. But I loved that little hunchback. I never overcame her." She took the puppet out of the proprietor's hand and kissed its hump.

"You know," he said, recovering the puppet and putting it gently into the basket, "in our country, we ask for the favor of touching a hunchback's hump. It is supposed to bring good luck. And what about the prince," he asked, "what did he represent?"

"He was the white knight in me. I was not surprised when, at sixteen, an old occultist and clairvoyant told me he saw the sign on me. I did not ask him which sign. I knew it was the mark of the chosen."

"So," said the proprietor, "you seem to have taken your mother's joke, that you were not your father's child, as a mark of distinction."

"I certainly did."

"That must have given you an unseemly arrogance."

"It certainly helped me preserve my personal reality in a time of mass exercises," the old woman smiled politely.

"Now here we come at last to the women—an Indian chief and a white girl," the proprietor went on, ignoring her comment.

"You must know them," she said, "Uncas and the girl Cora. I became an androgyne, half the young Indian chief in love with Cora, half Cora in love with the young chief. Again I become two in one."

"Anyway," muttered the old man, "you look like a woman here." He lifted from the rack a wide-lipped, blond-haired, blue-eyed, slim-hipped, and full-breasted puppet. "Time to become aware of it. At any rate, at this point you abandoned the white knight." He took the knight off the hook, handing her the puppet.

"Thanks," she said, throwing it into the basket.

"What about women lovers?" he asked.

"Oh," she answered nonchalantly, "there were only four or so, and all for different reasons. The first was the one who took *me* in *her* arms. The second was my way of participating in my brother's sweetheart. The third was an act of gratitude expressed in one fragile afternoon. The fourth was my revenge for my mother. The poor dear got a spanking, but she liked it."

"But," said the proprietor, "there is one more, the dark-haired Lesbian."

The old woman was amused. "That one," she replied, "could have been a veritable romance. I fell away from her into the arms of my Dionysus—cool Athena, learning sensuous games from the dark god."

"I won't speak of your married life," said the proprietor, "although there were dreams connected with it, dreams that rule life."

"Don't get philosophical on me," said the old woman.

"I see a lot of men puppets here."

"They are stand-ins to test the model," she explained.

"The model?"

"Yes, I seemed unable to find the one man who would fit all occasions—either he was too clever or too dumb, too ugly or too handsome, too humane or too male. I tried to make a composite photograph by laying a picture of my most recent lover over that of the preceding lover, hoping to combine the best of each in a single image of the perfect lover."

"And the bad sides?" asked the proprietor. He grinned from ear to ear. "They might have become a composite, too."

"What about the birdcage there beside the composite lovers?" he asked as he caught up the male puppets and dropped them into the basket.

"That was simple," she said. "I hated having demands made on me, either of sex or of love. In my dreams, the solution was to cage each one and visit him according to my whim."

"There were two who were special. On meeting the first, you experienced hate at first sight."

"He became my second husband," she said.

"And the other one, with whom you experienced love at first sight—he belonged to your dream life too, did he not?"

"Yes, that is so," she said.

"What did the one you loved at first sight do to you?"

"He unraveled my hates," she replied. "I feel toward him now just as I felt in the beginning."

"Love without knowledge," observed the old man. He scrutinized this last puppet before handing it to her. "Are you sure this one is not the spitting image of your own white knight, the androgyne?"

"Perhaps he is, but he materialized; he left the region of the puppets—to be! Besides, what was important was that our dreams clicked. I was the one who dared him to be himself. Even across oceans I could feel him. Even across oceans he could respond to me."

"No sex?" asked the proprietor.

The old woman smiled. "I see only a white knight who no longer belongs to my dreams. No sex."

The proprietor yawned. "Very unusual," he said, *"very unusual.* The basket is getting crowded.

He grabbed up this last puppet and threw it on the heaped basket. "One buck," he said.

The old woman pulled out nickels and dimes. "I am running short of money."

"I'll take it in small change."

"I'm cleaned out," she said, "And where does it leave me?"

"Do you want to go on to the next step?" he asked. He rattled a key on his chain as he moved toward a closed door behind the racks at the narrow, far end of the room, cursing under his breath, making his way through all sorts of litter, moving a skeleton aside. He bent down and inserted the key in the lock. It opened inward, pushing the proprietor against the wall. The old woman walked forward to enter.

"You cannot enter," cried the old man, "you can only look."

She stood at the threshold, twilight behind her, before her a star-lit night sky. The stars were not the faraway stars of her childhoodsky, they were prisms, softly shining from within like old-fashioned paperweights. Encased in each crystalline shape was a man or a woman. She knew all of them, she could have called them by name. The prisms turned slowly, their facets gleaming in rainbow colors. An unearthly sound issued from the circling crystals—an orchestra of singular voices, a disharmonic harmony. The old man pulled the woman back into the rack room, banging the door closed.

"Let me in, now that I've seen it!" she shouted, infuriated. She threw her hands up in outraged glee. "So that was it!" she shrilled. "What was the use of worrying all the time? *I am there!* We are ALL THERE! Why did it take me so long to understand?"

"Good things take time," said the proprietor, leading the way back to the street exit.

"You *will* let me in?" she queried.

"In your own good time," he answered.

The old woman turned at the threshold. "There must be another door," she said in a different voice, "a door leading into the great silence."

"That door," the proprietor said, following her out and then putting a key into the outside lock, "that door you have to find for yourself." He banged the door closed and turned the key. "The path is overgrown, too few people use it—ever." He turned to her, removing the key from the lock, but she had already departed.